GRAY SABBATH

GRAY SABBATH

JESUS PEOPLE USA, THE EVANGELICAL LEFT, AND THE EVOLUTION OF CHRISTIAN ROCK

★ ★ ★ ★ ★

SHAWN DAVID YOUNG

Columbia University Press
New York

Columbia University Press
Publishers Since 1893
New York   Chichester, West Sussex
Copyright © 2015 Columbia University Press
All rights reserved

Library of Congress Cataloging-in-Publication Data

Young, Shawn David.
  Gray sabbath : Jesus people USA, evangelical left, and the evolution of Christian rock / Shawn David Young.
     pages cm
  Includes bibliographical references and index.
  ISBN 978-0-231-17238-7 (cloth) — ISBN 978-0-231-17239-4 (pbk.) — ISBN 978-0-231-53956-2 (ebook)
  1. Jesus People—United States. 2. Evangelicalism—Illinois—Chicago—History—20th century. 3. Christian rock music—United States. I. Title.
  BV3793.Y685 2015
  277.73'110828—dc23

                                            2014045628

Cover Design: Jordan Wannemacher
Cover Illustration: Jessica Grieb

References to Internet Web sites (URLs) were accurate at the time of writing. Neither the author nor Columbia University Press is responsible for URLs that may have expired or changed since the manuscript was prepared.

For Martha, Wesley, and Camden Young

★ ★ ★

CONTENTS

✦ ✦ ✦

Preface and Acknowledgments ix

1. INTRODUCTION 1

2. THE LARGEST AMERICAN COMMUNE 20

3. THE BLESSING AND CURSE OF COMMUNITY 52

4. BIG SHOULDERS, BIG HISTORY: WHY CHICAGO? 103

5. THEOLOGY, POLITICS, AND CULTURE 130

6. THE CHRISTIAN WOODSTOCK: VERNACULAR RELIGION, INFLUENCE, AND CONFLICTING WORLDS 173

7. THE FUTURE: EX-MEMBERS, SECOND GENERATION, AND SOCIAL DYNAMICS 222

8. CONCLUSION 262

Notes 275
Bibliography 299
Index 309

PREFACE AND ACKNOWLEDGMENTS
✱ ✱ ✱

All that mattered was music. More important, all that mattered was good music with a deep message. That's the addiction that drove me during college. I played in bands, attended concerts, and remained active in a local church. My musical tastes were very specific. If Christian music, then it had to be heavy metal, progressive, alternative, indie, or avant-garde—anything interesting. I still remember when my wife (then girlfriend) suggested a music festival in the Midwest. This one, she insisted, was not your typical event. In fact, when we arrived at my first Cornerstone Festival, she warned me that I was about to see many odd things. And I did.

For the first time in my life I experienced something that was (in many ways) indefinable. My musical tastes were quite eclectic, ranging from Bach to the Beatles, Metheny to Metallica, Rachmaninoff to Rush, Kiss to King's X. For the most part, Christian music concerts and festivals did not offer the same quality as the so-called secular industry, at least in my estimation. Cornerstone changed that perception.

It would be an understatement to say I developed my worldview as a young adult as a result of this rather multivalent event. And yet the augurs of the written word began to complicate things for me. Graduate school brought with it a new understanding of text, people, and ideas. The study of culture cast new light on the peculiarities of popular religious expression. In

PREFACE AND ACKNOWLEDGMENTS

no small way, the Cornerstone Festival and its sponsors helped crystallize religious certainty. Then, throughout graduate school and my own crisis of faith, it served as a wonderful case study into the complexities associated with modernity, postmodernity, pluralism, and literary representation. For me, this book has been a labor of love. But it has also been about plain and simple curiosity.

I thank the following, whose mentorship and advice helped me reach this point in my academic career: Simon Suh, Gary Crites, James Noblitt, Mark Abbott, Rick McPeak, Richard Huston, Rich Beans, Jeff Wilson, Chris Woods, Norm and Carol Swanson, Karen Longman, Randall Bergen, Ivan Filby, Tom Stampfli, Debra Marsch, Louise Weiss, Yeeseon Kwon, Michael Johnson, Ani Johnson, Bill Archibald, Cary Holman, Jane Hopkins, Georgann Kurtz-Shaw, Warren Pettit, Jim Reinhardt, and a great many students at Greenville College, Michigan State University, and Clayton State University.

Special thanks go to my faculty mentor and adviser, David W. Stowe, who offered constant encouragement and kindness and challenged me to produce better research. Your work has been an inspiration. Brief as they were, our jam sessions were enjoyable! Thank you to Ann Larabee and Amy DeRogatis, who pushed me to become a better writer, highlighting various historical and theoretical points that needed greater clarity; to Jeff Charnley, who guided me through the process of conducting oral history; and to Arthur Versluis and Malcolm Magee, who took the time to offer instructive commentary that has, I trust, pushed me to present a concise history of a countercultural community deserving of an accurate oral history. I am grateful to Leonora Smith and Julie Linquist for their mentorship in WRAC. I especially thank Linda Gross, Matt Helm, and David Sheridan, without whose help I could not have effectively navigated my career search.

I owe gratitude to my fellow travelers and peers, with whom scholarship, writing strategies, and humor were often shared: Yuya Kiuchi, Morgan Shipley, Jack Taylor, Mike Spencer, Darren Brown, Christopher Chase, Kelly Myers, Ben Dettmar, Jesse Draper, Ernesto Mireles, Adam Capitanio, LaToya Faulk, Ted Troxell, Michael Blouin, David Schreiber, and

PREFACE AND ACKNOWLEDGMENTS

Paul Linden; to my former colleagues at Clayton State University: Delores Toothaker, Susa Tusing, Virginia Bonner, Steve Spence, Randy Clark, Jonathan Harris, Kurt-Alexander Zeller, Michiko Otaki, Richard Bell, Christina Howell, Kathleen Kelly, Susan McFarlane-Alvarez, Shontelle Thrash, Nancy Conley; to others who have offered insight, friendship, and support: Andrew Mall, Bruce Ronkin, Bob Batchelor, Ryan Terrell, Scott Hardesty, Linc Butler, Becky Butler, Rusty Butler, Liz Butler, Reed Thomas, Roger Hiduk; to music industry colleagues such as John Charlillo, Jorge Casas, Ty Tabor, Phil Ehart, John Lawry, and others, whom I fear I may have forgotten; and to Anthony Kolenic—I will refrain from including our oft-shared comedic salutation! Special thanks to Mark May. My family owes a great deal to you!

Many thanks go to my new colleagues at York College of Pennsylvania: President Pamela Gunter-Smith, Dean Dominic F. DelliCarpini, Kenneth M. Osowski, Grace Kingsbury Muzzo, Erin C. Lippard, James Colonna, Allison Altland, Brian Furio, Chad Perry, James McGhee, Jeffrey Schiffman, Kent Cyr, Lowell Briggs, Matthew Clay-Robison, Melanie Rodgers, Pamela Hemzik, Robert Mott, Ry Fryar, Thomas Hall, and Troy Patterson. I thank Jim Jabara for including me in the documentary (and for the free food!). I would also like to thank others who, along with my committee, helped me achieve certain clarity and organization: Benjamin Pollock, Bishop John Shelby Spong, Mark Abbott, and Brian McLaren. I am grateful for the advice, encouragement, and inspiration provided by notable scholars such as Larry Eskridge, Mark Allan Powell, Randall Balmer, Bart Ehrman, Heather Hendershot, Anthony Campolo, Jay R. Howard, Tricia Rose, George Marsden, Mark Noll, Melani McAlister, Lawrence Grossberg, Christian Smith, Jason Bivens, Lauren Sandler, Jon Pahl, Timothy Miller, Mark Hulsether, and David Di Sabatino. The Communal Studies Association provided a generous research fellowship. I also owe special thanks to Matthew Grow and Etta Madden.

I am grateful to the folks at Jesus People USA for opening their homes and their hearts to my project. I particularly thank the following, who offered their time, resources, and encouragement: Glenn Kaiser, Wendi Kaiser (great meatloaf!), John Herrin, Jon Trott, and Lyda Jackson. I am grateful to Columbia University Press, specifically to my editors, Wendy Lochner, Christine Dunbar, Ron Harris, and Anita O'Brien.

I am certain that Evangelical Christianity formed me in my youth. While I no longer fully identify with this worldview, I fully respect the positions held by my family, friends, and colleagues. I owe gratitude to all members of my family, without whom I could not have accomplished this: to my grandparents, to my mother and father, for their support and encouragement; to Shannon and Shalene and their families; to Shirley and Jerry (thanks for the great conversations, Jerry!); to Patty Turner for allowing her daughter to marry someone like me; To Julia (spin) Turner; to my two precious boys, Wesley and Camden, who occasionally referred to me as "professor daddy." Like your mother, you have sacrificed so much. Thanks for understanding when daddy was not always available. I love you (as Cammie would sing) "more than anything!!" Finally, thank you to my dearest Martha. (Yes, I said dearest.) Without you and our boys, none of this would have been possible. Thank you for weaning me off *The Andy Griffith Show* and inspiring me to read! Thank you for giving up your dreams to help me realize mine, and for working jobs that were quite undesirable, while still (somehow) maintaining a sense of what was needed for our family—for your realism in the midst of my idealism. Thank you for introducing me to the world of Jesus People USA and Cornerstone. And most importantly, thank you for simply putting up with me. Because of you, I was able to achieve what I never thought possible.

GRAY SABBATH

1
INTRODUCTION

✱ ✱ ✱

Evangelical Christianity has become a powerful force in American popular media, youth culture, and the political arena. Contemporary manifestations of popular evangelical culture remain connected to a history commonly associated with the American counterculture of the 1960s, specifically a revival of conservative Christianity among American youth. Though powerful in content and scope, evangelical Christianity appears to walk with a limp. New versions have been emerging in the United States, redefining the evangelical impulse, challenging the great American trinity of big business, big government, and big religion. And this has been accomplished to the sound track of the "Jesus freak."

We have been told that evangelical Christians lean on their right side, lumbering along, plodding their way through the so-called culture wars. And so it has become commonplace to associate American evangelicals with religious and political conservatism. Whether one views this group of believers as draconian or amenable, today's evangelical has become part of a larger conversation, a narrative thread that begins with Jimmy Carter and continues through the Obama years. At its best, evangelical Christianity is known for its ability to engage culture, meeting people where they are. And at its worst, it will go down as a juggernaut associated with televangelist escapades and Bush-era foreign policy. Regardless of how history will recall

INTRODUCTION

this version of the faithful, what will remain is the cultural synchronicity with which evangelicals have long operated. They have, in the words of the Apostle Paul, become all things to all people. But where did this version of Christianity begin? And how has it become so intertwined with popular media and, more specifically, youth culture? Although evangelicals have engaged pop culture since the Great Awakenings, our story begins with a group of hippies.

The year was 1967 and the hippie movement was at its peak. But as with any cultural revolution, there is a culling often fueled by disenchantment. For some, the break from the original revolution involved a deeper entrenchment into social radicalism. But for others, a return to some form of tradition quelled the angst felt toward both the establishment and the counterculture. Hoping to carve a new path, a number of hippies sought to resolve their own crises in the historical Jesus. The Jesus Movement was a significant American revival that changed the way many youth experienced Christianity. Disenchanted with mainline Christianity, the hippie movement, and the New Left, young evangelicals dubbed "Jesus freaks" sought emotional and spiritual security in the aftermath of the cultural revolution. Hoping to spread the gospel to youth of the 1960s, a number of conservative denominations adopted the cultural vernacular of "hip," pop cultural products. Jesus freaks were attracted to Pentecostalism, which piqued hippie interest in spiritualism. And the Jesus freaks' enthusiasm for conservative interpretations of the Bible appeased traditional religionists. Ultimately, conservative reclamation of popular culture was intended to rescue those caught in what many perceived as a decline of American values. This new version of evangelical Christianity became a powerful force, making its mark on publishing, film, television, festivals, and music, continuing the historical lineage of American evangelicalism as a dominant, complex, growing expression of Christianity. As this movement found what many deemed a significant lacunae between U.S. culture and Christianity, "new paradigm" churches provided Jesus freaks an institutionalized means to counter mainline liberalism's infectivity to deal with existential anxiety. As membership within mainline denominations declined, conservative evangelicals welcomed fresh-faced converts nursed on a mixture of revivalist Christianity and Christian rock music, reinforcing the movement's ability to combine contemporary "hip" Christianity with traditional forms of biblical conservatism.

THE JESUS MOVEMENT: A CONTINUED "SPIRIT"

The Jesus Movement certainly made its mark on conservative American Christianity throughout the course of the 1970s. But the effects of the movement can still be seen today in contemporary Christian aesthetics, new paradigm churches, communes, and new, emerging versions of the so-called Evangelical Left. Unbeknownst to scholars who once dismissed this movement as culturally irrelevant, the paragon for earlier evangelical approaches to culture (George Whitfield, Charles Finney, Billy Sunday, and Amy Semple McPherson) continued under the new auspices of evangelical hippies. These young converts had an enormous influence on the way evangelicals understood, produced, and consumed cultural products—though some historians and sociologists have maintained that this particular expression of evangelical Christianity was a ghost of its former self.

The mercurial Jesus Movement's core ideals were preserved in Jesus freak communities and have been celebrated in the largely Nashville-based Christian music industry. Although the movement has often been lumped into a larger history that associates evangelicals with the Religious Right, a number of Jesus Movement veterans went on to challenge the dominant paradigm of American evangelical Christianity as commonly associated (rightly or wrongly) with Reagan- and Bush-era conservatism.

This book explores a post–Jesus Movement "Jesus People" commune that does not conform to our common understanding of evangelical Christianity (at least in the United States) or popular Christian music. The community has diverged from the "cosmic" urgency that characterized early Jesus freaks. Still, to a certain extent they hold to the principles of the original movement, combining lived religion (in their model of community), evangelical activism, and the hippie aesthetic. But despite this triumvirate—seeming historical continuity of the puritanical—the group's epoch is nothing short of tattered, complex, and nebulous. To say their history is filled with a vast

INTRODUCTION

combination of wondrous humanitarian accolades and near-devilish missteps would be a gross understatement.

The book also offers an analysis of this community's social and cultural influence through the Cornerstone Music Festival, an annual multivalent event created by the community in 1984. Their political and theological ideals were often included as part of a larger conversation at the festival. This protean carnival evolved into a gathering where shared discourse served to create new understandings of what evangelical Christianity and faith-based music is or could become. Summer 2012 marked the final festival, creating an empty space where religionists and artists left-of-center once called home. For twenty-nine years Cornerstone created a ripple effect throughout the Christian music industry, changing the way a number of evangelicals have traditionally understood evangelical popular music—how it is defined, how it is produced, and how consumers perceive its relationship to evangelical Christianity. But the importance of this particular Jesus commune concerns more than the tepid nature of contemporary Christian music or the ever elusive consumer-demographic of evangelical youth.

An analysis of the community and the festival offers the reader a glimpse into a subculture that highlights an emerging disenchantment with the Religious Right and the Secular Left, as well as mainline liberal Protestantism. In short, there has been a sort of clarion call by a great number of evangelical ministers, activists, authors, and intellectuals who now embrace the various theological uncertainties associated with postmodernity and pluralism. In so doing they have attempted to reestablish left-leaning principles of social justice and articulate a cogent understanding of a new orthodoxy, now exemplified within the so-called Evangelical Left. And while it is easy to glean insight from a number of studies that consider the purely theological or historical nature of these sociopolitical developments, a study of the *organic* process of ideological change is far more informative and compelling.

EVANGELICAL PROGRESSION

This Jesus People community demonstrates how evangelicalism is continually reinvented as practitioners attempt to reconcile pluralism with what I

INTRODUCTION

will call "establishment evangelicalism." Thus an examination of the group sheds light on fundamental cultural problems related to pluralism. This was demonstrated at their music and arts festival, where music groups and guest lecturers challenged how art and ideas were represented and processed. And they even challenged the evangelical paradigm.

An analysis of Cornerstone (and the tensions between establishment evangelicalism and various countercultural Christian expressions) problematizes and nuances the ways in which religious commitment and "fanaticism" are depicted by parent cultures such as establishment evangelicalism. Using the festival as a case study, I explore how social discourse affects religious and political belief as members of the commune connect with an ideologically diverse population. Those who attended the festival were often challenged to reconsider basic assumptions about faith and the arts. For Cornerstone, "lived religion" exemplified reactions to and sympathies with cultural pluralism, further demonstrating how contemporary Christianity continues to evolve. The outcome of this multicultural experience was this: those who attended were exposed to various liminal moments; each situation—whether a concert or a lecture—encouraged the individual to reevaluate long-held beliefs and reconsider political and theological paradigms, which (I argue) are in many ways constructs of both establishment evangelicalism and the contemporary Christian music industry.

I offer an analysis of how the Jesus People community, Cornerstone, and (as an incidental consequence) the music industry experience ideological change in response to cultural pluralism. In the end I consider the community's longevity, their impact on the festival, how the festival contributes to shifts within the Christian music industry, and how the spirit of the Jesus Movement is maintained in the Jesus People community and expressed at Cornerstone. As such, the community and Cornerstone both demonstrate how conservative (establishment) evangelicalism is being challenged as veterans of the right-leaning Jesus Movement have been intersecting in unique ways with an emerging Evangelical Left.

To some extent, Cornerstone maintained the spirit of the original Jesus Movement as it nursed dreams of a simpler "tribal" faith, which connected religious commitment to a larger global community without overt focus on denominational loyalty or dogmatism associated with establishment evangelicalism. But this is also complicated by a number of competing sociocultural pressures: the rapid growth of individualism, the American tendency to mix evangelical Christianity with nationalism, and the commercialization of popular evangelical music. As a counterpoint to mainstream evangelical festivals and other "establishment" forms of Christianity, Cornerstone offered an outlet for musicians who would otherwise have been marginalized by the church. It provided a space where burgeoning faith-based artists experimented beyond the boundaries of the Gospel Music Association's gatekeepers. It nurtured up-and-coming musicians who did not conform to what is traditionally expected of contemporary Christian music. And it provided a safe space for consumers from both the right and the left to enjoy art and ideology in a common, friendly space for about one week. Ultimately, the social impact—the legacy—of Cornerstone and the Jesus People has been the music.

The Jesus People community has redefined how popular evangelical music is understood, defined, and performed. The record industry is now filled with artists whose beginnings can be traced to the evangelical subculture, and Cornerstone had a hand in remaking how consumers thought about faith-based music, radically altering how popular evangelical music is represented. But this community's cultural influence extends well beyond how the church perceives musical styles and lyrics. The reason evangelicals have increasingly reconsidered their popular conceptions about faith, politics, and music can be traced to the so-called culture war, as represented in our common political and theological binary.

Since the 1980s the Religious Right has garnered support and criticism from both secularists and religionists. In some ways, the average evangelical tends to view the Religious Right with the same suspicion it holds for both Republicans and Democrats. But despite its waning popularity it has not been declawed. On the contrary, as the political center continues to shift, the poles also shift, often widening the divide until one cannot locate a true center. On the other hand, there are other evangelical Christians who continue their search for a middle ground (a gray area) between conservatism and liberalism. The result has been a germinating discontent with the American evangelical paradigm.

INTRODUCTION

While the presence of an Evangelical Left is nothing new, the ideas espoused by adherents are being popularized among young consumers through an unlikely portal—the Christian music industry, a historically conservative arm of evangelicalism. Philosophies commonly associated with left-leaning politics now permeate a great amount of modern Christian music as artists muse over ideas once dismissed: they ponder the environment rather than puzzle over the Apocalypse; they explore the dangers of war and nationalism and avoid exploring Christian triumphalism; and they encourage listeners to mourn poverty rather than glory in the heavenly streets of gold.

The people in this commune are often encouraged to entertain and embrace ambiguity, but do so within the context of maintaining ideological order, a tall order to fill. Tensions commonly associated with existential anxiety and pluralism resulted in their reevaluation of the way meaning is understood and presented, a philosophical development often referred to as the "crisis of representation." Thus some leaders within the Jesus People commune began to sympathize with "postmodern" criticisms of how religious truth is represented and how the politics associated with art and society are defined, processed, and consumed. This approach to culture created a space for the community, one best defined as "progressive," without the historical baggage associated with theological liberalism. This progressive aspect of the community and the festival demonstrates a vastly different collective experience from the typical conservative megachurch or Christian music concert. Is this the quintessential left-leaning evangelical gathering? Unfortunately it's not that simple. Many who attended Cornerstone remained affiliated with conservative evangelicalism. Thus the community and the event have functioned interstitially, connecting two very different dichotomies.

Despite their dalliance with postmodernism and cultural pluralism, the Jesus People community self-identifies as evangelical. But what do we mean by "evangelical"? For historian David Bebbington, evangelical Christians have historically embraced four categories essential to the evangelical identity: dedication to Christian conversion, Biblicism, activism, and crucicentrism, the belief that the crucifixion of Christ atoned for the sins of humanity. To a certain extent, the Jesus People leadership read these essentials with postmodern eyes. Some academics and ministers have demonstrated that the term "evangelical" can be broadened to include a number of movements or individuals. Historian Randall Balmer's approach creates an ecumenical template whereby anyone who has experienced a spiritual "new birth" can qualify as evangelical—those who have been "born again." While specific theological positions are negotiable for the Jesus People community (as we shall see), their core principle involves some form of new birth (spiritual salvation), however nuanced that understanding may be. Despite their evolving theological paradigm, this community can be considered evangelical, but in a broader sense of the term. And in some ways, this complicates how evangelical Christianity in the United States is often understood (or misunderstood).

I offer three core arguments. First, historians have demonstrated that in most cases American communes are short-lived. But this community has continued beyond its 1972 genesis owing to various structural and organizational mechanisms. Furthermore, their ability to engage and evolve with American culture has fed into a sort of sustained commitment, which is often absent in other communal groups. Their longevity (to date) is a result of what sociologist Rosabeth Moss Kanter refers to as "commitment mechanisms," particularly the commitment of second-generation and younger members who are unaffiliated with founders. Second, the Jesus People and Cornerstone have offered us a new way to understand evangelical popular music. Third, the Jesus People and Cornerstone sustain a vestige of the original Jesus Movement. Despite the conservative nature of the original movement, this community represents the *general* ethos of "emergent" Christianity and the Evangelical Left and, through the festival, contributed to newly emerging forms of progressive Christianity.

Both the commune and the festival contribute to a growing counter-narrative to the Religious Right as emergent Christians and others associated with the Christian Left either reclaim what was purest about the Jesus Movement (before being absorbed by the Evangelical "establishment" Right) or now locate a livable space where both evangelicalism and cultural pluralism can coexist comfortably, despite paradox and existential tension.

INTRODUCTION

PROGRESSION AND ACCOMMODATION

The result of pluralism (or at least an increasingly multicultural society) is that to some extent American evangelicals often yield to popular opinion—reinventing a collective ethos, recategorizing cultural products with the hope of remaining relevant and authentic. In some ways this is the lifeblood of evangelical Christianity. While the populist impulse empowers and sustains American evangelicalism, says historian Nathan Hatch, the "movement" also thrives in the marketplace, indelibly linked to capitalism. In her own historical analysis, Colleen McDannell opines how mass evangelical gatherings often demonstrate "how a commercial American mentality has invaded the inner-sanctum of religion."[1] In contradistinction to fundamentalist Christianity, evangelicalism is naturally associated with cultural engagement and accommodation.

We will consider how this community has continued to be self-sustaining, marshaling enough cultural capital to actually have an impact on the evangelical subculture. Despite its theological inheritance from its Jesus Movement forerunners, this group now deemphasizes some positions long cherished by conservative evangelicals, creating a significant difference between the community and other Jesus-freak veterans. Moreover, their communal ethic (their government) places them outside parameters putative to conservative establishment evangelicalism, complicating the oft-held belief that the Jesus Movement was altogether a conservative movement. This community of "Jesus freaks" actually represents a parallel story to other narratives that explore the West Coast Jesus Movement.

My findings demonstrate that the social impact of communities such as this reveals how the evangelical subculture is rapidly changing and is on the cusp of a new reformation. This coming change has been made possible by a previously established context: a populist evangelical cultural activism nuanced by fundamentalist retreat and embattlement. Historians have devoted significant efforts to understanding the development of American evangelicalism and its relationship to the modern world and politics. Yet an examination of the Jesus People and the Cornerstone Festival reveals that evangelicalism goes beyond what many have considered complex, defying assumptions about the original movement. For example, many fail to recognize the complexity of transcommunal religious experience. Others offer reductive views of the marriage between the counterculture and (in this particular case) evangelical Christianity. Despite this, there is an emerging body of work indexing the larger, cultural impact of the Jesus Movement, as well as implications for a growing counterpoint to conservative forms of evangelical Christianity.

ORGANIZATION

Chapter 2 begins with an overview of American religious "countercultural" communities, covering nineteenth- and twentieth-century communalism and the threaded connection to Jesus freaks. It goes on to deliver a chronological history of this Jesus People group, beginning with its genesis in Milwaukee, Wisconsin, and the birth of the first known Christian hard rock group, the Resurrection Band. The chapter provides a close reading of the community's development. Initially settling in Gainesville, Florida, the Resurrection Band traveled extensively, growing in size as fans of the band (as well as spiritual seekers) followed. Originally dubbed the "Jesus People U.S.A. Traveling Team," the burgeoning community eventually settled in Chicago's inner city. After occupying a number of houses, their increase in membership and vision for inner-city outreach created a new need: the young group of believers needed a larger home.

In chapter 3 I detail the economic, organizational, and structural elements of life in the Jesus People and demonstrate how they have succeeded in outliving other communal experiments. The chapter explores daily life in the community and demonstrates how individual commitment to the group is connected to perceptions of democracy, control, and negative press; the community was castigated publicly, creating a maelstrom concerning leadership structure and the now discontinued practice of "adult spanking." Using Rosabeth Moss Kanter's theory of "retreat communes," I argue that tight boundaries serve to reinforce collective and individual commitment

INTRODUCTION

(if even to the detriment of individual maturation) to the communal ethic. While other Jesus-freak communes have faded into obscurity, this group of believers has managed to survive as a self-sustaining, inner-city village because of five fundamental commitment mechanisms: mission businesses, a plurality of leadership, a divine calling, denominational accountability, and a striking ability to affirm the individual within the collective. In the end, these elements are part of a core purpose connected to what Noreen Cornfield considers "norms of high involvement," activities made possible by the community's location.[2] And in some ways the rise and fall of communities such as this mirror the ebb and flow of larger communities such as evangelicalism.

In considering Chicago generally and the neighborhood of Uptown specifically, chapter 4 analyzes both the history and landscape that have contributed to the Jesus People's longevity. When juxtaposed against the New Left and Catholic models of social justice, Uptown's legacy of immigrant struggle and poverty demonstrates that the neighborhood continues to be an area in need of organizations willing to offer aid. This group's form of evangelical Christianity is unique, though in some ways they remind us of other expressions of evangelical social justice that have faded into the background of an assumed conservative mythology. Given Uptown's history of poverty, the Jesus People's choice to live communally was a reaction to problems associated with life in the inner city, though the initial thrust was a desire to construct a community modeled after the book of Acts. The decision to remain an *urban* activist group has contributed to their survival. In other words, the difference between rural, suburban, and urban communal living has to do with a particular location's ability to influence communards, who then marshal heightened levels of commitment and resources in service to social activism. Urban environments provide more interaction with society and a greater sense of urgency.

Ultimately their location reinforces a series of psychological processes connected to sustained levels of individual commitment to the commune and the neighborhood of Uptown. These processes are realized by what Kanter refers to as "disassociation" (a process that severs competing obligations) and "association" (a process that creates symbiotic relationships between communard and commune). In the end, the chapter argues that the community's political and cultural philosophy may prove inconvenient for establishment evangelicalism. Their presence, cultural influence, and urban activism all challenge the belief that the Jesus Movement was merely a faddish youth movement with little hope of affecting culture.[3]

Chapter 5 explores ideologies held by most members of the group, including personal accounts of ever-changing (if often ambiguous) political and theological positions. After providing an overview of "Rapture theology" (which informed much of the Jesus Movement), I explore this group's changing position on the topic of the end times. While the commune has, to some extent, always diverged from establishment evangelicalism, the two paths aligned during the 1980s as the Jesus People embraced rigorous theological models designed (ironically) to argue on behalf of fundamentalism. Then in sympathy with more liberal theological claims, the commune later grew suspicious of what they perceived as untenable arguments for faith that, for them, were too speculative, even counterintuitive to *true* religious faith. As a result, they entered the "postmodern" arena as leadership embraced literary criticisms associated with more quasi-liberal methods of biblical interpretation—but they continued to maintain a high view of scripture.

While Jesus People has held a left-wing fiscal position since 1972, the group remains sympathetic to views held by both the Right and the Left. Embracing the New Testament's model of community, members say their fiscal structure is most emblematic of socialism. But are they liberals? They oppose abortion, but they also oppose the death penalty. They are progovernment but remain self-sustaining through their many businesses. They engage in activist campaigns that favor feminism, protest weapons, affirm environmentalism, and question the war, but they oppose gay marriage. And they question categories such as "sacred" and "secular"—which allows them to embrace many musical expressions—but still use music to share the gospel. Categorizing this community is, to say the least, quite difficult. For all the possible labels we could assign, they remain an interstitial expression of evangelical Christianity, offering a counterpoint to both mainline liberalism and establishment evangelicalism.

INTRODUCTION

Chapter 6 demonstrates how the Jesus People have (so far) maintained the evangelical heritage of cultural engagement, embracing pop culture as a means of social outreach. The most visible example of this can be seen in the now defunct Cornerstone Festival. Originally intended to offer Christians something wholly different from mainstream festivals such as Creation and Fishnet, Cornerstone challenged the mainstream Christian music industry. A product of both the Jesus Movement and contemporary Christian music (CCM), Christian rock festivals are vestiges of the original movement's intent to reach the lost using the tools of pop culture. Yet the Cornerstone Festival worked to challenge an industry that bears little resemblance to early Jesus freaks, let alone the counterculture. Eileen Luhr says public space and consumer culture reveal how evangelicals' identities often converge. In response to what Luhr refers to as the "suburbanization of evangelical Christianity," Cornerstone (a Christian countercultural tour de force) re-established the subversive impulse that once inspired Jesus-freak aesthetics and notions of community, while also rupturing lines of delineation that often characterize establishment evangelicalism.[4]

Music groups showcased at the event were often incompatible with mainstream CCM. For example, popular Christian music has become a respectable niche genre, now enjoying moderate market success. Moreover, CCM artists often use celebrity status in service to humanitarian causes, often bundled as part of the larger category of Christian mission work. Consequently, these artists often play a part in what Melani McAlister elegantly refers to as "enchanted internationalism," an impulse that drives evangelical youth (and evangelical cultural agents) to engage the global village, Christianizing the lost.[5] In so doing, youth take part in a rite of passage that allows the missionary to experience the exotic Other, comforted they will return to the safety of the West or the global North. But while her claim is instantiated by groups within CCM proper, many at Cornerstone parted with establishment evangelicalism, particularly when considering the fragile distinction between evangelical missions and cultural imperialism.

Over the years Cornerstone played a role in redefining how popular Christian music could or should be understood. As a result, evangelical musicians now enjoy a presence in the general market without the signifier

INTRODUCTION

"Christian band," a significant development given the rising cultural capital held by evangelicals. Moreover, these musicians have increasingly distanced themselves from the Religious Right (or any official affiliation, for that matter), hoping to signal the presence of socially minded evangelicals; and at times these are disassociated from the stereotypical "brand" of right-leaning, nationalistic evangelicalism.

Chapter 6 ends by demonstrating how former members of the Jesus People view Cornerstone's evolution over the years—musically and theologically—and argues that the festival broadcasted an ideology perceived as incompatible with establishment evangelicalism. Yet as Cornerstone countered the establishment and the mainstream Christian music industry, it garnered support from festivalgoers and musicians who were *coded* conservative and evangelical. Both the Jesus People and their festival are thus unclassifiable in the strictest sense, demonstrating what Victor Turner refers to as liminality. Still, we can locate core principles of the community as related to larger movements or classifications. Avoiding what Jason Bivens refers to as "illegibility" allows us to classify the group within the larger framework of evangelical Christianity.[6]

Chapter 7 explores the future of the Jesus People. In considering the impact of rising generations within the commune, I note how younger members perceive the general administrative structure of the group. Individual stories of disheartened members (current and former) provide a tapestry of ideas that ostensibly demonstrate the fluidity of individual perception and the fragility of the commune. I also consider how the ruling council of the community maintains what Kanter refers to as "affirmative boundaries" in the face of cultural engagement, negative press, and perceptions of democracy. Some scholars venture that owing to the American premium placed on *personal* space, American communards often expect a certain amount of privacy and individuality, despite their choice to live a life of shared property and experience. The chapter highlights that tension and considers that commitment mechanisms can work in reverse, creating impetus for declining commitment in rising generations. This will become important as we consider how the end of Cornerstone might affect membership in the community.

INTRODUCTION

Individual testimonies share a common thread, one that affirms a consistent heritage of communal evolution. While some believe the commune has shifted from its evangelical roots, others applaud the leadership's efforts to remain true to their social calling. And as Jesus People has self-consciously adopted the model of what it refers to as "intentional community," its members continue to embrace a communal ethic that, on one hand, has served the group well, affording long life. On the other hand, the American appeal to the *individual* has influenced other members, many of whom make up the future foundation of the commune.

While my findings confirm that commitment mechanisms are valuable for calculating communal longevity, in the end I argue that these mechanisms are relative to time and culture. Second-generation perceptions of communal living actually have undermined the purpose of boundaries necessary for communal dedication and longevity. Along with chapters 2 and 4, chapter 7 demonstrates that these "mechanisms" have contributed to disenchantment among the second generation. While this has little bearing on the status of the greater evangelical subculture or the inimitability of Protestant Christianity, it goes without saying that similar trends can be identified when one examines the waxing and waning of evangelical youth and the impetus behind new movements such as emergent New Monasticism and the New Evangelicals, contributing to what theologian Scot McKnight called "the biggest change in the evangelical movement," nothing less than the emergence of "a new kind of Christian social conscience." This new conscience emerged in brisk response to the George W. Bush administration's approach to foreign policy, humanitarianism, social inequality, and cultural issues. Contrary to the Religious Right, new evangelicals evince antimilitarism, anticonsumerism, and antitorture. "These new evangelicals" notes theorist Marcia Pally, "focus on economic justice, environmental protection and immigration reform—not exactly Republican strong points. The religious right remains a potent political force, but where once there was the appearance of an evangelical movement that sang out in one voice, there is now a robust polyphony."[7]

INTRODUCTION

THE EVANGELICAL LEFT

The book concludes by arguing that the Jesus People represents a significant expression of the American Evangelical Left. The community was founded as a Jesus-freak commune, oriented around principles often associated with rightist, parachurch movements such as the Moral Majority, the Christian Coalition, and the Religious Right. Understandably, journalists have labeled them conservative. But what follows is an account that proves otherwise. While members of the Jesus People are "conservative" on some noteworthy points, their affiliations and overall ethic defy ideas commonly associated with the Right and with liberalism.

Jesus People remain committed to a social ethic quite similar to ideals commonly associated with the New Left, a movement founded by visionaries whose goals bore similarities to the evangelical paradigm. In this fashion the existence (and influence) of groups such as the Jesus People ruptures the way religionists of any stripe are often coded. A common mistake among historians is to locate potential categorical rubrics in hopes of identifying where the studied group falls within a historical and ideological continuum. But this is a redundancy that serves only to reinforce what we already know, and it sheds little light on newer expressions of religious faith. If we consider the community to be merely part of the broad swath of the American evangelical experience, we risk a totalizing view of the whole movement, without regard for nuance or dissent. In like manner, if we particularize this group as unique (to the extent they can no longer be categorized as evangelical), we must reinvent a new category entirely. While in many ways they remain uncategorizable, we can still locate traces of multiple traditions, most notably the hippie movement, progressive forms of evangelical Christianity, and the New Left.

This work assumes a certain amount of causality as it connects the Jesus People to the Cornerstone Festival and extends that influence outward to the Christian music industry. Put another way, ideological symbiosis holds the community and the festival in an orbit, one always feeding off the other. The result is fourfold: (1) In ways quite dissimilar from other forms of baby

INTRODUCTION

boom evangelicalism, Jesus People maintains the original spirit of the Jesus Movement and injected that spirit into its festival. Similarly, the festival refreshed the Jesus People community by keeping the group culturally and ideologically engaged with a world disassociated from their inner-city sanctum. (2) Given the desire to challenge the mainstream Christian music industry's tendency to maintain a strict dichotomy between the sacred and the secular, members of the Jesus People align with a music movement largely independent of gospel music gatekeepers, contributing to new ways of defining evangelical pop music. (3) Given their ethic of social justice, various radical associations, and an evolving ideology, the community is best classified as part of the contemporary Evangelical Left. (4) Given their interest in "postmodern" theology, a growing suspicion of Christian apologetics, and ambiguous positions on sociocultural values, the community challenges establishment evangelicalism, offering us a case study in how evangelical Christianity is changing in U.S. society.

Unfortunately when research is conducted on any group of human beings (religious or secular), there remains the possibility, even likelihood, that a great number of sins will be uncovered. This is true of the Catholic Church, Pentecostals, mainstream evangelicals, mainline Protestants, and a number of groups associated with the Jesus Movement. It is also the case with this group. But while the sins of a community often result in gross negligence, deceit, and broken relationships, leaving a trail of victims to find healing (often on their own), the depth of American religious history remains. Terribly, the dark side of the human experience has touched every religious institution, but there is also light.

A WORD ABOUT CURRENT SCHOLARSHIP

The paucity of historical and theological works that dwell on the evangelical identity has effectively demonstrated that evangelical Christianity is simply too complex to categorize. However, scholarship on evangelicalism either has tended to focus on how one defines the *particulars* of belief by which one is labeled "evangelical" (to the exclusion of radical postmodern nuances

INTRODUCTION

of those beliefs) or has examined canonical works, theologians, evangelists, and denominations (to the exclusion of countercultural groups such as the Jesus People). Moreover, the ethnographic element of communal studies—a focus on individual "radical" communities that self-identify as evangelical—is often mentioned in passing, nestled within larger studies on sects, communes, utopian theory, or biographical works on politically driven Jesus rockers. Thus there are few demonstrative works concerning the breadth of diversity within *countercultural* evangelicalism, particularly those forms that lean to the left.

A WORD ABOUT TERMS

Throughout this book I use the word "postmodern" as members of the commune use it. The term is intended to communicate a reaction to modernism. For the sake of this book, the term "modernism" will be understood not as a temporal distinction or as a valuation of human progress, that is, "modernization." Rather, it serves as a reference to the Enlightenment's emphasis on humanity's ability to fully ascertain certainty on matters pertaining to science, religion, philosophy, psychology, economic systems, cultural systems, and various subjects related to human ontology. As a reaction to modernism, postmodern philosophy (when applied to JPUSA and the so-called emergent church) accomplishes the following: (1) it recognizes that competing truth-claims are part of a pluralistic society; (2) it challenges totalizing metanarratives and assumptions about universal truth; (3) it challenges (or at least reconsiders) truth-claims linked to "received" authority—whether written, oral, experienced, or tested; (4) it attempts to reconcile Christianity with the aforementioned.

The term "establishment evangelicalism" is intended to convey the presence of an officially sanctioned version of evangelical Christianity. I do not intend to suggest that evangelicalism is a monolith. Indeed, as a movement or an ideology, evangelical Christianity is part of a complex historical development that is tremendously diverse. But despite its many expressions, there remains a "core" to what many Americans perceive as "evangelical," regardless of debates offered by theologians and historians. Thus the term "establishment evangelicalism," for this study, is intended to convey what is most commonly associated with evangelical Christianity.

Emergent Christianity represents a "conversation" among evangelicals who are disenchanted with traditional, conservative evangelicalism and the Religious Right. Though defined by their desire for ideological evolution, emergent does not represent any sort of fungible example of theological reform. But it does signal a growing desire among young evangelicals to engage a new conversation about ideas and culture. More significantly, emergent represents an attempt by evangelicals to engage postmodernity and cultural pluralism, while retaining a tweaked version of Christian orthodoxy. Some emergent Christians describe themselves as "postevangelical." But more often they are considered, in some fashion or another, connected (or at least sympathetic) to the Evangelical Left.

It is within this space (and even in concert with the complexity of these rather peculiar terms) that the Jesus People community exists. Inasmuch as one can locate the core of a community (or a belief, for that matter), I hope to tease out the peculiarities associated with these terms and ideas as they relate to this specific community and the new approaches to music that emerged out of their story. My attempt to do so within these pages merely represents one interpretation of a larger cultural phenomenon. What makes this manageable is that conclusions have been developed in conjunction with a historical trajectory long established by social activists—evangelicals and hippies alike—and the wildly fascinating study of American communes.

2
THE LARGEST AMERICAN COMMUNE
✶ ✶ ✶

The war in Vietnam raged; the antiwar movement swept college campuses; the civil rights movement was thoroughly under way; love-ins, sit-ins, and be-ins became commonplace among the flower children; sex, drugs, and rock 'n' roll fueled a cultural revolution. It was the sixties. But something else happened amid what is often considered the decline of Western civilization. As the revolution grew, so did a new version of evangelical Christianity, one linked to the counterculture. In the late 1960s there was a revival, one that brought conservative evangelicalism to American youth. While this included a number of backgrounds and traditions, hippie Christians entranced the media to the point of making headlines in major publications such as *Time* and *Life*. Commonly referred to as the "Jesus Movement," this revival—two unlikely worlds sutured together—challenged traditional Christian aesthetics but also embraced a conservative interpretation of the Bible. Dubbed "Jesus freaks," hippie converts represented a group of Christians who displayed impulses often associated with the Great Awakenings. Donald E. Miller has considered the impact of the movement, arguing that it had the makings of a second Reformation: "Many of the principles of the Reformation were reborn as ordinary people discovered the priesthood of all believers, without ever reading Martin Luther."[1] Similarly, Jesus freaks questioned the authority of the church,

FIGURE 2.1 Johnny Cash performing at Explo '72.
© Used by permission of CRU archives.

FIGURE 2.2 Billy Graham preaching at Explo '72.
© Used by permission of CRU archives.

reinstated biblical authority, but retained a countercultural aesthetic, often sporting the hippie image while using pop music to spread the Gospel.[2]

To a certain extent the Reverend Billy Graham made the Jesus Movement acceptable, offering a bridge for countercultural youth to return to evangelical Christianity. As the revered leader took the stage at the movement's tour de force, Explo '72, Graham's endorsement went a long way in assuaging parental concerns about mixing Christianity with the counterculture.

The message of evangelical Christianity began to surface in popular media such as publishing, film, television, festivals, and music, later becoming a powerful force in American pop culture. This continued the historical lineage of American evangelicalism, affirming what historians have long considered a complex, growing movement. But in the midst of a theologically and socially conservative Jesus revolution, a parallel story developed.[3]

Jesus People USA (JPUSA) is an inner-city commune of post–Jesus Movement Jesus freaks located in Uptown Chicago. Timothy Miller refers to JPUSA as "one of the largest single-site communes in the United States."[4] The fact that such a large commune is still around raises the question: how? This chapter is a brief foray into the historical context from which the community arose. In many ways this community is emblematic of the original movement; in other ways, they diverge. Founded in 1972, JPUSA has thrived owing to its somewhat flexible approach to communal government that (for its members) served to stabilize the community. Its survival can also be attributed to a number of outreach efforts that serve to keep communards engaged in a social cause that requires continued commitment. Simply put, JPUSA has continued since 1972 as a result of two factors: collective commitment and individual freedom. Moreover, commitment to some higher *concrete* purpose has allowed this group of Christians to adapt to a series of events that otherwise would have dissolved them. But collective commitment to purpose does not undermine individuality; community members are able to retain a sense of "self" within the context of collective purpose.

Inspired by the Book of Acts, members of JPUSA have created a unique communal environment. Housing an average of four hundred members—

old hippies, young punk rockers, "straights"—the group embraces a form of socialism: all earnings generated by JPUSA businesses are relinquished, placed in one common purse. The total population of the commune can be broken down into three categories: individual members attached to "nuclear families"; young, single, transient persons; and individuals living in the commune's low-income senior housing. The group operates several ministries and businesses throughout Chicago and abroad, the most visible being Lakefront Roofing and Siding Supply, Cornerstone Community Outreach (a homeless shelter), Tone Zone (a recording studio), Grrr Records (a record label), and a once significant music festival. For years the Cornerstone Festival tantalized the faithful with unique approaches to arts, song, and ideas. The myriad services provided by JPUSA are evidence of its attempt to continue the evangelical heritage of social and cultural engagement. But didn't other Jesus Movement communes also illustrate this reformation commitment to touching the hearts of the people?[5]

Although earlier communes were often evangelical, this particular group has often been conflicted over its religious identity. Though moderately evangelical, JPUSA does not completely identify with the Religious Right or liberalism. Its political affiliation places it outside of what has largely defined mainline evangelicalism since the late 1970s. And yet the group not only continues as a Jesus freak intentional community, it continues with the approval of its parent denomination, the Evangelical Covenant Church (ECC), and various evangelical publications such as *Christianity Today*.

JPUSA has enjoyed success in the wider culture due to its enigmatic Cornerstone Festival, its cutting-edge *Cornerstone* magazine, and continued outreach to the homeless population of Uptown Chicago. But the future remains uncertain. As second-generation members have reached adulthood, many have chosen to chart paths wildly different from those of their elders, making estimates about future leadership or community growth uncertain.

The Cornerstone Festival once afforded JPUSA a significant tool for recruitment, though that was never the group's intention. But it was discontinued in 2012. How will this development affect JPUSA's longevity? For many readers this is as uninteresting as it is irrelevant to their own lives. Though seemingly unrelated to the perils associated with models of church growth or the future of evangelical Christianity, the fundamental nature of popular religious music is, in fact, intimately connected to the way people of faith engage each other and the world around them. This book offers a story about how JPUSA and Cornerstone's evolution signals the coming of newer forms of evangelical Christianity, despite JPUSA's somewhat sketchy past.

This is a sociocultural history that seeks to understand JPUSA's relationship to evangelical Christianity and music, using personal testimonies and historical data. For Rosabeth Kanter, two types of communes exist. "Retreat" communities remain largely isolated, whereas "service" communities engage society, hoping to bring about some sort of greater good. While both types embrace a larger purpose, service-based groups work to create sustainable organizations able to meet the needs of those unaffiliated with communal groups. Kanter argues that for a service commune to remain vibrant, various "commitment mechanisms" must be established. These mechanisms are

> specific ways of ordering and defining the existence of a group. Every aspect of group life has implications for commitment, including property, work, boundaries, recruitment, intimate relationships, group contact, leadership, and ideology. These pieces of social organization can be arranged so as to promote collective unity, provide a sense of belonging and meaning, or they can have no value for commitment. . . . Abstract ideals of brotherhood and harmony, of love and union, must be translated into *concrete social practices*.[6]

This approach creates a symbiotic relationship between the individual and the community, strengthening a collective ethos that inspires everyone to achieve a larger, concrete (measurable) purpose. It comes as no surprise that communes in the United States have often been met with skepticism owing to communitarian dalliance with either socialism or apocalypticism. And it comes as no surprise these groups have often been associated with rogue, wild-eyed leaders who would lead followers to an early grave. But despite this common depiction (often exacerbated by media), the connection between how evangelicals on both the right and the left view their own unique traditions is unswervingly stuck in the mire of the American tendency to champion the rugged individual, even at the expense of the greater good.

COMMUNALISM

Existential angst inspired countercultural activists throughout the 1960s. Some young existentialists, writes Doug Rossinow, "concluded that the way out of anxiety was through disruptive, challenging political activism." Countering this cerebral approach to life's greatest questions, young people sought practical answers. For Rossinow, "The sense of anxiety and the need to comfort it, the preference for the concrete over the abstract, the importance of decision and personal responsibility, the attractiveness of situational ethics, the desire for a sense of vital life, and, above all, the search for a life of authenticity in touch with the 'really real'" peppered American campuses and rallied youth to action.[7] In some cases intentional communities (communes) provided solace for those who sought escape from a meaningless, materialistic world. In other cases they provided a template for a form of social activism that for them existed only in the *minds* of the Old Left or in the *rhetoric* of Christian preachers whose doctrine often trumped the needs of the poor. Communes provided a quick fix for those whose earnest desire for change was never fully met.

Communal living has been widely practiced in the United States (particularly during the nineteenth and twentieth centuries) and continues to fascinate sociologists and historians. Communal experiments built on religious belief reveal something about the American quest for purpose, as well as the natural complexities associated with any attempt to combine democracy, individualism, and community.

There is something about communal living that remains attractive. Of course the concept of "community" often refers to local expressions of citizens who gather to share the milestones of life (church, dinners, celebrations) to the point of reaffirming collective myths and values. But some extend this to encompass the totality of life. Defined as a "relatively small group of people who have created a whole way of life for the attainment of certain goals," these people choose to live in collective fashion, relinquishing worldly goods in service to the greater community.[8] Humans seek a deeper experience in life and often do so in community, says Anson Shupe: "Monasteries, religious retreats, and communes are perceived by many as exotic or antisocial. After all, they reject many of mainstream society's norms. Yet the existence of such groups suggests that for some persons, a *communal imperative* exists. They have a desire to reach beyond 'normal' society for something deeper and more spiritually rewarding."[9]

Despite heartfelt attempts to create utopian worlds, these groups have mostly ended, leaving little legacy and precious few historical examples. Although communities such as the Shakers and Oneida Perfectionists left their mark on American culture, they did not last, nor did their presence affect the way the majority of Americans actually live. Very few have enjoyed even a modicum of consistency, longevity, or significant social influence. While the more noteworthy examples such as Mennonite and Amish (the communal ones) continue to thrive in their own right, they remain cozy leftovers of a bygone era and are anachronistic products of older expressions of Protestant Christianity. But these examples cannot be appropriately analyzed for longevity in the face of pluralism in contemporary U.S. society since they can be best understood as expressions *against* the dominant culture. It has been well established that the more successful Protestant expressions are the result of cultural assimilation. As we shall see, the positive developments associated with the contemporary Evangelical Left, emerging forms of Christian pop music, and the growing fascination with "collectivism" can best be understood when examined as new products of cultural pluralism.

Arguably the more intriguing examples of twentieth-century communes have been those founded on the basis of a "countercultural" ethic, established during the 1960s. A significant number of communes developed in the United States throughout the 1960s and 1970s, amounting to what historian Timothy Miller refers to as a "watershed moment in American communal history."[10] Offshoots of the cultural revolution, Jesus Movement communes retained the hippie aesthetic, adopted a conservative position on evangelical theology, and proclaimed the second coming of Christ. And they were everywhere. Miller has observed that "so many of them erupted that the Jesus movement communes may have been, in terms of sheer numbers of communes and of members, the largest identifiable communal type during the 1960s era." But few remained successful.[11] While it is difficult to pinpoint the reasons so many communes failed, recognizing the initial draw of communal living might provide insight into the reasons for failure. Regardless of the criteria used to determine communal success, the overarching goal remained the same—communes during the 1960s represented a core human desire for community, engagement, and dependence.

In the beginning, various Jesus freak communes were sponsored by local denominations such as Calvary Chapel of Orange County, California. Others spawned larger networks, the largest and most notable being the now defunct Shiloh Youth Revival Centers. As these urban, service-based communes developed, they were often met with various challenges, such as zoning laws that affected multiple-occupancy status. Not to be undermined by the general American thrust toward legal definitions of "family," some groups actually found favor with local authorities that granted the status of "legal family."[12]

A commune of note, Shiloh was "a remarkable example of the manner in which the Jesus People movement had grown and prospered," writes Larry Eskridge, becoming "one of the largest communal groups to emerge out of the hippie counterculture, much less the Jesus movement." By 1977 the group had over one thousand adult members in their headquarters near Eugene, Oregon, managing a network of nearly fifty communal houses across the United States. The owner of multiple properties (including farms and apartment buildings), Shiloh also sponsored traveling ministry teams, published a monthly journal, operated a credit union and medical clinic, and owned a two-engine airplane. "Shiloh had a *net* worth of probably more than $2 million dollars," writes Eskridge, "and was running an annual budget of more than $3 million dollars."[13] Despite its ubiquity and apparent force within the Jesus Movement, Shiloh did not weather the effects of hierarchy. After a heavy turnover in membership, the community "remained viable by changing its programmatic emphases in response to altered circumstances," notes Marion S. Goldman. However, board members became increasingly disappointed with how founder and leader John Higgins handled business. By 1989 the group had officially disincorporated.

Kanter has provided a model from which other historians of communitarianism have gleaned knowledge, offering a clear thesis of how and why this sort of group succeeds and fails. To understand this is to understand why the Religious Right has (seemingly) so vigorously opposed any attempt to focus on the collective over the individual. As a service commune, JPUSA is a case study that supports Kanter's notions of sustainability. The events leading to JPUSA's current residence contributed to reinforced levels of commitment, shoring up allegiance from individual members.

Conservatism has played a lengthy role in ferreting out systems and traditions that appear to usurp fundamental liberties afforded individuals whose country values human agency. But JPUSA appears to strike a unique balance, bolstering individual identities (inward service) while, as a community, providing rescue services to persons in the neighborhood (outward service). In keeping with its vision of activism, its structure is such that symbiotic relationships between individual communards, the commune, and the Uptown neighborhood strengthen communal solidarity. JPUSA's genesis set the stage for its raison d'être.

THE BIRTH OF JESUS PEOPLE USA: BRADY STREET HIPPIES

Just as the Haight-Ashbury district of San Francisco is commonly associated with hippies, Brady Street in Milwaukee, Wisconsin, is considered ground zero for one of the most significant Jesus freak communes of the Jesus Movement. JPUSA formed out of a larger Milwaukee group headed by Jesus Movement evangelist Jim Palosaari. Along with wife Sue Cowper, Palosaari assisted Linda Meissner to form the Jesus People Army (JPA) in Seattle, Washington. Meissner later joined forces with the controversial Children of God, leaving Palosaari to form a counterpart to JPA. Jesus People Milwaukee (later renamed Christ is the Answer, under the direction of evangelist Bill Lowrey) formed in 1971 after a "Jesus march" in the city, culminating in the founding of the Jesus Christ Power House, a coffee house in the countercultural neighborhood of Brady Street. John Herrin Sr. (formerly affiliated with the Advent Christian Church, Assemblies of God, and the Methodist Church) and Dawn (Herrin) Mortimer were profoundly attracted to Jesus People Milwaukee. The Palosaaris went on to found Jesus People Europe, which spawned the community's first music group, the Sheep. Jesus People USA began in 1972 as a traveling "Jesus music" group. Palosaari's son Jedidiah recalls that his dad wanted to "spread the wealth and John Herrin [Sr.] wanted to leave with a group of people and start his own thing with JePUSA [sic]." Jim Palosaari "decided to just go ahead and bless that, and send them out."[14]

The Jesus People U.S.A. Traveling Team began touring with approximately sixteen members, traveling the United States in a painted school bus with the word "Jesus" painted on the side, holding "ad hoc revivals in small towns"[15] referred to as "Jesus rallies." Glenn Kaiser (who joined in 1971), Herrin, and the Jesus music band Charity (later the Resurrection Band, then Rez), eventually developed their own identity and purpose. The group finally landed in Gainesville, Florida. Using a combination of rock music and street witnessing, the fledgling JPUSA began to spread the gospel to the tune of rock 'n' roll.

Now a transient community, JPUSA embarked on a journey that was merely the beginning of a series of temporary houses, the first a ramshackle house previously owned by the Vietnam Veterans Against the War, and then one formerly occupied by Hare Krishnas. Community member Jon Trott has recorded the changes undertaken by the young group: "With the house also came an old synagogue next door which served us as a coffeehouse; in addition, we briefly ran the one-night-a-week 'Harvest House' coffeehouse located in the basement of Rawlings Hall dormitory on the University of Florida campus. Meanwhile, the church folks had a hard time relating to us Northern hippies."[16]

Along the way, this band of believers picked up followers (between twenty and twenty-five) who felt transformed by what they heard and experienced through public concerts. The music group continued touring and, after extensive travel, was forced to consider the future. Longtime member

Tom Cameron recalls events that inspired the community's decision to relocate: the band "never expected to be gone as long as they were gone, so they lost their lease on the place . . . so the first six months I was with them we lived in the big red Jesus bus driving around the upper-peninsula of Michigan doing concerts."[17] JPUSA founder John Herrin (son of John Herrin Sr.) offers an account of travelers whose purpose shifted:

> So we ended up kind of retracing some of our steps of where we had been earlier in the year and doing some concerts. And then when we got up to Duluth, MN. We kept getting more and more invites to come across the upper peninsula of Michigan. So we spent that whole winter [of 1972] just going from little town to town across Michigan and it was a great time. I mean you know everybody just had a little simple bedroll. Matter fact we'd left . . . pretty much everything we owned (which wasn't much) . . . in Florida, cause we thought we were going to be back in about three weeks. But we ended up staying up here and went from town to town, and I remember like a little town called . . . its name is Ontonagon.[18]

Herrin recalls rumors that the West Coast Jesus Movement was making its way to the Midwest. Rumors quickly spread about the coming of Jesus freaks and their invasion of small-town America. But the music group was well received in Ontonagon. Herrin notes how the group of Jesus freaks must have, at the time, appeared to be a "pretty raggedy looking bunch" to rural, middle-American towns. Then, in February 1973, JPUSA was in Michigan once again, spearheading revival efforts. The towns of Ontonagon, Houghton-Hancock, L'Anse, Baraga, Ironwood, and Marquette each "experienced the Jesus movement's full power," recalls Jon Trott.[19] A local newspaper in the Houghton-Hancock area of Michigan wrote an impressionistic entry, descriptive in the sense of small-town exposure to something already occurring on a national scale: "A large bus and several cars with Jesus painted on the side roll into the Houghton-Hancock area. Thirty-six freaky-looking kids spill out onto the streets. The girls with ankle-length dresses and long-haired boys fortified with armloads of papers scatter and start rapping with the closest passerby."[20]

FIGURE 2.3 Commune members performing in front of the "Jesus bus." © 2010 Cornerstone Press/Jesus People USA Evangelical Covenant Church; all rights reserved.

The article goes on to identify the young JPUSA as "people from all backgrounds" including college students, high-school drop-outs, and "'heavies' who have smoked, and dropped shot their way out of reality." The common denominator, the article reported, was the transformative aspect of conversion to Jesus. The account also demonstrates how JPUSA diverged early on from other communes that were isolationist and captures the zeitgeist of the larger Jesus Movement:

> Each morning the group assembles to pray and study the word of God. Classes include studies in Romans, Apologetics, Old Testament Survey, Life of Paul, the Study of Cults, Christian Leadership and various leading Christian teachers. The afternoons are spent on the streets witnessing person to person. In the evenings, the group gathers for rallies which feature the "Resurrection" Jesus Rock Band.... Their purpose is to help build

up the Christian community here. The Jesus People U.S.A. have worked with all kinds of churches, schools, and many different Christian organizations. They are available for programs in churches, youth groups, ladies circles, classes, and prayer groups. Jesus People U.S.A. is a ministry totally supported by the faithful giving of people concerned about the "drop out" generation.[21]

Herrin has particularly fond memories of the time spent in Ontonagon:

And I remember we went out that afternoon passing out flyers—of course this is the dead of winter—you know at least probably late February or something in the upper-peninsula—so cold and snowy in this little town. We're passing out flyers to the kids after school and then that night we held our first rally there and I remember thinking, "You know, I don't know if anybody's going to come to this dinky town." And here we are in the middle of nowhere and it's freezing cold outside. . . . There [were] probably about eight hundred people showing up that night at that gymnasium. And this is a town of a thousand! I'm thinking, "Holy cow where did all these people come from?"[22]

These experiences were formative on a different level, as the band considered increasing its own power of the countercultural vernacular. Between the late 1960s and early 1970s, Jesus Movement music groups (often dubbed "Jesus music") showed a clear connection to folk-rock. Others went on to mirror mainstream pop in burgeoning (though infant) contemporary Christian music. Quite distinct from the young Jesus music scene, early JPUSA members were influenced by the rock music stylings of Jimi Hendrix, Cream, and Led Zeppelin. Recalls Herrin:

We had kind of switched the band from being a little more of a folk rock kind of a sound—almost a Crosby Stills and Nash kind of an early sound—to where Glenn's heart always was [Glenn is a member of JPUSA's Rez Band] . . . a full-blown rock-and-roll band for the Lord. And we really switched it over and I started playing drums in the band that fall of '72, and we . . . traded in all the acoustic instruments for electric ones and just went for it. So we ended up traveling all through that winter and early spring, and we ended up in Chicago on a break.[23]

This shift laid a foundation that would significantly affect how popular evangelical music would be conceived. The band's decision to adopt hard rock would later prove seminal in the history of Christian rock, as it went on in 1978 and 1979 to produce "two blistering hard rock albums that surpassed anything the Christian music culture had produced," recalls Mark Allan Powell.[24] This change in genre represented an entirely new stylistic orientation, later inspiring the creation of JPUSA's edgy Cornerstone Festival, an alternative to the slicker festivals that have peppered the landscape of evangelical pop music.

The group remained on the road for approximately one year, wondering about their end-goal, their purpose. JPUSA faced a crossroad. After a lengthy stint of traveling, it would later come to understand its lifestyle as "intentional community." The revival concerts eventually led the small group to Chicago.

SETTLING IN CHICAGO

The political battles and mythologies commonly associated with Chicago are formative, when considering the epoch of any community or social movement; in some ways, socially conscious groups that call Chicago home are influenced by sociopolitical ghosts. Its history as an industrial city is one of both success and failure. A bastion of international culture, the "city of big shoulders" is known for gothic structures, the University of Chicago, high-rise apartment slums, Victorian houses, great factory systems, ghettos fraught with gangs, and homelessness.

For some founding members, the choice to settle in the city was unexpected. John Herrin is a bearded, earthy sort with long hair. His demeanor is disarming, indicating his familiarity with being interviewed (and his abilities as a leader). A gravelly voice gestures at storms weathered. Herrin's persona is more like that of a ranch hand than one who has spent his life with a groundbreaking urban hard rock band. A lover of backpacking, he has a rough exterior that is perhaps a byproduct of inner-city community life and frequent visits to JPUSA's property in Bushnell, Illinois; Herrin likes to hunt on the Cornerstone Farm. This veteran and founding member cherishes the commune, noting the simplicity of life lived without collared shirts or slacks. His primary position in the community once placed him at the pulse of the music industry as he directed one of Christian music's more edgy and controversial festivals.

Although stopping in Chicago proved serendipitous, the group's original intention did not include an urban setting. Herrin recalls thinking, "If we are going to find someplace to put down roots, we [want] to live in the country where our kids [can] run around barefoot in the grass and . . . do whatever young hippies do."[25] But the pastoral ideal of communalism did not come to fruition for JPUSA, at least in the conventional sense. While they chose to live in Chicago, the commune was still able to secure land in a rural area. Around 1977 a reader of JPUSA's publication, *Cornerstone*, offered 230 acres of land near Doniphan, Missouri, to be operated as a retreat center and farm. Veteran member Jon Trott writes: "What old hippie, saved or not, had never dreamed of having his own cabin snuggled in the woods? We accepted the offer and soon reported in C-stone [*Cornerstone* magazine] that we'd begun constructing a massive log lodge."[26] For years the community used the center for vacations and communal retreat functions; then the caretaker of the land became ill. In 1991 JPUSA purchased land in Bushnell, Illinois, offering the ever-expanding Cornerstone Festival more space and freedom. The timing was right—JPUSA sold the retreat center circa 2005.

While the group has had ample opportunity to enjoy country living (albeit intermittently), JPUSA's home has, since the beginning, been about offering outreach within an urban environment, a grand gesture that, for them, evinces a level of social justice that is on par with biblical teachings on community and economics, despite the "socialist" implications. Evangelicals have not always been credited for progressive social tendencies, let alone attempts at shared communal living. Given the Midwest's history of evangelical reform and countercultural activism, Chicago seemed the perfect fit.

The stop in Chicago was simply another event, but the community needed a base from which to work and plan the future. Originally JPUSA planned a brief stay, but members remained for about two weeks in an old converted building, which was at one time a "gambling house of some sort," recalls Herrin. The council was approached by the head of the Chicago Full Gospel Businessmen's Association, who offered the group modest living space in the basement of Chicago's north side Faith Tabernacle. Once merely a traveling rock group, JPUSA's heartfelt band of believers truly felt they could save souls. But the indigence they witnessed was life changing. After talking with people and listening to their problems, the team considered divine guidance: "Maybe God wanted us to stay in Chicago, maybe that's why we came here."[27]

For the leadership, Chicago provided a supportive environment. Herrin believed some city officials appeared to maintain a "Catholic understanding" of intentional community and social justice and offered a supportive environment for JPUSA's choice to live communally. But why would a commune feel *less* supported in another city? Yes, the Reverend Billy Graham had essentially endorsed the Jesus Movement. And yes, the idea of Christian communalism was hardly groundbreaking, considering the many groups that popped up throughout the nineteenth century. But the idea of a Jesus freak commune still appeared anathema to many within the American mainstream. JPUSA's *Cornerstone* captured public sentiment:

> To the public mind a commune is either a group of drug subculture freaks, or radicals who have copped out on reality, living in cloistered protection. Most people rarely think of the possibility of a community living by Christian standards. . . . [They] are probably repelled at the idea of having to share their lives with so many other people. However, we have found it highly rewarding as well as demanding.[28]

Despite negative perceptions, JPUSA adopted a communal model and continued an identity in keeping with Jesus People Milwaukee's original vision: a "discipleship school, street-witnessing, and rallies with the band."[29] Having been an elder with Jim Palosaari's Jesus People Milwaukee, John

Herrin Sr. (originally referred to as "Papa John") assumed the leadership role of Jesus People USA from the beginning. Although Herrin Sr. was considered the primary elder, JPUSA maintained the council model previously established in Milwaukee, including deacons and deaconesses: Dawn (Herrin) Mortimer, Richard Murphy, Glenn Kaiser, Karen Fitzgerald, Mark Schornstein, Janet Wheeler, and Denny Cadieux. However, it was clear the bulk of responsibility fell on one man, the death-knell of many communes.

Attracted to another communard's wife, Herrin Sr. fell into disrepute with the community after refusing to repent. Encouraged to seek help, he was asked to leave the community on March 18, 1974. This led to a change in leadership structure. The council had been active under Herrin Sr., but after the elder's departure it carried a new sense of power as the idea of plural leadership emerged, which proved pivotal in JPUSA's success as a community. JPUSA decided it would never operate under a singular leader again. Richard Murphy and Glenn Kaiser became the new leaders, and the council carried a renewed sense of authority.

Finding a tenable organizational structure proved challenging as JPUSA entered a new chapter in its history. Along with Kaiser and Murphy, the council would later grow to include John Herrin, Jr., Denny Cadieux, Victor Williams, Tom Cameron, Neil Taylor, and Dawn (Herrin) Mortimer. Jon Trott (former writer and contributor for JPUSA's now defunct *Cornerstone* magazine) has considered the difficulties faced in the early years:

> The older members of the community searched the Scriptures for answers to what had taken place. It wasn't as though there were plenty of people to ask. Christian community among evangelicals is almost unheard of, and was even more so in the mid-seventies. The Book of Acts, which had provided a sort of blueprint for living in community for the Jesus People, painted plurality of leadership as a norm."[30]

Glenn Kaiser and Richard Murphy relied on the Book of Acts and their own sense of collective need. For Kaiser, the need to live communally amounted to a desire to hold one another spiritually accountable while living what they argue is the truest model of the "Jesus way." But as we shall

FIGURE 2.4 JPUSA, circa late 1970s, near Montrose Beach at Lincoln Park, Chicago. © 2010 Cornerstone Press/Jesus People USA Evangelical Covenant Church; all rights reserved.

see, this new structure of authority would not come without its own set of challenges.

The fall of a leader often signals a community's downward spiral. But JPUSA regrouped, seeking to avoid the pitfalls of what it considered isolation and extremism. Moreover, it began to experience what Trott calls "sociological detritus" as the community evolved from a group of single hippies to married couples. As young families emerged within the growing community, JPUSA's pioneering spirit yielded to the call of stability. The young community became settlers.[31]

For a commune that developed during the Jesus Movement, the idea of settling down was, in many ways, at odds with the apocalyptic thrust of other Jesus freaks. According to research conducted on JPUSA between 1974 and 1975, the group demonstrated a sense of balance largely absent in the Jesus Movement. David Frederick Gordon argued that balance was a major theme in JPUSA's theology and lifestyle: "structure and spontaneity, submission and love, criticism and praise, teaching and worship, and recreation and work." Gordon's findings note the oft-held belief that early Jesus People (the larger movement) were often "presented as proof-texters who quote Bible passages out of context, accept every word of scripture as literal truth, and generally have a simple-minded approach to the Bible." Challenging this, Gordon found that JPUSA members admitted "the Bible is ambiguous and requires interpretation, that context is crucial to understanding passages, that the Bible does not contain all answers (although it does contain all necessary answers), and that careful study of the Bible and commentaries is necessary for full understanding."[32] Even in its early stages JPUSA demonstrated a measure of flexibility crucial to its survival.

Having chosen Chicago as home, JPUSA had to identify lodging suited to its long-term goals. Faith Tabernacle's basement served immediate needs, allowing the group to grow as the search for a permanent home began.

THE SEARCH FOR HOME

After its inception on Brady Street, JPUSA engaged a world already experiencing a groundswell of countercultural ethics and spiritualism. For this young community any sense of home or stability was associated with temporary scenarios that prioritized evangelism, including life on the road in a "Jesus bus" and a lengthy stay in the basement of a church. After growing out of Faith Tabernacle, JPUSA landed in a house on Paulina Street in the Ravenswood neighborhood of Chicago. The quarters were cramped. Lacking space, the community had to rent a number of storefront offices to run their burgeoning businesses.

In 1977 the growing community purchased a two-story house across the street, a new dwelling quaintly dubbed "the Yellow House." While these living conditions did not appear optimal, they were, after all, part of a shared experience encountered by other Jesus communes and houses. People who chose to live in the community viewed this arrangement as their only hope.[33] But life was not lived in a bubble. JPUSA's impact was felt in other neighborhoods, creating awareness among other like-minded communities.

FIGURE 2.5 A community gathering in the basement of the house on Paulina Street. © 2010 Cornerstone Press/Jesus People USA Evangelical Covenant Church; all rights reserved.

The leadership had been developing a relationship with another intentional community on Chicago's south side. New Life was an African American–based community that saw in JPUSA a vision similar to their own. Cognizant that the Jesus Movement was largely white, JPUSA longed for an interracial community but was careful not to co-opt the existing body or structure. Then, in 1978, New Life elder Ron Brown, his community, and the leaders of JPUSA decided to merge.

Even in the early years JPUSA's modus operandi appeared flexible and adaptable to the group's surroundings. In his research on JPUSA, David Gordon advanced an argument that the community's ability to value both the individual and the communal contributed to their sense of ideological balance:

> One reason that this particular Christian identity is so compelling is that it simultaneously locates the individual at each of these various levels [a

hierarchy involving God, Jesus, and various Christian expressions]. Each identity focus gains reinforcement and legitimation from the others. The search for personal identity becomes intertwined with God's will and with the fate of the world.³⁴

This ticklish line between the good of the collective and the individual continues to mark the landscape of American politics, particularly during the 2012 election and debates that surrounded President Obama's proposed polices on health care and taxes. And it continues to haunt evangelical Christianity as the two poles rip at the fabric of the evangelical electorate. It goes without saying that both the American political system and American coreligionists continue to polarize, as any true center either dissolves or shifts into something largely unrecognizable. And while most concede that this attempt to balance individual need with the collective good is both noble and possible, efforts to articulate the ways this can be truly realized are often blunted, each argument swallowed up, then lost within cascades of sound bites, punditry, and attempts to wrangle the base. What to do?

Those on the left often estimate that fortune has never been shared. In some ways, analyzing JPUSA might help us locate new, inventive approaches to our country's political system, shared values, and the challenges associated with democracy and pluralism. Indeed, as with other communities of faith, JPUSA might not serve as the most robust model for responsible human behavior. Similar to other evangelical communities (as well as the Catholic Church), this group has had its fair share of moral missteps. But this in no way invalidates the fact that JPUSA has managed to make its communal experiment work. For starters, it's worth mentioning that communities often succeed when there is a collective agreement about a shared "higher purpose," whether religious or secular, a common cause. But having a purpose is not enough. Successful communities must maintain a number of ideological structures that collapse both higher purpose and personal identity into one holistic being. In other words, when the goals of the community and the "reinforcement and legitimization" of the individual become synonymous, both individual and community become indelibly linked, thus driving commitment to the extent that leaving the community seems unthinkable. Gordon's observation is revealing. His findings suggest that JPUSA demonstrated early on a commitment to affirming individuals *within* a communitarian context. And in this case, individuals were affirmed in their own unique expressions (hippies, punk rockers, goths, etc.) and provided a grand mission with which they identified and to which they fully committed. God's call to help the less fortunate galvanized the community.

It became evident that Uptown would become JPUSA's mission field. Considering the diversity of the neighborhood, JPUSA's *Cornerstone* offered a depiction of the area, highlighting Uptown's historic multicultural milieu:

> Uptown truly is unique. It is the home of the most complex culture of people anywhere. Carlos Plazas, Ph.D., Executive Director of Edgewater Mental Health Center, states, "For many years Uptown has been considered a kind of port of entry for people who are coming from different areas of the country and even different countries of the world. . . . For example, at this moment there is a 40% white population, 30% Latin American, 20% from different countries in Asia, about 18% are blacks, and 8% native American people."[35]

Based on David Fremon's analysis, Chicago is "the most segregated major city in the nation." There are "two Chicagos—one black, one white."[36] And yet those from disparate backgrounds live within walking distance. Overall the wards appear to be largely organized around community need, business, class, race, and ethnicity. Considering the demographics of Uptown, Fremon writes: "The rich and the poor live here, and it is uncertain which group will dominate the area over the next decade." Gentrification has been "given a boost." Charges have been made that "historic district status was being used as a tool to force low-income people out of the area." It is no surprise that "poor people abound in uptown." The 46th Ward has been "a port of entry and home for transients ever since the first apartment hotels appeared in the 1920s."[37] Given the cultural and political climate of the 46th Ward, it is little wonder that JPUSA's fledgling Rez Band considered the needs of Uptown when seeking a permanent home base.

By 1979 the community relocated again, to 4707 North Malden, a move that marked a new chapter in their epoch. The local paper, *Uptown News*, commented on JPUSA's purchase:

> A Christian missionary group has purchased the Chapman hotel, a former halfway house at 4707–4711 N. Malden, and says it plans to help Uptown's poor and needy. The religious order, which calls itself Jesus People, U.S.A., bought the hotel complex at an undisclosed price [it was approximately $300,000] from the owners of the Traemour and Stratford nursing homes—two institutions which have been in and out of hot water with state officials because of building code and health code violations. The Chapman also has a history of housing code violations.[38]

As the 1980s unfolded, JPUSA discovered new, increasing needs in Uptown. Poverty was very real. The sense of urgency increased as Uptown's homeless population reached critical levels. Writes Jon Trott:

> As "Reaganomics" took hold in the early 1980s, homelessness suddenly became one of Uptown's most noticeable features. Entire families had nowhere to go. The total number of those we provided dinner for grew (to between two hundred and three hundred a day), and the complexion of those eating with us changed as well, from predominantly single men to entire families. The vast government cuts in housing programs also created a tremendous demand for temporary shelter of any kind. It was obvious that housing had become Uptown's most pressing problem, and we were compelled toward finding solutions.[39]

The 1980s proved difficult for the struggling JPUSA and for Uptown. President Reagan's policies were "immediately visible on the street. . . . Whole families were homeless" owing to the Reagan administration's chopping of the welfare system, according to Trott.[40] The rising population of homeless persons and the dispossessed seeking aid made the search for real estate an ongoing challenge. But this was simply part of a larger lurch toward increased privatization. Ronald Reagan "all but promised to dismantle federal housing programs in 1980," notes journalist by Ben Joravsky, "and he was elected president. Once in office he kept his promise, and he was reelected."[41] Not surprisingly, the politics of the day crystallized JPUSA's purpose as it undertook what amounted to swaths of social justice crusades; *Cornerstone* launched spirited protests through critical journalism. But this recognition of social inequity went beyond mere musings about class struggle. Resembling the practical activism of the New Left, JPUSA's hearty determination distinguished its approach to social justice from that of so-called limousine liberals. Along with considering (and often challenging) economic policies supported by fiscal conservatism, in grassroots fashion the community became publicly vocal, resulting in a growing influx of homeless families seeking refuge in JPUSA's lobby. And *their* version of the Left would soon be heard through music.

In 1980 the community moved yet again. As is the case with communes experiencing growth and mission (particularly urban-based groups), finding appropriate real estate is always problematic. To efficiently accommodate their congregations, successful communities deal with problems associated with growth: local expansion or the creation of satellite groups. JPUSA chose the former. Once again the group packed and moved, relocating from the house on Malden Street to 4626 North Magnolia, only one block away. "Though the building's front facade rose in beautiful castle-like minarets," writes Trott, "its rooms were studies in squalor, infested with both rats and cockroaches."[42] The new home was livable within two weeks. But this location was dependent on the community's ability to negotiate with the socioeconomic culture emerging around them. In 1984 JPUSA delivered a mailing that referred to the rising housing crisis, stating,

> A mother losing her welfare check needs us to watch her five kids for three months, another mother having to move out of a bad living situation has to have a place for her two children until she can move. We continue to feed 200–250 people from the streets each day; also many additional food baskets go out. . . . The need for emergency housing seems to be on the upswing with people coming nightly for a place to sleep. We will be helping with the overnight shelter when it opens again this winter.

If Trott's estimate is accurate, JPUSA was positioned for the perfect storm. By 1985 "nearly fifteen-thousand units of low-income housing vanished in Uptown."[43] Then urban renewal created a mess—gentrification.[44] The needs of low-income persons in Uptown began to reach critical mass. Trott's account of that season is sobering: "Winter is nipping at our heels; it may be discomforting for us now and then, but for others their very existence is at stake. This is one of the reasons we, as a community and church, provide emergency housing."[45]

By the end of 1985 a developer purchased a number of buildings with hopes of turning Uptown into an upscale neighborhood. The incentive was a 20 percent tax break. Then by 1986 housing occupied by nearly forty Laotian and Cambodian families, according to Trott's count, had been marked for gentrification. Protests began, but with little effect. "This was the first any of the families had heard about being evicted," writes Trott.

> Fearful but determined, they told us about their plan to stage a march on the developer's offices. On August 16, 1986, we stood at the end of Malden and watched as a determined band of refugees holding signs came toward us. We added 150 JPUSAs to their number, armed with our own signs: "Uptown NOT Yuptown," said one. Seeing us, one of the march leaders burst into tears. "Many of us were afraid to come. The police in our country. . . ." He didn't need to say more.[46]

The march did little but yield a gesture of recompense—one thousand dollars relocation money offered by the developer in an attempt to sell a cleaner political image. The *Chicago Sun-Times* highlighted what the displaced felt, quoting a member of Uptown's Lao Association: "We have started rebuilding our lives here. . . . Sometimes I start feeling: What is the promise of America if hard work doesn't mean anything, if someone with more money can come and push you out."[47] Rent was doubled and poorer residents were forced out.

As the problem escalated, JPUSA joined forces with various religious and social service organizations to form the Uptown Task Force on Displacement and Housing Development.[48] The community began discussions with former member of Students for a Democratic Society and Black Panther supporter Helen Shiller. JPUSA chose to align with her campaign for alderwoman, a close race ending in Shiller's victory, which is attributed to JPUSA's collective vote. David Fremon observed that "in the end, it might have been an unusual constituency which decided the election. Jesus People U.S.A., a religious group with many members living in the ward, supported [Jerry] Orbach throughout his career. They suddenly switched to Helen Shiller in the run-off. Orbach supporters charged that a city official had offered the Jesus People's construction firm city contracts if Shiller was elected—a charge the group denies."[49]

JPUSA would later feel the effects of its decision to support Shiller as other evangelicals voiced dissatisfaction over the community's socialist leanings, now made public. But despite conservative dissention toward JPUSA, members reasoned their expression of socialism was fully in line with Christian teaching, particularly when identifying political candidates whose positions on class struggle clearly evidenced greater sympathies toward the wealthy elite. Adding insult to injury, many within the Evangelical Right often belied their own affirmations of so-called Protestant uplift, often more fearful of would-be Trotskyites than empathetic toward classes who lived on the receiving end of unchecked corporate power. Orbach stated that "every vacant building in his ward either was renovated or scheduled for rehabilitation." Shiller countered, arguing that "Orbach was attempting to drive out low-income people and senior citizens," and that his funding came from "large developers."[50] For members of JPUSA, this was serendipitous.

The politics of gentrification forced the growing community onto a path that inspired grassroots activism, eventually leading to their current home and well-managed shelter for the homeless. But the journey was far from over. Two worlds came into conflict when the neighborhood's new, upscale residents found the lines of homeless dinner guests to be unsightly. JPUSA pastors sought new solutions. In 1987 they secured a two-story 21,000-square-foot industrial building, which served as a meeting place for Sunday services and the hot meal program. Then in 1988 they obtained a building at 939 Wilson to house the Crisis Pregnancy Center, which included free screening and alternatives to abortion.

After steadily building coalitions for radical resolutions, JPUSA joined with the Chicago Union of the Homeless and the Heart of Uptown Coalition to construct a tent city on October 8, 1988. Hoping to raise awareness about housing and gentrification, the new caucus set out to send a message. Complete with pup tents and houses constructed out of wood scraps and cardboard, the makeshift town included outdoor grills, fire barrels, and lean-tos that sported messages; one amounted to a written gesticulation against the virulence of city developers: "We refuse to freeze to death quietly."[51]

The last evening of the tent city brought with it the presidential debate between George Bush and Michael Dukakis. Chris Ramsey, comanager of JPUSA's homeless shelter, noted community-perception as the debate was watched on a portable television in the makeshift town: "The sheer irony of sitting outside in October," he quipped, "watching our Presidential candidates talk about what is important to them would have been laughable if it wasn't such a serious matter." Neither candidate mentioned homelessness.[52]

Helen Shiller and Jon Trott were both arrested. And the problems were not resolved, despite news coverage provided by Channel 9 (WGN). As Ramsey began patrolling the evenings, looking for homeless persons in need of rescue, the first-floor lobby of JPUSA's North Malden location housed fifty to seventy men and, by summer of 1989, ninety women and children. As the house became overcrowded, their own faith and commitment was tested: "How long would we love our neighbor when he smelled like urine and liquor, cursed at us, or defecated on the floor?" Despite the difficulties, the homeless became real—they had names, personhood. Now JPUSA simply needed more room.[53]

In late 1989 an old hotel located on 920 West Wilson Avenue was placed on the market. John Herrin recalls the events that led to JPUSA's acquisition of what was formerly the Chelsea building, stating that the previous owner was the classic slumlord who operated a building in violation of city codes. Unwilling to deal with the city's expectations, the former owner left, creating a situation where the building had no official owner on record, resulting in bankruptcy. In a violation of safety protocols, the old hotel was occupied by a large number of low-income senior citizens; the city stepped in, drawing media attention to the gross negligence of previous owners. JPUSA approached the city in an effort to place a bid on the property. Given the multiple liens, city officials decided on a public auction, seeking to award the building to the highest bidder. The JPUSA council feared what could have been potentially competitive. Herrin expected local developers to enter the picture, and they did.

> We got approached twice by a big named developer in the area [asking us] to go away. I got a call one day and a guy wanted to know if he could meet with us. And . . . I didn't know who he was. And I said, "Well sure, come on over." And we met and he basically made an offer, saying, ". . . we know that you guys are interested in this building too, and all you're going to do is drive the price up, and you're going to hurt us all. But there's no way you're going to buy it, because we have deep, deep pockets." So he basically wanted to know how much money it would take for us to go away. He was trying to buy us off and we were like, "Whoa dude, whoa hey, you've got to leave. . . . We were here praying, 'Maybe God will provide this building for us.' And I don't think what you're doing is legal and I think you need to go. So, please don't call."[54]

After being confronted by the developer on more than one occasion, Herrin began to believe JPUSA was in a battle with big money. Thinking the purchase was going to be a lost cause, the community decided to appear in court. Herrin recalls the moment vividly: "There were people standing all the way around the edges. I thought, 'Oh brother, there's like two hundred people here to bid on this building. We're sunk, you know, we're sunk.' But of course, there had been so much media attention." A $100,000 cashier's check was required to register as a bidder, which JPUSA had. An attorney (who represented a buyer) requested that the judge postpone the proceeding for thirty days. The judge denied the request, opening the bid at $250,000, which was cheaper than what JPUSA had originally offered.

JPUSA accepted the offer, no one raised the amount, and 920 West Wilson Avenue became the community's new home. They moved in 1990.

Finally settled and able to bring what would be titled "Friendly Towers" up to code, JPUSA could realize its larger goals as a community. It's easy to see how members (at least the founders) grew profoundly connected to a home discovered after years of struggle—a promised land, as it were. Both the new building and the inner city provide JPUSA with a sense of purpose. But their struggle is not unique. The United States has a history of revivalism and social reform, making JPUSA part of a larger story.

CONCLUSION

Although the Herrin family essentially founded JPUSA, the council structure evolved into a model of shared leadership. And the mantle of leadership can be handed down. Ronald Enroth (JPUSA's primary critic) has intimated at a sort of "family business" controlled by its founders. But JPUSA remains, in my estimation, a "collective" in the sense of shared responsibility. This is not to suggest that veteran members do not enjoy certain benefits. It is egalitarian in attempt, but hierarchy still creeps in. Some are afforded special privileges, to the chagrin of others. Furthermore, newcomers must prove they are serious about committing to the tasks at hand before enjoying special privileges, while veteran members (those who have weathered JPUSA's epoch) take vacations to visit family or hunt wild game on the Cornerstone Farm. Still, longtime members enjoy the same freedoms afforded founders; they qualify for consideration as council members. As members of the council leave or pass away, says John Herrin, new members can be invited by the council to join, as has been done in recent years. As we shall see later, JPUSA's leadership structure has evolved over the past ten years from a centralized to a decentralized structure, allowing different committees to provide oversight for various communal areas.[55]

Has JPUSA's genesis and journey provided clues to its longevity and, by extension, knowledge about how evangelicals must wrestle with pluralism?

And does the location contribute to recruitment and retention? Given what has transpired over the years in Uptown, a space has been created that welcomes any community willing to make a difference. Members dedicated to locating a final home found a sense of purpose in Chicago's inner city. This is "the old country church model," says founding member Glenn Kaiser. His depiction of daily life suggests some are drawn to the sort of communal authenticity largely absent within a world now defined by the rupture and fragmentation associated with social media. In other words, while social media undoubtedly connects us to the world and reconnects us with long-lost friends, it also removes the organic element of human interaction. JPUSA works, says Kaiser, because it is organic, yielding a small community that continues to experience all aspects of life together—a sort of barn raising.[56]

JPUSA's reach has extended beyond Uptown. The community was at once able to remain an active force of neighborhood rescue while maintaining a strong presence at their music festival. Categorizing the community remains challenging. But it's possible to locate their core impulse, one best found in the Evangelical Left, a socially liberal branch of evangelical Christianity. A quote from Howard Zinn best captures the connection JPUSA has to the spirit of social movements like the New Left. Zinn once observed that the New Left tried "to create constellations of power outside the state, to pressure it into humane actions, to resist its inhuman actions, and to replace it in many functions by voluntary small groups seeking to maintain both individuality and co-operation."[57] An enclave of resistance to establishment capitalism, JPUSA aligned with Jesus Movement Christianity, revealing nuances of how evangelicals are commonly understood or represented. The community is dedicated to avoiding the status quo of the evangelical subculture, challenges corporate greed, and interpositions itself where government leaders and programs prove incapable or unwilling to provide assistance to "the least of these."[58] What's more, the group affirms the individuality of each member and absorbs the unique qualities offered by newcomers, assimilating new cultural and ideological trends, allowing the commune to remain culturally relevant. But how does their desire to serve as a counternarrative to establishment evangelicalism actually work?

The community embraced socialism. But they have remained self-sustaining owing to an agreement with *industry*—an admitted connection to capitalism. Put simply, JPUSA businesses thrive as a result of the free market. So how are they socialists? Since the beginning, the commune's council decided to allocate money based on individual need, not effort. All assets earned by members are relinquished to the community. And over the years the group has grown in number and ambition, allowing for its social mission to transcend mere rock concerts or street evangelism. This commitment is tied to a collective suspicion of big business and corporate interests. Thus a kind of über dedication defines the community's core impulse. But can it continue?

To date JPUSA has enjoyed greater longevity because of its dedication to a grand cause and to cultural relevance. Theories of sustainability offer cogent reasons for its success. Despite the fact that few evangelicals know about JPUSA, its epoch may tell us something about why social and political pressure-points appear to levy power for special interest groups in the United States. As we continue to explore the group's relationship to the theological, the political, and the musical, a few gems that encapsulate this triumvirate will highlight a larger possibility: a gesture toward what is possible (even likely) for the greater evangelical subculture. The next chapter explores life within JPUSA's commune—how it's structured, how other evangelicals might categorize it, and how JPUSA's form of socialism appears to work. In short, the story of these Jesus freaks developed while the Religious Right simultaneously co-opted the Jesus Movement. In no small fashion this unlikely community is part of a larger story—the emerging Evangelical Left.

3
THE BLESSING AND CURSE OF COMMUNITY

✶ ✶ ✶

Images of rural farms spring to mind when one considers the idea of a commune. But in the case of JPUSA, "urban collectivism" is a more accurate description. Its location contributes to the retention of members and serves to attract new followers eager to find a sense of purpose. Chicago's 46th Ward is what David K. Fremon describes as an area that evokes images of "derelicts, flophouses, vacant lots, storefront day-labor agencies, resale shops, and taverns, with a social worker on every corner."[1] This hardly squares with the staid, romantic sentiments of communes often associated with *Walden Two*. The ten-story Friendly Towers is located at 920 West Wilson Avenue, a relatively dangerous neighborhood that has nonetheless improved over the years.

This chapter explores daily life in the JPUSA community and considers reasons the members were attracted to communal life, the importance of JPUSA businesses, and strengths and weaknesses of the group's government. It also looks at how second-generation and former members view this lifestyle, offering historical and impressionistic (at times anecdotal) accounts of life in JPUSA. The chapter ends by returning to the question of sustainability and longevity, putting forth possible reasons for JPUSA's survival since 1972, a major feat considering American evangelicalism's high valuation of private property and personal space.

FIRST IMPRESSIONS

An aging hotel looms over a street packed with cars, pedestrians, and sidewalks that could repel the foppish or the dandy. Some people stand near the entrance asking for spare change. Some hustle by, talking to themselves. And then the same person walks by again. Sirens. Car horns. Music blaring from cars. Jaywalkers weaving in and out of cars on the street, eager to make way to the other side. Friendly Towers and the street are quite unassuming when measured against the enormity of America's first Christian hard rock band.

Sporting a blue awning with white lettering that simply reads "Friendly Towers," JPUSA's building conveys a welcoming message, complete with planned graffiti on the walls and psychedelic images in the windows. The front door opens to a hallway covered by an ornate ceiling (a relic of what was once a hotel) ending at a locked door; people are buzzed in by those holding post at the front desk. Regardless of the time of day, one can expect to see a gaggle of activity involving a mix of old hippies, young punk rockers, goths, and senior citizens making their way to the senior's dining room or back to their ninth-floor apartments. At times one might notice those whose social interactions carry the unmistakable signs of mental illness. While an outsider might write the scene off as chaotic, it is readily apparent that all are members of a tight-knit community dedicated to shouldering the burdens of its members, many of whom display a certain sanguinity one might expect from utopian hopefuls. But in this case, utopia comes with expectations most would rarely consider. Those in need of aid often frequent Friendly Towers, a location known for its social outreach. JPUSA veterans recall the early days when the homeless even camped on the doorstep of the community. As we shall see later, this issue has (for the most part) been resolved through JPUSA's homeless shelter and soup kitchen.

With the exception of senior citizens, all communards live rent-free in small, modest apartments. Unlike in commercial apartments and motels, multiple tenants who walk the halls of Friendly Towers are treated in ways reminiscent of family members interacting early in the morning or late at

THE BLESSING AND CURSE OF COMMUNITY

FIGURE 3.1 JPUSA's current home, Friendly Towers

night. They exhibit a familiarity with one another in such fashion that constant greetings or common civilities are simply not needed. I was struck by how parents and grandparents trusted fellow communards as children ran down hallways to visit neighbors. (Where are they going, and can the neighbors be trusted around children?) And they are always ready to be approached by transient drifters and seekers. But is this safe for the children?

I approached, hoping for an interview. I've known various members for a number of years (particularly those in leadership) and continue to enjoy their friendship. But those whom I did not know at the time of my visits appeared wary, noting other works of journalism and research that had apparently misrepresented them.

At first blush each floor of the building functions as its own neighborhood, a kind of necessary stratification. While newcomers are housed in fairly basic rooms unmarked by the flavors of home and personal décor,

JPUSA veterans and leaders occupy their own floors and enjoy modestly equipped apartment rooms, allowing comfortable interaction between families and children who have lived together for many years. Individual apartments often reflect the personality of the tenant if he or she is a long-time resident. Small as they may be, apartments are decorated with images familiar to both the cultural mainstream and subcultures: bookshelves are constructed to accommodate limited space; mounted deer heads temporarily displace minds conscious of the inner city; guitars and pictures of religious icons share flat, vertical spaces; wooden frames combine the utilitarian and the romantic in bunk-bed, kitchenette combinations; apartment entries display artwork depicting music groups, hippie sentimentalities, political affiliations, biblical references; gothic iconography is reminiscent of a mausoleum, complete with plaster of paris tombstone hinting at fascinations with the macabre. Indeed, JPUSA shares money, food, and space, but individuality is still clearly prized as a countercultural badge of honor.

Unlike earlier communal experiments of the Jesus Movement, JPUSA no longer focuses on full-time street evangelism. Instead its members have no choice but to knuckle down if they are to survive. This sense of practicality has led to various domestic and foreign businesses that sustain the community. Indeed there are other post–Jesus Movement groups that also engage the wider culture. Among the more controversial include the Children of God (COG). Now the Family International, this debatable group has become ubiquitous, displaying a website that sports all the familiar attributes common to mainstream evangelicalism. The Family International remains ambiguous, taking care to avoid rhetoric that might implicate the community in practices that media already depict as unseemly. Jesus People USA made certain to delineate its community from those of other radicals such as COG. Ironically, JPUSA must now defend itself against accusations reminiscent of COG's own media onslaught.

In spite of recent developments, to the visitor life in JPUSA can seem rather mundane. Meals are prepared in a central kitchen and served in a central dining hall; those who live in senior housing have a separate dining room. Communards can choose to have meals in the main dining area or, as is the case with many veteran communards, retreat to individual apartments

FIGURE 3.2 JPUSA communards eating a late-night snack

after going through the food line. Along with the primary kitchen and communal dining room, each floor has its own common area, complete with sofas, chairs, and a small kitchen. Aside from meals prepared for the community, individuals are free to prepare their own food. If newcomers miss a meal and do not have a supply of their own, peanut butter and bread are always available in the main kitchen facility.

In some ways it might seem JPUSA has retreated into its own world of a large, extended family. But given its mission, it would be difficult for the community to become isolationist. And retreat has never been the organizing principle. The choice to settle in one location differentiates JPUSA from the Children of God and other radical groups. But haven't other communes also settled down and interacted with the wider culture? Unlike many of the isolationist communes that garnered media hype throughout the 1960s, other groups engaged their surroundings while remaining interstitial. Much like JPUSA, these hopeful utopians often worked regular jobs, returning to their communes in the evening.[2]

As will become clear, JPUSA's overall purpose differentiates it from other communes that were either isolated from mainstream culture or focused all attention on the end of time. This placed the group outside a common mythology, one associated with conservative organizations such as Calvary Chapel, Vineyard, and Shiloh Houses, evangelical fellowships that sympathized with the Jesus Movement. While these organizations had both communal and noncommunal members, each asserted an ethic common to the period and the movement: revivalism linked to apocalyptic urgency, political conservatism, and a strong sense of individualism. These three flagship organizations of the Jesus Movement all exemplified a near sectarian revivalism throughout the 1970s and 1980s, later becoming part of establishment evangelicalism. In comparison, JPUSA occupies a very different space, one somewhere between the isolationist impulse of groups such as the Children of God and Tony Alamo's Alamo Christian Foundation[3] and the establishment evangelicalism of Calvary Chapel and Vineyard.

Despite its own unique subcultural existence, JPUSA has remained open to the public, offering Sunday services to the residents of Uptown and to students attending local seminaries and Bible colleges. But the neighborhood of Uptown has changed over the years. Gentrification has caused many of the homeless to be relocated, and gang activity is in decline. However, my own impressions concur with Fremon's description of the 46th Ward. As I walked down an alley to visit Cornerstone Community Outreach, JPUSA's shelter program, I was struck by how dilapidated the area still appeared to be. The signs of poverty and mental illness were unmistakable. My effort to photograph the shelter's sign was met with obscenities from a man who joined the line for the evening dinner. "Rather than taking pictures, why don't you help?" The scene inside the shelter was little different from the one on the street. Single mothers, children, and a few men filled the dining room waiting to eat. Middle-class volunteers received instructions from a JPUSA communard who comanages the shelter with his wife.

As I tried to return to Friendly Towers before nightfall, hoping not to brave the streets alone, I considered the commitment it must take to keep JPUSA communards engaged in such a massive effort. The decision to commit oneself to such extremes must involve an attraction to a way of life that usurps the attraction of any particular group. So what's the attraction?

THE DRAW OF COMMUNITY

Members of JPUSA are drawn to a life of service and communal living. But given the nature of collective living, what's the appeal? Why do people (especially Americans, and particularly Christian conservatives) remain fascinated by communal living while still valuing private property, personal space, and the various edicts that have come to define American culture? Why are we supposedly more in danger when left to our own devices? And if living in a commune is better and healthier than our attempts to go it on our own, why do we appear to have a simultaneous need for and aversion to collective living? This answer is connected to the way communalism is commonly understood. Following the logic of Timothy Miller, how does one actually determine the communal ethic? Does it include street gangs, tribal villages, terrorist cells? Does it include apartment communities? While Americans remain unflinchingly individualistic, the communal ethic continues to attract interest. Americans still consume books and documentaries that explore the glories and failings of communal life. Yet there remains a conflict between communalism and individualism. Indeed, the communal way of life still captures the imagination. But it does so in the shadow of negative media depictions of collectivist cults.[4]

Our popular understanding and representations of communal living tend to be overly reductive, linking collectivist efforts to cultish hippie experiments or obscure nineteenth-century doomsday sects, not to mention those little-known groups infatuated by the predications associated with the Mayan calendar and the so-called apocalypse of 2012. When considering the reasons for attraction or revulsion to the communal ethic, we must think about the ways in which communes can be appropriately understood. As discussed earlier, "retreat" communities are defined by negative boundaries, while "service" communities are defined by affirmative boundaries.

The former seek to retreat from the evils of the world, are occupied by isolationists, and often lack the proper commitment for long-term sustainability. The latter engage society, are mission-minded, operate based on shared values, and often prove more successful than retreat communes.[5] This same formula can be applied to other spheres of life, including urban, suburban, and rural neighborhoods, businesses, educational institutions, and so on. JPUSA's model of community proposes enclaves, "voluntary small groups," which Howard Zinn maintains will "create constellations of power outside the state." In this sense (and within the context of our thoroughly embattled elected officials), the middle ground of the political can be found on the edges of corporate and state control. Against the rancor of concentrated power, JPUSA's arrangement is a kind of fiduciary model, whereby the property-owning powers are localized enough to (perhaps) avoid the sort of totalitarianism associated with unchecked government or big business. And while their model smells like an anarchical form of socialism, their inspiration comes from a Catholic luminary.

A twenty-first-century example of a service commune, JPUSA's organizational structure is inspired by the writings of Jean Vanier, Catholic founder of L'Arche communities. Vanier's *Community and Growth* (1979) has been a seminal document in the community's key principles. Its public statement demonstrates commitment to those in need and indicates religious inclusiveness:

> L'Arche enables people with and without disabilities to share their lives in communities of faith and friendship. Community members are transformed through relationships of mutuality, respect, and companionship as they live, work, pray, and play together. In these ways, L'Arche USA gives witness to the vision that people of differing intellectual capacity, religion, and culture can come together in unity, faithfulness and reconciliation. While some of our communities were founded in the Roman Catholic Church tradition, today L'Arche USA communities are ecumenical and welcome people of all faiths.[6]

JPUSA draws organizational inspiration from L'Arche. But true to its evangelical commitment, JPUSA maintains stricter boundaries of religious distinction. Vanier remarks that *"the secret of L'Arche is relationship: meeting people, not through the filters of certitudes, ideologies, idealism or judgments, but heart to heart; listening to people with their pain, their joy, their hope, their history, listening to their heart beats."*[7] *JPUSA, on the other hand, adopts a more modest form of ecumenism. Like L'Arche, members of JPUSA are drawn to a life of service toward those less fortunate. While they differ from L'Arche on religious pluralism, they also differ from other like-minded urban co-ops.*

Another group, Reba Place, was founded in 1957 as a Christian communal house. Initially the group included three people who shared in all aspects of life and possessions. After occupying one house just north of Chicago, Reba Place grew into "several communities and many ministries," according to its online statement. Members currently live in an "urban village" in Evanston, Illinois, "a mix of apartment buildings, single family houses, and commercial buildings sheltering a variety of cooperative ventures," seeking to share life and to live simply together in households.[8] The difference between Reba Place and JPUSA concerns location and purpose. While both groups seek cohabitation and simplicity, JPUSA's location warrants specialized outreach to the homeless. And although Reba Place shares JPUSA's vision of collective living and social justice, the location of Uptown forces JPUSA to engage the neighborhood in ways Reba Place or other evangelical communities cannot.

Geographical location and a sense of practical urgency reinforce a concrete sense of purpose for JPUSA. "The orientation of [service] communes," Kanter writes, "is toward service to a special population; they have a mission." But this does not suggest that Reba Place is not service oriented. Citing the Georgia-based Koinonia (founded in 1942) and Reba Place, Kanter argues that these communities have adopted a model of affirmation rather than negation, defining themselves by a set of values and belief-systems, insisting that "all members share them. . . . Service communes often control information across their boundaries as part and parcel of their mission to serve. They incorporate new information from the outside that will further the group's ability to perform its service. Rather than finding the continual intrusion of communication from American society to be threatening, a service commune may consider it useful 'data.'"[9] Although both JPUSA and

Reba Place share many commonalities, their respective locations create different impetuses for activism and different levels of social engagement.

INDIVIDUAL STORIES

Members of JPUSA have noted that life in the commune amounts to a call from God, one that includes a crucible, of sorts. Their stories often combine quaint memories of family life with the truculence associated with inner-city poverty and shared living. Nathan Cameron, a second-generation member and son of founding member Tom Cameron, appears to be correct in his own assessment of what attracts new communards. The most significant attraction JPUSA offers is that it conveys an interstitial lifestyle, attracting curious nomadic travelers. They hear about it from friends, says Cameron. And though people have not always come as a result of JPUSA's Cornerstone Festival, some show up to get a meal after the event and, at times, have chosen to remain, if only for a brief stay.[10]

The stories of older members highlight JPUSA's connection to the Jesus Movement. Now seventy-one, Curtis Mortimer was married to Dawn Herrin. Pleased to learn of a continued presence of Jesus People, he joined JPUSA in 1992. During the original movement Mortimer was a student at Saint Paul Bible College in St. Paul, Minnesota, with the Christian Missionary Alliance, where he trained to be a minister. He became disappointed early on with what he viewed as a false image often put forth by clergy but also believed that the movement was merely a passing fancy, a fad. But hasn't every generation nurtured the wildly disenchanted? Dropouts, antiestablishment types, longing for meaning and purpose. For Mortimer, the plastic, pastor-parishioner relationship was inauthentic and symptomatic of something wrong with the mainstream church.

Mortimer discovered a group of Jesus People sometime between 1970 and 1971 in a country farmhouse, where he became the ex post facto teacher. Following the teachings of theologian Watchman Nee, Mortimer gained a background in the concept of community and multiple eldership. Since Nee taught against the proliferation of denominations, Mortimer's first Jesus

People group avoided becoming a new church, hoping to live as part of a larger order. His discovery of JPUSA proved beneficial for both the commune and himself. Now having lived with JPUSA for a number of years, Mortimer notes that the leadership council exhibits an ability to interpret communal rules based on individual need—an important distinction from other collectives dedicated to one charismatic (at times despotic) leader with a single mission. Many who have been drawn to JPUSA are disillusioned seekers, spiritual zombies jonesing for acceptance. And they found JPUSA through the music festival.[11]

Crisis and quest are themes that appear in many stories told by members of the community. Now in her fifties, Dorena's five-plus years with the commune have met a deep need in her life. Her gothic attire contributes to the subcultural aesthetic ubiquitous throughout the community. The daughter of an itinerant preacher, Dorena rebelled and dabbled in the occult. Though she lived in a large home in California, her life felt empty, leading to her eventual conversion to Christianity. But despite her newfound faith, she felt estranged from God. With a history of cancer in her family, Dorena received her own diagnosis a few years back and was later miraculously healed. After an abusive marriage and a number of family deaths, she considered joining JPUSA, a decision that would reunite her with her daughter, who was already a member of the community.[12]

A young woman in her twenties, Raye Clemente has been a member for less than five years. During her spiritual quest she considered Buddhism and Unitarianism, ending her search with Christianity. Though she accepted the tenets of faith, she remained conflicted, hoping for an expression that was not, in her words, "greedy and Republican." Raye has struggled with how faith has been traditionally represented in the mainstream evangelical world. JPUSA offered something she could not find elsewhere, a kindred spirit felt at Cornerstone.[13]

A need for training inspired JPUSA to seek extrabiblical texts for theological guidance, unlike other isolationist communes associated with the Jesus Movement. In the early days JPUSA explored teachings designed to provide a needed ingredient if they were to avoid the overt experiential ethos common during the Jesus Movement. Training was mixed with practical application as members spent hours sharing their faith and meeting the needs of those outside the immediate community. Stories provided by founders demonstrate how the initial draw of community life involved a *crisis moment*, some sort of epiphany, and then a sense of divine directive leading to full commitment, which provided a strong familial base often lacking in precommunal life. Like Clemente, copastor Neil Taylor viewed life as unfulfilling until his conversion to Christianity in a "Jesus house" in Jacksonville, Florida. For him the concept of community was attractive. And like others, Taylor's attraction to JPUSA involved the Rez Band. His father accused him of throwing his life away when he joined in 1972. But according to Taylor, he narrowly escaped Hell.[14]

Tom Cameron was a "directionless college student" who needed to dedicate himself to some sort of spiritual vocation. After joining in 1972 as a "roadie" for the Rez Band, Cameron assisted the band with the heavy lifting associated with touring concerts. Now a pastor, in-house attorney, and director of JPUSA's Grrr Records, Cameron was allowed to attend Northwestern University Law School.[15]

Most members of JPUSA are drawn to practical expressions of faith. To that end, they have constructed their lives around serving others. Hoping to live with like-minded people. Lyda Jackson joined in 1975. Living "in community" was both a religious and a vocational conviction. She began by serving in the kitchen, mending clothes, and taking part in street evangelism. Now in her fifties, Jackson coordinates volunteers at Cornerstone Community Outreach, JPUSA's homeless shelter.[16]

A native of Modesto, California, Joshua Davenport has always been restless. In fact, he's been in and out of JPUSA since he was nineteen. But his story began earlier, a time marked by a growing anger toward organized religion. Feeling stagnant, trapped in a system adopted by his family, Davenport sought something new—an unfamiliar place where God could be found—if God was real to begin with. Now in his thirties, Davenport considers stability a viable option (finally) and hopes to remain settled. He and his wife are attracted to the way the commune supports their own ministry, marriage, and music, amounting to what he refers to as an "overwhelming sense of family." Simply put, JPUSA is a place where they feel safe.[17]

Susan joined after having been involved with another communal experiment on the south side of Chicago, the New Life Fellowship. This largely African American group was not linked to the Jesus Movement but still wanted to live Christianity within a communal context. In 1976 New Life secured a house and tried to "live out the Bible." Despite all efforts, its small size made the attempt difficult. After meeting JPUSA, members of New Life noticed similarities and then chose to combine efforts by joining in 1978.[18]

Living between two uniquely American dichotomies can be challenging for anyone, particularly if the Religious Right has nursed your leftist heart. Colleen Davick is from Dallas. She converted to Christianity at the age of eight. In the aftermath of her collegiate exploration in a Bible college, Davick experienced what she calls a "wandering period," a time when she was in search of a sense of purpose—a job that actually meant something in the grander scheme. After a period of self-analysis, Davick was drawn to communal living: "I wanted a deeper way of living besides . . . the typical American—live in your house in the suburbs, do a job—I wanted something, a deeper experience than that. I figured after coming to visit here, that . . . I would find that deeper experience here." Aware that JPUSA's community had something to do with Rez Band, *Cornerstone* magazine, and the Cornerstone Festival, she viewed the commune as a "cool place to go," one that offered that deeper way of life. Davick joined in 1992 and has never looked back.[19]

Many communards join while they are relatively young. Consequently, this requires a certain level of commitment to two different families. Not surprising, some parents of young communards often remain suspicious of a group that chooses to raise children in abject poverty. Others are sympathetic to any expression associated with the Jesus Movement, recalling their own storied past. Aaron Tharp is in his early twenties. His parents (affiliated with the Vineyard Church) had no conflict with him or his decision to join JPUSA. They simply asked him to research the community before joining. Tharp moved in 2008. He works on the "home crew" (where many newcomers begin), washing dishes, sweeping and mopping floors, doing the laundry, cleaning restrooms. And while he is not paid, Tharp insists that his true inspiration (his payment) comes from the knowledge that his services provide his friends with a nice clean home.[20]

These stories tell us something: attraction to JPUSA's radical way of life is a result of a number of factors. They illustrate that those who live in JPUSA all share common experiences, hopes, and dreams. Not all revealed are struggles with depression or crisis. But for most, JPUSA offers something largely absent from the cultural mainstream, particularly the church. For these members, there is a common binding thread. This manner of shared living underscores how leftist Christians can differ so greatly from the modern paradigms advanced by Christian conservatism. Put another way, travelers, seekers, and the marginal are attracted to JPUSA precisely because they reestablish the subversive elements of social activism while also offering what is strangely absent from the American mainstream. But even though the Jesus Movement's spirit has been sought after and celebrated within this community, JPUSA's structure diverges from its communalist forebears. And somehow it is able to combine the socialist ethic with free-market capitalism.

COMMUNITY BUSINESSES

JPUSA is good at assimilating culture, adapting to its environment, and remaining flexible enough to alter its approach when warranted. It has undertaken a number of business enterprises and ministries over the years, some successful and some not. Commitment to fiscal longevity and cultural relevance has kept it vibrant, in some ways belying the common notion that communal living breeds impoverished beggars. Yes, JPUSA is a socialist expression of evangelicalism. Yet there remains a commitment to engage free enterprise for the financial good of the immediate community (JPUSA) and the broader community (the homeless population in the 46th Ward). Some members seem to revel in the idea that they remain virulent anticapitalists. However, they still enjoy the fruits of the free market. While this dichotomy appears contradictory or Pollyanna-ish, this "agreement" with capitalism can simply be attributed to the way American society is already structured. JPUSA members chose to live in an urban area, which (in the absence of farmland) created the need to engage industry. So how is it socialism?

It's possible to reconcile the two seemingly incompatible systems simply by considering their economic structure on the micro level. JPUSA had to engage in industry to generate income since the government would not provide all needs. Then, to remain true to its own biblically inspired form of left-wing government, it had to embrace a "common purse arrangement," which placed it in a different category. Essentially, when considering matters pertaining to daily life in JPUSA, the council acts as the government, deciding *how* monies are distributed and to *whom*. Granted, this still amounts to a church-funded scenario (a conservative, business-friendly thrust) with little acquiescence to the state. But in the absence of socialism on the national level, JPUSA leaders have chosen to employ a left-wing paradigm within their own, local community, maintaining a system of government based on their interpretation of the New Testament. Thus the community is able to operate mission businesses (much like the tent-making venture of the Apostle Paul) while meting out monies according to individual need.

The most notable JPUSA businesses include Lakefront Roofing and Siding Supply, Belly Acres (a t-shirt printing company), Friendly Towers's low-income housing for senior citizens, Grrr Records, and the Tone Zone recording studio. Grrr Records signs a number of artists, earning most profits from revenue generated by the Rez Band and the Glenn Kaiser Band. With the exceptions of Tone Zone, Grrr, and Lakefront Roofing, the ventures are considered forms of ministry. And while both Grrr and the Cornerstone Festival have been the public faces of JPUSA, the roofing supply company remains its bread-and-butter.

Lakefront Roofing was established in 1985. The company has nurtured a steady stream of dedicated clients, despite competition. Advertising is largely accomplished through word of mouth, signage, and radio stations. Ads mostly target the user, not the contractor, creating leads and relationships, which generates work for customers. This has been a successful approach to business, says Chris Spicer, a leader in the company who joined JPUSA in 1983. Lakefront currently has five locations: three in Chicago, one in Schereville, Indiana, and one in Waukegan, Illinois. In an effort to extend JPUSA's ministerial arm, Lakefront also operates a business in Romania. Nehemiah American Romania Company (NARCOM) is a distribution center that deals in roofing supplies and other products. NARCOM functions as a "mission business," allowing JPUSA to maintain a location that partners with Osana Foundation, an orphanage that cares for children with AIDS. Given Lakefront's multiple locations, many employees are not members of JPUSA, and they are paid a salary. But JPUSA employees are paid a "virtual payroll," which goes back into the community purse.

The company often refers customers to contractors, stating that they "know the good guys," who are defined as "an insured, professional and licensed contractor that agrees to our Contractor requirements." Lakefront's Contractor Referral Program is a free service intended to satisfy home and building owners.[21] The web advertisement reassures the potential customer that they are ethical and will offer free advice:

> "We Know the Good Guys!" is a free Chicagoland roofing referral service sponsored by Lakefront Roofing & Siding Supply. Everyone benefits—Homeowners and Building Owners, Contractors, and Lakefront! Re-roofing your home or building doesn't happen every day. It usually only occurs once every 15–20 years. We work hard to help homeowners and building owners with free advice. In return, the business is usually placed with us, through the contractor.[22]

JPUSA continues to expand its borders, trying new ventures considered culturally relevant to its overall mission or potentially lucrative for the community. Over the years it has attempted a wide array of business ventures. The list of "experiments" is a telltale sign that it continues to seek out every possible method of remaining fiscally responsible, a wise move in the wake of Cornerstone's demise. The variety of businesses is both diverse and interesting: typesetting, a boutique store, carpentry, painting, moving, masonry, tree planting, hog farming, insect extermination, carpet cleaning, roofing, saw sharpening, electrical work, clothing design, sheet metal, window repair, human resources, cabinets and office furniture, printing,

Guatemalan window products, self-storage, a skateboard shop, and candy sales. Throughout successes and failures, members of the community have garnered skills important to maintaining their own dwelling. And while it is true that members are required to work for JPUSA-owned companies, and while there is a common purse that dictates an individual's ability or inability to function outside of communally established structures (lodging, food, health care, etc.), JPUSA's emphasis on individualism within communitarianism creates a certain measure of freedom.

Members are allowed to take modest side jobs outside of the commune, within certain limits, to earn extra money for a trip or a television by agreeing to complete a fellow communard's kitchen duties, haul equipment at a local bar, perform carpentry, or do other minor tasks. But they are not permitted a full-time career in a non-JPUSA business unless it serves the community.

A MODEL FOR EVERYONE?

Higher purpose notwithstanding, one may wonder how a worker's dedication can remain unfettered when confronted by American materialism. Rosabeth Kanter has considered the future of corporations, suggesting there are emerging "vanguard companies" operating on a level that exceeds merely maintaining the bottom line, seeking to instill certain values, hoping to contribute to changing the world for the better. Thus some Americans (particularly the younger generation) often demonstrate what amounts to a growing commitment to social justice, even at the expense of material gain. That this impulse can also be seen among young evangelicals indicates a fundamental shift in the post-1970s American evangelical paradigm.[23]

Kanter goes on to imply that the same social convictions that inspire communities like JPUSA (purpose transcending materialism) might become more prevalent throughout corporations. Any development such as this will prove exacting in its tidal-wave effect in the wake of corporate scandals and economic crises that have defined the past few years. But while this research implies the possibility of a mission-minded future—where corporations consider the needs of society over monetary gain—what is more intriguing about Kanter's research for our purposes is that it reaffirms that fiscal longevity, whether in business or in a community, is often determined by values that transcend the immediate goals of a particular business or community. This forms strata of values-based commitments that hold both large and small units to standards defined by the needs of the collective over and above those of the individual, *while simultaneously* affirming the validity and importance of individual need, value, and circumstance. This approach to community would seem to bridge the now widening gap in the United States between the community and the individual, public and the private.

COMMUNITY MINISTRIES

Although JPUSA has always been involved in social activism and outreach, the initial mission concerned its own version of Christian evangelism. But its understanding of evangelism is broader than that of other evangelical mission groups, particularly those formed during the Jesus Movement. After touring the country, JPUSA extended its idea of Christian outreach to include social justice in Chicago's inner city. Its list of ministries is as diverse as its business ventures: discipleship training to community members, care for older people, street witnessing, housing for the homeless, soup kitchen, low-income senior housing, Big Brother/Big Sister (mentoring), outreach to Mexico, Cambodian Outreach, Bosnian Outreach, Romanian Outreach (business supporting missions in Romania), Guatemalan Outreach, Pro-life Action Counsel, Crisis Pregnancy Center, new women's shelter building for homeless women, host for youth groups, a boy scout troop, Imagine DAT Model hobby building with kids, Cornerstone Festival, Grrr Records, and the now defunct *Cornerstone*, an edgy publication (1971–2003) that once offered analyses of music, film, and articles pertaining to theology, philosophy, culture, sexuality, global events, and various controversial topics often not found in other evangelical publications. Including a vast canvass of styles such as rock, heavy metal, punk, rap, black gospel, and Celtic, JPUSA's music groups encapsulate both the old and the new: Rez Band, the Glenn Kaiser Band (GKB), the Grace and Glory gospel choir, The Crossing, Cauzin Efekt, Crashdog, Brothers & Sisters United, Seeds, Sheesh, Ballydowse, Scientific, Leper, The Blamed, and Aracely.[24] These ministries are all important to members of the community, but they ultimately exist to serve JPUSA's most important outreach.

Just as Lakefront Roofing is the primary source of income for JPUSA, the shelter program Cornerstone Community Outreach (CCO) is the motivating mission for members of the commune. Functioning as a primary commitment mechanism, the shelter program inspires members to persevere in community life as they work for the communal paradigm, shouldering the responsibility of caring for those who need food and shelter. Obtained in 1989, CCO, a nonprofit organization, seeks "to raise the quality of life for low-income residents of the United States and the rest of the world through social, educational and economic development programs that include: development & preservation of decent & affordable housing for the poor, job training & creation, educational & social programs, and feeding & sheltering the homeless."[25] CCO offers housing for single women and men, single mothers and their children, other family units, and women who have been abused. (Note that CCO's housing for single mothers is not considered a battered women's shelter.) However, it has become "Uptown's own version of the Salvation Army," according to former alderman Jerome Orbach.[26] There are two large buildings under the umbrella of CCO. One operates as the cafeteria and houses women and children, while the second houses families, functioning as a daytime drop-in center for single men. A twenty-four-hour shelter, CCO's buildings house between 300 and 400 people, serve three meals per day, and average 125 for breakfast, lunch, and dinner.

A member of JPUSA since 1976, Sandy Ramsey manages the shelter program, along with her husband Chris. For Sandy and Chris, the Bible offers a divine mandate to feed the poor. The free-market social policies known as "Reaganomics," argues Sandy, created a dangerous scenario, which resulted in an increase in Chicago's homeless population throughout the 1980s. Sandy Ramsey and Jon Trott have both argued that throughout the 1980s, Uptown's homeless population in no fashion represented stereotypes associated with urban poverty. Substance abuse and addiction were not the only causes of poverty or homelessness, at least according to CCO. Products of Reagan's policies, working-class families became homeless in the wake of urban renewal. But urban renewal was not the only culprit here. Mental illness played a role in shaping Uptown, as well as other urban centers. When President Carter signed into law the Mental Health Systems Act on October 7, 1980, he sought to establish a program to encourage the creation of new community mental health services, an initiative that was to be administered by states but with federal funding.[27] At first blush this appeared to be a healthy direction in which to proceed, despite involvement by conservative special interest groups and "law and order" Republicans, who viewed imprisonment and involuntary institutionalization of mentally ill individuals as expedient ways to alleviate homelessness. But the opposite occurred. First, although involuntary commitment was usually reserved for those whose mental conditions warranted concerns over safety, laws that governed involuntary commitment were later expanded to include those who did not pose a threat to themselves or to society. This bolstered the business and income of health care professionals, maintains sociologist Alexandar R. Thomas. But the effect of this still feathered the caps of those interested in treatment for the mentally ill. One step at a time, bureaucratic processes led to a system that finally valued ongoing treatment. And this, says Thomas, was "counter to the financial goals of the Reagan administration . . . to reduce federal spending, reduce social programs, and transfer responsibility of many if not most government functions to the individual states." Then, on August 13, 1981, Reagan rescinded the law Carter had signed. "In accordance with the New Federalism and the demands of capital," writes Thomas, "mental health policy was now in the hands of individual states."[28]

Mental health services continued to be subject to budget cuts throughout the 1980s, reinforcing Reagan's philosophy that provision of services should come from the private sector. The result was catastrophic. The number of beds available to mentally ill people, according to Thomas, "dropped over forty percent between 1970 and 1984." As the 1980s wore on, the number of available beds increased in psychiatric wards and private hospitals, slowly privatizing the U.S. mental health care system. Ongoing treatment began to benefit private professionals rather than strap taxpayers with the burden. Patients, however, would benefit only if they had health insurance. As the private sector grew, a greater emphasis was placed on how mental illness produced profit. Those without insurance simply did not receive ample care. This, combined with the reduction in funding for public hospitals, hastened the premature release of mentally ill patients, many of whom would end up homeless. Economic redesign of health care and gentrification were two parts of a puzzle that would lead to the perfect storm. Writes Thomas:

> The concerns of the general public were also mobilized in the context of fear over the possibility of a patient committing a violent or otherwise antisocial act. Media attention paid to the problems of the mental health system tended to concentrate in two areas: the growing homelessness problem of the early 1980s and the possibility of criminal acts committed by deinsitutionalized patients. Throughout the 1970s and 1980s, hundreds of thousands of mentally ill people concentrated in the inner cities. With the rise of gentrification during the 1980s, many of them became displaced from their relatively affordable housing and were unable to find new accommodations. Many of these patients had lost contact with family members and were unable to work, and many did not have health insurance. Thus, they were unable to receive mental health services in the private sector. Media coverage of the growing homeless problem helped to pressure legislators in many states to rewrite commitment laws to extend the net and make the streets "safer."[29]

As homelessness concentrated in the inner cities, both religious and nonreligious activists marshaled their resources, hoping to alleviate the growing problem. Along with other activist groups seeking to resolve the issues connected to inner-city poverty, JPUSA began to house the growing homeless population in 1987. Its tent-city moment with its alderman was one effort to increase public awareness. Once it ended, homeless families remained, finding their way into JPUSA's lobby and living rooms. The Department of Human Services (now the Chicago Department of Child and Family Services) started unofficially dropping people off. Then the community struck critical mass: the need outweighed what JPUSA was able to provide. Approximately fifty men huddled in JPUSA's lobby. One hundred women and children were fed nightly, each sleeping on floor mats in the community dining room or on unoccupied couches. The situation was further complicated by the lack of funding. In 1989 elder Neal Taylor spoke with the commissioner of Chicago's Department of Human Services, indicating the difficulty. The result was a grant of $75,000. CCO was simply a natural outgrowth of human need as JPUSA's community became overwhelmed with individuals in search of shelter on their doorstep, in their cafeteria, and at times in their apartments.[30]

Along with outreach to Uptown's homeless, care for the elderly has remained a concern for the group since they obtained Friendly Towers. When JPUSA initially purchased the hotel the group agreed to take on the responsibility of senior housing units already part of the building. In so doing, the leadership council inherited a number of structural problems, which had to be resolved with expediency. Now up to code, the building houses approximately one hundred senior citizens. Senior housing manager David Baumgartner says residents are expected to pay $430 for rent and $25 for food per month, and JPUSA staff members are responsible for cooking meals and cleaning the rooms. Fifty-one units "receive subsidies from the low income housing trust fund, 4 are subsidized by the Chronic Homeless Initiative Grant (HUD & low income housing)," and "1 unit is a CHAC Section 8 voucher."[31]

I wondered how these senior citizens fare with so many hippies, punks, and goths in their midst. How do they coexist? In fact, many aging tenants welcome the most radical of neighbors. In the twilight of their years, they seem less concerned with appearances, simply valuing the diversity offered by neighbors: pierced, tattooed, sporting a myriad of hairstyles. For them, the comfort of friendship outweighs social mores established by the cultural mainstream. Eileen Freed, for example, is seventy-three and has lived in a senior unit for some five years. She moved to the community hoping to find an inexpensive place to call home. Freed is on Medicaid. While the community is free to use the public health services offered by Cook County Hospital, some opt for the house visits offered by a physician and psychiatrist who frequent the community.

THE NECESSITIES OF LIFE: BASIC NEEDS AND COMMITMENT TO COMMUNITY

JPUSA's organizational structure has provided elements that make sustainability possible, at least for the foreseeable future. Leaders are able to parlay the familial structure of interconnectedness into a network of community families, all dedicated to the cause. For example, whether married or unmarried, members are assigned to a family that is related to the council, which creates a nexus of multiple extended families within the larger community framework. Each council member is assigned ten to fifteen couples and unmarried persons. These extended families serve to maintain accountability for those who would otherwise fade into the background, which for JPUSA would be detrimental to spiritual protection and development. New members are particularly dependent on their assigned families to learn about their respective roles in the community, as well as guidance on matters pertaining to communal life. But for some this level of familiarity can amount to uncomfortable erasures of personal space. And according to some second-generation members, a few adult members of extended families have actually overstepped their boundaries, assuming the role of parent.

Extended families meet for dinners, celebrate holidays, go on picnics, and take vacations together. This may appear to be, in some sense, a replacement for an individual's real family. But members can visit their biological families, if they have the money. Jobs outside the community are allowed, providing they do not conflict with the commune. Much like the industrious swapping of lunches or baseball cards among siblings and friends, these communards can pay others to complete chores, which offers a modicum of holdings for the enterprising communalist. And if a member needs to purchase a costly item, he or she visits the office coordinator, who doles out money on an as-needed basis. Guidance also extends to personal lives. For example, if couples wish to date or marry, they must seek permission from family heads, who in turn seek permission from the leadership council. While couples hoping to marry may also seek guidance from biological parents, JPUSA's requirement for communal approval functions as a safeguard against behaviors deemed unsuitable or harmful to community cohesion.

JPUSA's location and socioeconomic context require certain levels of austerity, bearing in mind the enumerable fragilities that accompany this sort of subcultural community. Newcomers often exhibit elements of dysfunction, hoping to find healing through reorienting their lives under the guidelines of communal living. In an effort to protect these individuals from "temptation," JPUSA guidelines remain a tacit reminder of what is expected of all members. In some ways there is a continued sense of interrelational attachment within the community, one that demonstrates a certain consilience. And this model of living may very well offer evangelicals and other coreligionists hope as they struggle uphill to locate the perfect balance of democracy, pluralism, and stability. But given society's premium placed on materialism and individuality, why would one be attracted to any situation that requires giving up one's sense of a guarded self? For JPUSA, communal living deemphasizes material possessions and a personal agenda in hopes of identifying with the poor. Moreover, while individual needs *are* considered (everyone is allotted items or money according to their need), the overarching purpose is to realize the larger goals of the community. Perhaps this is precisely the attraction. Young members point out that mainstream society's pursuit of individuality merely serves to bolster an ideology of self-reliance. The result, according to JPUSA, is a society that is not "other-centered," or at least a culture that considers tepid attempts to darken the doors of the poor somehow worthy of recognition. And this, it argues, encourages social apathy.

The choice to adopt this way of life cannot be taken lightly. In fact, the expectations set forth by the founders are encapsulated in a more or less binding statement. Written in 1986 and revised in 1989, the *JPUSA Covenant* outlines the community's financial expectations and functions as an official document:

> JPUSA is taxed as a large partnership according to the Internal Revenue Code, section 510(d). Each provisional member becomes a partner upon

signing this covenant. All income goes toward food, housing, utilities, and maintenance costs, as well as our stated community purposes of evangelism, helping the poor, and discipling believers, all of which are paid for by our financial department.[32]

JPUSA leaders do not believe this way of life is for everyone. But they do maintain that their social activism exemplifies a kind of humanitarianism that was demonstrated in the life of Jesus, a perspective largely associated with left-leaning positions on social justice. Through her life, founding member Dawn (Herrin) Mortimer, who passed away in 2014, believed the church misunderstood the totality of the Christian mission. The mainstream evangelical church often evangelizes, she argued, without regard for the poor. When she considered whether the concept of evangelism includes social justice, Mortimer replied with shock, "How can it *not* mean that?"[33]

To be clear, members of JPUSA do indeed recognize the presence of other socially active communes and churches. But there is a genuine belief that a great number of faith-based communities merely define Christian evangelism as a means to share the gospel, to the exclusion of social justice or grassroots activism. Mortimer said that if "secular" society were to simply consider sharing resources (doing with just a bit less), they could better contribute to eradicating poverty.[34] But this community seems to be living with far less than they actually have to. Although members enjoy the basic necessities of life, they agree to a sort of vow of poverty, which affects the community's health care. In its attempt to identify with the poor in Uptown, JPUSA makes use of the free medical services offered by Cook County Hospital. And what of the wandering newcomer? The community has chosen to avoid tackling every health issue financially since a high percentage of membership tends to be short-term seekers.

They face a number of challenges concerning medical treatment, problems best resolved with universal health care, argued Mortimer. When asked which presidential candidate she favored, she was quick to endorse President Barack Obama, stating, "Is there any other?" For her, identification with the poor is an essential part to life in the community. In an effort to avoid slipshod activism or mere lip-service evangelism, JPUSA became poor to identify with the homeless. A radical move? Certainly. But the founders are still haunted by the failings of their evangelical brethren on the right.[35]

Noting that JPUSA lives based on the ideal—"everyone according to their need"—Mortimer recalled a situation where someone suggested dividing money up according to the needs of their Crisis Pregnancy Center. When one worker (it is unclear whether this was a member of JPUSA or a volunteer) shouted, "That is Communism!" Mortimer was dumbfounded. For her, this was a simple biblical principle, one that is organic and lived, as outlined in the *JPUSA Covenant*.[36]

As can be expected, some on the right have questioned JPUSA's harsh austerity measures. Offering a fairly leavened response to critics, Pastor Neil Taylor explained that while the letter of the covenant is not absolute in its authority, the spirit of the document informs communal commitment:

> The two-week stay is still suggested for any visitor, especially if they are thinking of staying long term. At this point, we do offer P-12[37] as a 10-month internship with JPUSA. The term commitment document was an attempt to say to those who have lived long term in the community that we should all continue to assess our commitments to life in community. The document became lifeless or ineffective as something we could manage and/or keep up with, but the heart of the document is still very much alive in that all members of our community are encouraged to stay in touch with their commitment to life here.[38]

The spirit of the *JPUSA Covenant* is explicit, according to Taylor. "We have seen many 'covenant communities' draw up a detailed covenant, then attempt to live that covenant out, resulting in either outright failure or (what's worse) sterile religious legalism. For ourselves, we find a covenant more an outgrowth of relationships than their cause." While the covenant is binding in terms of relationship, the council does not dictate lifetime commitments. Every few years each member must read and sign term commitments, but they are not required to commit for life. If someone breaks a term commitment, the breach is handled on a case-by-case basis. This acts as glue, encouraging members to give serious consideration to communal life before they act in haste. Simply put, the community counts on every person to contribute to jobs that keep JPUSA functioning. Term commitments serve as a covenant—built on tight-knit relationships—intended to ensure that all members are fully aware of the cost associated with a breach. And if someone wants to return after leaving, the council proceeds with caution.

When someone leaves, everyone feels it. Scott Jones (his real name has been withheld) left in 1998. For him, members who choose to leave often experience emotional trauma, and they create pain for the rest of the group. He writes:

> [I]in a way it was like being married to 500 people (there were about 500 members when I joined). And the understanding was that you would stay there for the rest of your life. That wasn't always preached in so many words, but it was clearly the subtext. And to leave was to break your commitment to your brothers and sisters, like a giant divorce. At the time I first joined, (1982) the people who left did so in the middle of the night. And it was never addressed. A person, or family, would be gone and you would hear whispers of "so-and so split the ministry." It was a big deal, but very hush-hush . . . no one in leadership said "So-and so left to sin" but that was the subtext.[39]

Living communally was about dedication to one's "brothers and sisters," says Scott. Throughout the 1980s and 1990s sermons in JPUSA were often preached about commitment to the cause, which was a directive received from the Lord. They were to live in this unique way without looking back. "To answer that call," he continues, "meant a sort of vow to living your life together." Many communards tended to be ephemeral. But if you hoped to "move beyond visitor status" you had to "pledge to devote your life to 'the ministry.'"

Some former members recall acerbic responses from leadership, and they continue to struggle with what was for them a difficult separation. Now communards leave under better terms. "Like a divorce," Scott writes, "it could be amicable and it could even be for the best, but it was always messy and never easy. Through the years I was on both sides of the divide. When members would leave, I would feel hurt and abandoned.... And then when we left, we made people feel abandoned." Scott fondly recalls his own departure, which was met with a party involving storytelling, the sharing of memories, and the signing of a book. The community has, he quips, come a long way from the "splitting in the middle of the night" years.

Stephen (his real name is not revealed) left JPUSA in 2002 to pursue a Ph.D. degree. He's now an atheist. For both Stephen and his wife, the separation was amicable: "I spoke with Pastor Neil the day I told the community we were *leaving*. I told him first. I asked about how we could raise money to leave and they gave me all the opportunity necessary for us to get enough money to move. I never felt judged. People were still as kind as ever. I think it was a very healthy departure."[40]

Unlike other communes, JPUSA's designation as an "intentional community" emphasizes a personal choice to join or leave. Officially the *JPUSA Covenant* makes allowance for anyone to leave and suggests a level of assistance from the community:

> Any individual member may end his or her membership and leave the community at any time. We encourage anyone wishing to do so to communicate with older members of the community as to his or her reasons, not so we can "convince" him or her to stay, but so that we can together pray over God's continuing will. As that person's Christian family, and as friends who have lived and learned together, we want to be honest and open even in a time that may be taking us different directions. A person who has come for "rehabilitation" purposes and decides to leave or give up their faith in Jesus Christ often finds it hard to face fellow believers and tell them the truth. Nonetheless, we would rather have their departure be with good wishes and our prayers.

THE POWER OF COLLECTIVE CAUSE

If the 2012 presidential election was any indicator, we appear to be on the brink of two extremes emerging in the United States: partisan ideologues, on the one hand, and noncommittal quasi-nihilists, on the other. If we are to continue this American experiment—life within the balanced sweet spot of democratic pluralism—we must find a way to tether ourselves loosely to our communities of belief and our extended, often disconnected worlds. We must live within the gray! In the wake of a political system teetering on the brink of losing its base as moguls continue to posture rather than resolve partisan bickering, we must consider how to continue the American dream realistically. Part of this concerns how we choose to commit ourselves to a collective cause. Historian Timothy Miller notes how communities (particularly religious ones) that are organized around high-commitment and authoritarian structures of varying degrees might experience greater longevity.[41] And Kanter has demonstrated the value in locating a common, overarching purpose shared by everyone. But Hugh Gardner takes issue with this, arguing that less-structured communities actually enjoy greater longevity.[42] Though his particular thesis concerns overall communal longevity, his argument may have merit when considering JPUSA's own unique situation. In other words, while its members' levels of commitment shore up physical and emotional resources (storms weathered, etc.), theirs may represent a sort of "overcommitment" to a grand cause, which would affect solidarity among up-and-coming generations. Simply put, in previous years JPUSA did not live in the gray.

The way JPUSA maintains its boundaries (only to be changed) has contributed to a pattern of disenchantment, or at least a lack of complete dedication from drifters hoping for solidity. In the early years a great deal of pressure was placed on members. But these expectations have softened. Some have experienced tension when deciding to leave. Others emphasize the family-like nature of JPUSA, an emotional nexus often difficult to break. Thus while the power of commitment often inspires founding members to remain dedicated to the community, rules associated with this commitment have not always worked for those who joined as adults, or for the second generation. Put another way, JPUSA's founding members were part of the original Jesus freaks, a once marginal and extreme affiliation. In short, they did not perceive communal commitment as confining or "radical." But those who joined during the 1980s did so within a social context that was unfriendly to the communal ethic. Kanter's theory may account for JPUSA's success since 1972. But it is here where Gardner's counterthesis proves true, accounting for why nonfounders often bristle at notions such as lifelong commitment and covenant contracts. What's more appealing about this realization is that it demonstrates how unyielding commitment might lead to stalemates and increased division, an unpleasant specter that also haunts Congress.

CONTROVERSY: PERCEPTIONS OF COMMUNITY GOVERNMENT

As with any religious community, JPUSA's epoch also includes a number of controversial episodes and negative press in the wake of former members who have in a number of cases experienced a great deal of distress—and some who have attempted to capitalize on this. But this is not surprising. The word "commune" often carries a pejorative connotation. Americans who have been raised on the concept of rugged individualism tend to struggle with the idea of shared property, especially if it involves religion. For JPUSA, perceptions held by ex-members have been an ongoing source of conflict. Allegations of physical abuse, sexual assault, and excessive authoritarian control have all given rise to media sensationalism and critical journalism, which has understandably soured the community on any attempt to position themselves within the broader swath of American religious history, as this researcher quickly learned.

JPUSA's castigation is in part a result of negative publicity created by public iterations about the community. Sociologist Ronald Enroth's *Recovering from Churches That Abuse* contained allegations from former members who noted incidents of abusive situations that happened in JPUSA's past. Sociologist Anson Shupe later scrutinized Enroth's work, charging that his methods were unsound as he tended to affiliate with the victims, and that he never actually paid a visit to observe the community firsthand. Thus Enroth's findings, according to Shupe, did not conform to acceptable sociological methodologies. But for Enroth this analysis concerned those abused by churches, which warranted a different approach to data collection.

Other publications began to surface, attempting to sensationalize life in JPUSA. These focused on allegations by former communards who have been negatively affected by their experiences in the commune. On April 1 and 2, 2001, journalist Kirsten Scharnberg published a two-part article in the *Chicago Tribune*. Scharnberg's account of JPUSA included testimonies provided by former members who shared their perspective on what amounted to excessive control by JPUSA's leadership. Moreover, she questioned the community's business practices. Scharnberg concluded the article by highlighting Enroth's book and musing over the decline in JPUSA's membership, particularly as it applied to older members who have chosen to leave. While Scharnberg notes that Ruth Tucker, a professor at Trinity Evangelical Divinity School in Deerfield, Illinois, defended JPUSA, her account also included oppositional statements by Paul Martin, director of Wellspring Retreat and Resource Center, who allegedly received requests from former members who needed treatment. Martin argued that JPUSA "displays virtually every sign that I watch for in overly authoritarian and totalistic groups."[43] Critiques of the community created a veritable firestorm. But Enroth's assessment of JPUSA (albeit intended to bring forth the stories of former members) was met with other suspicions. Paul Larsen, former president of the Evangelical Covenant Church, argued that Enroth's study was based on a bias, which was a "middle-class one, aimed squarely at a group of people living as a countercultural community."[44]

The publications by Enroth and Scharnberg affected the community in a number of ways, troubling current and former members and sparking suspicion among countercult organizations. Distressed former members have included references to both Enroth and Scharnberg on various websites. But JPUSA has had its equal share of supporters. Intent on educating the public (as well as Enroth), letters were written in response to the *Tribune* article. These letters outlined how communes are often structured, and why some forms of communal government have simply been misunderstood. An expert on American communal history, Timothy Miller, wrote an official response to the *Tribune*, as did other academics, church leaders, and members of JPUSA. "Most Americans, young and old," wrote Miller, "are devoutly unwilling to give up their personal possessions and privileges in favor of living from a rather threadbare common purse." After establishing a disconnect between the lifestyles of many American clergy and those in need, Miller (while admitting that JPUSA is not perfect) exonerated the community, stating that

> by any rational standard there is little public evidence of major wrongdoing in the organization. Members are free to join and free to leave; the poverty in which they live is pretty much shared equally; the vast wealth that the organization is accused of amassing is greatly less, on a per-capita basis, than that of the average American family. $2 million per year is hardly a luxurious income for 500 persons [which includes monies funneled into aid for the homeless].[45]

Scholars representing the Communal Studies Association also submitted a letter to the *Tribune*, pointing out that former members of any group are frequently bitter, particularly if their lives were defined by a total immersion experience. But what is most telling about the letter is that it challenged one of the more frequent accusations presented by former members of JPUSA. Most continue to note their struggle with the authoritarian nature of JPUSA—its undemocratic governance and unelected leadership council. But in defense of JPUSA and communal experiments generally, the Communal Studies Association made two arguments that desensationalize JPUSA's form of government. In contradistinction to what some Americans may believe, "religion and democracy are not co-terminous," and "clergy in some major denominations are not democratically chosen."[46] But for many ex-members, the absence of democracy within a religious context is tantamount to cultism.

Some former members and journalists have scrutinized the American tendency to overvalue wealth, private property, and personal space, calling into question the limited ways freedom is often defined. While these arguments appear to exonerate JPUSA, they do not fully engage the underlying thrust of ex-communard discontent. The way these former members perceive structure has (at least in their words) indicated that they measure communal life against the "normatives" of American culture. And faithful members, they say, can be victimized if these norms are breached by authority figures. This argument can be found in the mind-control paradigm, largely advanced by organizations such as the Cult Awareness Network and the American Family Foundation.[47] JPUSA communard Jon Trott has commented on this in the edited volume *Bad Pastors: Clergy Misconduct in Modern America*. In considering the mind-control debate as related to new religious movements, observes Trott, psychiatrist Robert Lifton has been a key figure for both the school of mind control and how cults are generally understood. Examining Lifton's concept of the protean self, Trott challenges Lifton (and to a certain extent, Enroth's application of Lifton), noting that mind-control theories, which suggest hegemonic power, are founded on principles associated with individualism. He writes:

> What Lifton, in all his articulate (one might say romantic) longing, seems to be saying is that the human self is not a reality grounded in any absolute truth, but rather a self-defined entity. The problem (among others) with this is that one ends up with the self defining the self. Further, as a self defines itself, it inescapably begins defining *all* selves. Lifton does not escape this tendency. And in spite of discussing his protean model for an entire book, he is unable to formulate how human beings find self-definition. This view is profoundly individualistic, and nowhere in *Protean Self* does Lifton explain just how such men build a family, church, or society together.[48]

Despite Trott's challenge to the mind-control paradigm, perceptions held by former members of any organization are often widely varied and held in wide regard by countercult groups. A quick Internet search will reveal the number of sites dedicated to ex-members of JPUSA. Some include private forums on Facebook designed to offer former members a space to reconnect with others who still nurse deep psychological wounds and bad memories. One even explores "JPUSA diaspora." The reasons for their anger and disappointment are many. Some have voiced concern over how leadership roles were decided. Others recall painful memories of being spanked with "the rod." Many have recalled the horrors of sexual abuse. And there are those who zero in on the lack of privacy within the commune. Still others, with combined humor and frustration, quip about JPUSA's fiscal policies.[49] Blogs associated with "ex-JPUSAs" offer evidence that there are two sides to this story. And those sides are rooted in fundamental disagreements about democracy, structure, mission, personal space, and property, the sort of debate that fuels political engines and pundit fodder.

Disputes over leadership and power have resulted in the public airing of grievances for a number of years. Websites offer statements made by former members of JPUSA, some pointing to hidden items in the JPUSA Bylaws and Constitution, which are (they argue) inaccessible to the public. According to one former member, "Power is concentrated in such a way that one's landlord, pastor, CEO, one-purse manager, community leader—even (for some) marital counselor—are found in the same 8 members." Leaders control romance and marriage, and the finances are under strict governance:

> Financially, the community is represented to outsiders as living out of "one purse." What is not mentioned is the reality that the purse-strings are held by those same eight leaders (who hold perpetual terms of office). What would have been an individual's bank account, salary, pension, unemployment compensation, and the payments that would have been made into Social Security—as in any other para-church or missionary organization—are all combined into that purse. Leaders have no financial accountability to the members who earn the money that goes in to their purse. . . . The leaders' unquestioning faith in their "plurality of leadership" has made them accountable only to themselves.[50]

Indeed, many have argued that the community uses excessive control and secrecy. In response to the statement above, Trott argues that communal life and the American life are not always synonymous:

> What the paragraph really wants to do is to transform JPUSA from a uniquely surviving communal group which is an alternative to the American Dream into a standard congregationally-governed church. [This] isn't what most of us want. If we HAD wanted it, we could at almost any time simply rise up and take it. . . . it seems obvious to me that a Christian

communal life in America is threatened most by the same forces threatening Evangelicalism itself.[51]

Contrary to those who argue that the leadership structure is not made public, the bylaws are actually defined in the *JPUSA Covenant*. In a section containing information on finances, the document outlines the commune's tax status, stating that while JPUSA is tax-exempt (with the exception of the businesses), individual workers (since they produce profit) are not. Thus each communard is allotted an equal share, and those in leadership pay the taxes on that share. But if that share reaches a certain threshold, the communard bears the tax burden. The document clearly explains the communard's relationship to the community and to income:

> While members are allocated a share of the JPUSA net income every year they do not receive this amount in the form of salary. Most of this income goes toward food, housing, utilities, insurance and maintenance costs, as well as our stated community purposes of evangelism, helping the poor, and discipling believers, all of which are paid for at the community-wide level by our financial department. In addition, members may individually requisition money for entertainment or specialized needs from the money office as funds are available. Members do not need to separately report these discretionary monies on their tax return as these amounts are included in the pro-rata member's share of JPUSA income.[52]

Regardless of particular arguments brought by former members (especially those concerning statements made by Enroth and Scharnberg), most critiques of JPUSA have been rooted in understandings of community governance and boundaries, the very things that account for longevity within most social contexts. So why is there such grievance toward this method of organizing a community? The same forces that threaten communal living, argues Trott, also threaten evangelical Christianity; he identifies those forces as American materialism and the Christian Right. For Trott, people influenced by these forces live based on the myth of a lost "Christian America." And they preach a radical return to that myth. In so doing, rightists secure military and monetary safety, securities a commune cannot offer—at least on a grand scale. According to Trott, the continuation of right-wing materialism will only result in churches governed by leaders who appear more like corporate CEOs and less like ministers. This is not too much of a stretch, given the constituents who rallied around Mitt Romney's appeal to the American heart of corporate governance (the corporatization of the United States) in 2012. And this peculiarity can also be extended to specific areas of American culture: food, health care, and so on, and the music industry, now shopworn by its daily struggle against the competing forces of the corporate monolith and a community of "independents." Each entity vies for a seat at the table, only to pray they can avoid being swallowed up by the digital flood.

The similarities among the trials of a commune, the trials of a country, and the trials of the music industry are striking. JPUSA's epoch is thus a barometer. In short, Trott and Timothy Miller advance a singular argument: those who have complained about JPUSA's style of government, financial structure, or lack of privacy and property do not understand communal living. Ex-communards (and, by extension, JPUSA's critics) are not ready to forgo the safety net offered by the forces of American materialism.[53] Still, ex-communards Eric and Barbara Pement appear to fully understand the thrust of communal living, as they spent many of their adult years within JPUSA's leadership inner sanctum. But they feel the emphasis placed on collective control not only contributed to stunted growth of the individual but extended into proper management of the seemingly mundane. "No one owned their personal car," recalls Eric Pement, "and vehicles were corporately shared but poorly maintained."[54]

The Pement family has a grasp on what a commune is meant to do, and their account bears this out. In the group's infancy, those considered rebellious were seen as "unfit for the purposes of remaining in Jesus People,"[55] writes Barbara Pement. They had little patience for people who did not want to remain obedient to God's call. As a measure intended to stifle resistance, the disobedient were asked to leave. This method of pastoring/management was used to create boundaries for those who bucked authority in their pre-Christian lives. "The rule was a good idea at the time," she recalls, "because it weeded out those who were not serious about their commitment." Put simply, this sort of heavy-handedness discouraged laziness and provided an incentive to work. Contrary to Trott's assumption that dissenters simply did not understand how communes are supposed to operate, the Pements are fully cognizant of the stakes: this sort of communal structure was, to a certain point, necessary. But there came a point where members were pushed too far. "There could be no honesty in raising serious discussion about certain long-held practices," says Barbara Pement. The leaders were immovable. Challenges were viewed as mutinous and dissenting. "Maintaining the structure of the commune," she continues, "took precedence over the architecture of our lives." The original intent of the group changed, she reasons, yielding a community that seemed more committed to their own structure than to Jesus, strengthening the commune more than the individual.

Trott's argument notwithstanding, disagreements that led to dissent are connected to how power has been perceived. Council member Neil Taylor admits that JPUSA does not adhere to congressional polity. But the sense of openness and flexibility, he says, comes from working within a plurality of leadership. And how does a plurality of leadership work, particularly when all voices have equal weight? Given the value placed on every council member's opinion, meetings often end as issues are tabled, awaiting consensus. Like Taylor, most members view this form of government (rarified as it might be) as good for the whole.[56]

When measured against what is considered normative by American culture, it is not a stretch to see how these people could at times perceive their growth as stunted. Trott argues that many members have assumed that democracy might lead to a better community. But history proves otherwise. Politicking, he reasons, will lead to ill-conceived leadership, mere products of a popularity contest.[57]

Ironically one ex-member website points out that Jean Vanier outlined healthy leadership structures in *Community and Growth*, a formative document in the life of JPUSA:

> Structures call for mandates and accountability; they define how leaders are voted or nominated and for how long. They set out how major decisions are

to be made and by whom. They define the limits of power and the areas of responsibility. They define also the relationship between the leader and the community council. Such structures can sometimes appear heavy, but they are necessary for a healthy community life. If each and every person is called to be responsible for the community, then all must know how decisions are made, *even if not all can participate in the process of decision-making*.[58]

Vanier's model is intended to create a salubrious environment. The ex-member website interprets Vanier's guide as a means to *limit* the terms of those in leadership, that is, "they define the limits of power." But given the totality of the paragraph, Vanier actually affirms a governmental structure similar to that of JPUSA. However, over the past ten years, says John Herrin, a new approach to leadership has emerged. Writes Herrin:

> What we have done is decentralize the decision making process. Most everything we do here is actually overseen by some committee or team other than the Council/Board, i.e., budget committee, school committee, kitchen, business, housing, visitors, web, Abbey Team (they are directing the new building project which will be the major thrust of the community going forward), transition committee, church, etc. The official Board/Council is really more of an oversight team these days. We don't interfere into much unless asked to or feel we absolutely have to.[59]

The complaints advanced by many former members may have been warranted, grounded in the assumption that the council exercises absolute control. But it seems the new decentralized approach to leadership now offers more agency to rank-and-file members.

MORE CONTROVERSY

One of the more controversial chapters in JPUSA's history involves the practice of "adult spanking." In its youth, JPUSA sought leadership in the wake of the departure of J. W. Herrin, Sr. Having to deal with Herrin's lust, the leaders began to confront community problems head-on. "The confrontation with J. W. Herrin" recalls Trott, "had reinforced our belief that forcefully confronting sin, whether in ourselves or others, was a necessity." Then in 1974 Jack Winters, pastor to a suburban charismatic community, Daystar, attempted to fill the void left by Herrin, Sr. Trott's account of the adult spanking incidents highlights how the young community acted out of deference to Winter's system of behavioral correction.

Jack Winters's weekly class, which usually dealt with counseling, healing, and deliverance, eventually wandered into some pretty interesting territory. His teaching, according to those who were there, went something like this: *This is a rebellious generation—young, rebellious people who didn't grow up having any discipline or love from their parents. Sometimes, they need to go back and experience discipline to deal with that rebellion in their lives. You need to go back and walk through those steps, receiving parental discipline to heal the rebellious adult.* In short, what Winters was talking about was giving spankings to "rebellious" adults![60]

According to communard Curtis Mortimer, this practice came about during a time when psychological theories such as regression therapy (where one regresses into infancy and then matures) were in vogue. For JPUSA, adult spanking was viewed as a method of ensuring humility before God. It was also a chance for adult members to submit to the authority of senior leadership, purging sin in the process. But spankings were not reserved only for the rank-and-file. On one occasion, two JPUSA pastors drove to Daystar to "request" their own discipline. Against spanking generally, Dawn Mortimer blamed herself, recalling that she viewed the whole matter with suspicion. Still, she was concerned about the community's need for concrete leadership and teaching in the wake of her former husband's departure. And members trusted Winters.[61] In the years that followed, the practice waned to the point that individual members no longer availed themselves of the "discipline," nor was the practice widely discussed. In 1978 Trott noted:

> Glenn Kaiser announced to the fellowship that Winters' teaching had been in error and that we were discontinuing the practice. His rationale was that (1) the teaching was outside the evangelical mainstream, that no one else we

knew of (besides Winters) was practicing this teaching, and that JPUSA didn't want to be involved with anything which would bring reproach to Christ; and that (2) that people were using "getting the rod" as a cheap alternative to serious repentance, which ought to be about stopping wrong behavior and pursuing righteous behavior.[62]

Complaints by ex-members notwithstanding, the structures and practices of JPUSA are not dissimilar to those of Catholic monasteries, convents, or nineteenth-century Protestant communities that required complete devotion from adherents through corporal punishment. Given that their purpose was not defined by American democratic practice, these religious enclaves chose to install leaders based on criteria established by ecclesiastical mandates. The call to complete devotion, the concentrated power in a few nonelected council members (installed based on character and spiritual maturity rather than democratic vote), member term commitments, and positions of power held in perpetuity are all part of a larger tradition that defines intentional community. But while some practices continue (in the spirit of communal living) and some have been discontinued, there remains a disconnect between some former and current members, each recalling the history a bit differently. Put simply, some feel nurtured ("discipled") while others feel violated.

In the end, many of the controversies (particularly allegations involving excessive control of members) are based on perceptions of breached boundaries. But Kanter's work on successful communes reveals that boundaries simply must remain in place.

> Whereas retreat communes impose no limits, service communes that work effectively tend to impose many limits. The model of discipline and direction is an appropriate one. Service communes define behavior that is acceptable; they make coherent choices of life style and expect them to be adopted; they do not shy away from making demands, developing organization, and creating rules—though not all the rules may be formalized. The group has work to be done. Whether decisions are participated in by a whole group or by single individuals acting for the group, it is important

that decisions be made. Even helping individuals with their own growth is interpreted as requiring the imposition of limits, the acceptance of order from the group.[63]

Despite arguments against this sort of "fencing in" made by of Enroth and sociologist Hugh Gardner, high-commitment values, reasons Kanter, are absolutely necessary. "The group has work to be done," she says. For JPUSA, its ministry, it seems, has often eclipsed the needs of individual families. And it goes without saying that the sort of discipline ex-members recall may appear extensive, even brutal. However, Kanter's argument is less concerned with the end-result of individuals than with the end-result of the community. But as we shall see, the group has evolved to the extent that there is now an ongoing effort to appropriately balance the needs of the many and the needs of the few. The bottom line is that the community (for good or bad) has survived, in part, as a result of strict expectations.

SUSTAINABILITY

Any group's success is largely dependent on how it envisions a larger purpose. But for most communes throughout the 1970s, lofty goals and dreams were not enough for a sustainable community. For Kanter, "The primary issue with which a utopian community must cope in order to have the strength and solidarity to endure is human organization: how people arrange to do the work that the community needs to survive as a group, and how the group in turn manages to satisfy and involve its members over a long period of time . . . commitment thus refers to the willingness of people to do what will help maintain the group because it provides what they need." Commitments are then realized when individuals express or fulfill something that is part of their individual personalities (tattoos, hair styles, piercing music, etc.), while still nurturing the connection between the individual and the community to the extent that communards can no longer meet their deeper needs elsewhere. For Kanter, "Through commitment, person and group are inextricably linked."[64] But this dynamic should not lead the reader to assume a lack of agency on the part of these people. JPUSA's choice of the signifier "intentional community" is intended to distinguish its commune from isolationist groups; those who remain in JPUSA do so voluntarily. And those who choose to leave are now encouraged to develop life-skills, which will serve them on the outside.

In considering long-term sustainability for JPUSA, there has been resounding agreement among leaders and rank-and-file communards. Jean Vanier believed that each community must have both a general and specific mission, providing examples such as Mother Teresa's mission to the lonely and the dying in Kolkata (Calcutta) and Benedictine communities whose general mission is prayer. JPUSA's general mission has been about offering an open door and an open heart to anyone—and to a certain extent, exemplifying alternate ways of being "evangelical." For example, while JPUSA maintains general rules for the community, application is based on the individual, allowing nuanced interpretations of community guidelines, politics, and theology. Members often note that longevity is merely a result of ideological flexibility and a continued ability to accommodate (absorb) the surrounding culture. Yes, it is widely held that communes typically disband if they are built solely around charismatic leaders. But Taylor believes that communes also fold because of their inflexibility on ideas. An apparent credit to the power of pluralism, JPUSA has always been able to reinvent the community to align with cultural and philosophical trends viewed as unwieldy within evangelicalism proper.

Every decade brings a new generation into the halls of JPUSA. And with each generation, new stylistic expressions emerge: spiked or green hair, body piercings, tattoos, and those who avoid bathing in an attempt to identify with those who do not have running water. More than this, new philosophies trickle in. Before its untimely folding, Cornerstone leaked these ideas into the fabric of the evangelical subculture by way of Christian rock. Newness stretches thin the layers that insulate JPUSA members from potential heresy, but this newness also continues the spirit of the Reformation—ecclesia semper reformanda. Veteran member Susan argues that this increasingly flexible structure manifested as greater freedom for youth. The result, she says, may have contributed to a decrease in membership among the second generation. Simply put, after tasting the accoutrements of pop media (as one example), younger members end up leaving, hoping to enjoy what has been denied.[65]

Aesthetic freedom notwithstanding, the immediate concerns of Uptown Chicago keep JPUSA actively engaged. But in previous years there was a different kind of immediacy, according to Lyda Jackson. Ready for the Rapture, she fully anticipated that she would not die. And this is what fueled the early Jesus Movement. A clear departure from the Jesus-freak dalliance with doomsday, JPUSA's vision changed as it attracted those who simply needed practical assistance. Yes, the doctrine of the Rapture remained, but it lost its formative influence on daily purpose; the mission to the local community transcended doctrinal particulars such as millenarianism. In this manner, JPUSA differs from earlier communes. The needs of the neighborhood made it necessary to move beyond esoteric musings about the end of time.[66] Those who remain all feel a tug, a calling to serve the homeless in Uptown, exemplifying commitment to both God and location. And for Raye Clemente, a community will be strengthened when it looks outside of itself, focuses on *external* needs, and develops rescue scenarios to help the homeless.[67]

Nathan Cameron feels his life is interwoven with those of others in the community. As a result, he remains committed, recognizing the integral connection between all members. Like a link within a larger chain, he believes his absence would have an effect on others. If Cameron's responsibilities were ignored, a ripple effect would occur. In this sense, everyone's place in the community fits into a larger whole. This is why term commitments are valued, as leaders count on members to carry their weight. It is this sense of interconnectivity that makes leaving the community a daunting possibility for those who derive a sense of identity from the overall mission.[68]

For Neil Taylor the focus on evangelism has been central in retaining members who are committed to one cause, but he qualifies how he actually defines evangelism. Unlike other early Jesus freaks, Taylor does not define evangelism in the narrow sense of ministering to the soul. While part of JPUSA's goal has been to lead individuals to Jesus, these pastors continue to view the concept of missionary work as holistic. Unlike Rapture-minded evangelicals (particularly those during the Jesus Movement), Taylor also defines evangelism as the ability to maintain an open door to new people, young mothers, and prostitutes with children. This was distinguished early on, notes Taylor. "Back in those early seventies . . . we were learning about how to . . . live out the gospel, how to visit the widows or the shut-ins, and continue to care for them." He credits Dawn Mortimer—who had twenty years of life experience on the rest—as the leader who provided the community early on with a sense of ideological balance, imbuing the commune with a sense of urgency to engage matters concerning social justice.[69]

A BARN RAISING

This family has some of the dynamics of a small town, where communards help those who might experience crisis. People rally around members who are in need, a scenario similar to an "old-fashioned barn raising," according to some. This aspect of community is undergirded by a sense of continuity of communal vision. Put another way, communards collectively share in goals outlined earlier in this chapter. But mission by itself is not enough. Along with Neil Taylor, communard Tom Cameron notes that cultural adaptability has greatly contributed to JPUSA's ability to sustain an ongoing commitment to serve God and the neighborhood of Uptown. And this continues to attract drifters, many of whom remain for a brief three or four months. Leaders are then able to adjust to what amounts to a community that remains in a constant state of flux, simply because the core members remain committed to a life of service. Moreover, to some extent the transient provide JPUSA with new lifeblood (culturally) as well as a work force for communal businesses—a revolving door of sorts.

Cameron's assessment of communal strength is largely sentimental, if not wholly romantic. But it is accurate. Two cultural worlds inform JPUSA's modus operandi. The first concern's Neil Taylor's assessment of its members' evolving ethos of aesthetics; the community has for many years accepted all manners of sub- and countercultural expressions. The second concerns their sentimentalities for simple living, where postindustrial scenarios such as suburban living (a model that isolates the self and ruptures community) do not continually fragment identities. Cameron describes their vision in a manner reminiscent of a bygone era: "In some sense, this has some of the dynamics of a small town fifty years ago. If your husband or your wife comes down with a serious disease or something, [there are] half a dozen people at your door ready to help you with whatever things you need help with."[70] This combination of subcultural sensibilities and 1960s "small town living" might appear anachronistic, but the mix seems to work.

Freedom to express individual aesthetic taste, familial ethics, and the small-town feel have strengthened the larger mission. These aspects of the commune made bearable what has otherwise been a threadbare existence. But ultimately resilience is bolstered by a measurable aesthetic flexibility, as well as the ways in which leadership is structured. As former members have argued, the council's overly authoritarian hand hastened the departure of many communards and exacerbated the already ticklish situation created by Ronald Enroth and the *Chicago Tribune*. But despite this, many maintain that a robust mixture of centralized power and a plurality of leadership are necessary. Any organizational scenario evidences this. When a mission is built around one powerful individual, or when that mission is compromised by the rule of willy-nilly law, community decay is not far behind.

After John Herrin, Sr., fell into disfavor with the community, they were forced to reconsider the leadership structure. Both Neil Taylor and Curtis Mortimer (husband to matriarch Dawn Mortimer) note how the move from a single-leader model to a plurality of leadership (nine co-equal council members/pastors) was important, resulting in consensus-based decision making rather than majority-rule democratic vote. Mortimer maintains that a number of factors have contributed to JPUSA's survival thus far, and he has identified what he believes to be five core reasons for JPUSA's continued existence, as well as their potential for longevity:

1. Mission-businesses solved the problem of finances, eliminating the need to solicit donations.
2. The group shifted from a single-leader model of governance to a model of multiple eldership, with nine members (other communards feel they

THE BLESSING AND CURSE OF COMMUNITY

are well represented as the council is occupied by men and women, each coming from a different background).
3. The community operates based on individual need. The person with the most needs gets the most resources (everyone according to their need), not "we each get equal." All accept this, with compassion for those who need extra resources. This also includes an emphasis on personal decision making (choice to remain or leave).
4. There is a shared sense of calling and purpose—ministry, not just a paycheck. For example, *Cornerstone* magazine went out of print, reallocating the magazine budget so JPUSA could purchase a new building for the shelter.
5. There is external accountability (affiliation with the Evangelical Covenant Church).

Mortimer has observed the direct relationship between the mission businesses and the shelter, which reinforces a collectively agreed upon purpose. Put another way, the relationship among mission businesses, social outreach, and the authority granted the council is predicated on a higher purpose that transcends the mundane. And the mundane is simply necessary to carry out God's plan to rescue those in need. At times these people seriously consider the reasons for their common-purse arrangement and relative threadbare existence. "If they have that sense of commitment and that sense of ministry," urges Mortimer, "that's when they're happy to go to work . . . they have that sense of ministry that their work is definitely supporting our work at the shelter." And the shelter is the emotional life-blood of JPUSA as it attracts outsiders who feel called to social activism, warranting JPUSA training programs such as Project 12, a new undertaking whereby youth anywhere can obtain training in inner-city activism.[71]

The two pillars that provide a practical foundation for JPUSA—purpose and the plurality of leadership—are a reoccurring theme throughout the community. Glen van Alkemade runs the sheet metal department of Lakefront Roofing. Before joining JPUSA, van Alkemade was a civil engineer with Illinois Department of Transportation. After reading the Bible on a dare, he found it persuasive, reached a personal crisis, and then took a leap of faith. Finding his career wanting (diverging from the values learned in his discipleship group), he sought change. Van Alkemade agrees with what appears to be a consensus among members. Basing his understanding of community structure on JPUSA's oral history, he considers the shift from a "single strong leader model" to a "plurality of leadership model" as the "make-it or break-it moment" for the community. For him, JPUSA is a "large, motley, rag-tag, unruly, difficult-to-lead group" that needs to be led by a motley, rag-tag council.[72]

Van Alkemade believes that group decision (consensus) often ranks closer to optimal survival ability. This model ends with better decisions, though reaching consensus often takes longer. If consensus is not reached, the topic is tabled. And at times the result amounts to years of deliberation, with no decision in the foreseeable future. JPUSA is not democracy. In this case (according to his account), communism works only when group need and individual need are balanced (individualism within collectivism). And communism only works within smaller groups.[73] There have been consensus-based communes that have grown weary of decision by consensus. But others, such as the Quaker-founded Alpha Farm, remain vibrant even as their epoch began in the 1970s.[74]

Regardless of the manner in which decisions are made, commitment remains a matter of choices made by those who feel connected to others who hold all things in common—particularly the overarching goals of the collective order. But how communards perceive and interact with one another has always been both a strength and a weakness for any commune. Veteran communard Chris Spicer emphasizes that JPUSA's focus on humanity and Jesus—two core organizing principles—is unwavering. After all, communes have often failed simply because the focus changed. But then there's the paradox of "life in community" in an oft-stated aphorism: "the joy of community is all the people," Spicer quips, "and the curse of community is all the people."[75]

While it is true that change of focus tends to cloud the vision of any communard on the brink of departure, ironically the idea of change (or flexibility) also serves to galvanize groups. Others within JPUSA maintain that the willingness to change focus is actually a major contributing factor to sustainability. Second-generation communard Tamzen Trott has argued that JPUSA always seems to be open to what is new—what the younger generation is about—holding to what they believe Jesus requires. For example, *Cornerstone* magazine was one of the more significant reasons JPUSA that remained culturally relevant for so many years. Part of its purpose was to push boundaries and challenge ecclesial comfort-zones held by establishment evangelicals, encouraging them to reexamine their own assumptions about politics, theology, music, and various taboo social issues.

Beyond the cultural relevance of the magazine, social outreach has always protected the community from sinking into insularity. The community has always been about discipleship and evangelism, notes Stu Heiss (former guitarist for Rez Band), impulses that remain "important grounding points for the community" that keep them from "withdrawing into [their] own world and becoming cut off from the larger community."[76] In other words, communities err when they withdraw from the world. Heiss echoes the sentiment that unaltered focus remains important, so long as it is tempered with an ability to reexamine ideas. "As God has revealed himself and as history is played out and cultures changed, I think that JPUSA has adapted, and that's part of the reason why that there's still vitality." The death of any social group begins when it attempts to stop history, seeking to maintain a particular way of living without regard to the larger culture.[77] Founding member Wendi Kaiser agrees. JPUSA members are "world Christians." And for her, flexibility is key, but within a broader understanding of culture and Christianity. As a striking example of how some on the left view "Americanization," her opinion of American Christianity hints at JPUSA's aversion to narrowly defined boundaries: "One of the things that really distressed us is confusing patriotism with Christianity and confusing the American-Manifest-Destiny-we are-the-second-Israel type of mentality into Christianity, and we just can't go there. We just can't go there at all."[78]

Cultural engagement and relevance notwithstanding, this community has sustained itself owing to multiple variables. The five foundations provided by Curtis Mortimer might account for JPUSA's survival thus far. If so, these reinforce communal purpose and dedication. Financial stability, a council marked by diversity, respect for individual need, and the immediate sense of purpose all contribute to the commitment mechanisms necessary for a healthy, sustainable commune. But Scott feels differently. He joined in 1998 and views the general structure as overly controlling. Early JPUSA was a grassroots effort, without clarity of planning or structure—simple trial and error. While he concedes that the leadership strove for the good of everyone, he says that a government with too much power emerged:

> To be fair, I think the leaders did the best they could, under the circumstances (being untrained and learning on the job), but of course, mistakes were made. In hindsight, I think it was not a good idea for a small group of leaders to make all the decisions for everyone else. The same few people decided where you lived, where you worked, how much spending cash you could (or couldn't) get, when (if) you could date, or marry, or have kids. Basically your boss was also your landlord, your counselor, your pastor—everything. That was just too much power for one brother to hold over another (or another several hundred.) I'm amazed that it worked as well as it did, truth be told. A testimony to the grace of God.[79]

Scott has voiced what other former members have—the desire for privacy and allegations of excessive pastoral control. While history demonstrates the effectiveness of authoritarian structure (such as convents and monasteries), Scott does not link communal government to success, arguing that JPUSA's location and spiritual focus account for its longevity. Indeed, the fact that the commune is urban-based has allowed members to come and go freely. Location also forces the group to maintain an outward focus on the poor, thus avoiding insularity or self-preservation.[80]

Noting that a large percentage of communards are travelers and nomads, long-standing members agree that membership has been in constant motion over the years. But location is not the sole reason, though the group's location makes it more accessible. Many travelers have heard about JPUSA over the years through Rez Band, *Cornerstone*, or the Cornerstone Festival. But while location in and of itself might not attract members, it clearly serves to retain many of them. The revolving door of travelers provides fresh workers to occupy positions paramount to JPUSA's survival. As newcomers arrive, they take post on kitchen and house duty, freeing other members to expand into other parts of JPUSA interests. So, for this wonderfully complicated group, the inner city has saved them, as much as they have saved the homeless.

CONCLUSION

In their unique, atavistic manner, JPUSA has succeeded in maintaining the zeitgeist of the Jesus Movement. The compelling thing is it has managed to maintain something long expired, or long lost in the vacuous materialism once embraced by coreligionists, whose view of the homeless was obscured by their skyward gaze. Original Jesus freaks were absorbed by the Right, tuned into apocalypticism, and dropped out of *practical* activism. Yet this community has, in some ways, revitalized the dreams of the New Left, if only partially. More to the point, they have outlived other left-leaning groups whose goal was nothing less than restructuring U.S society in hopes of instilling a class consciousness that highlights the futility (even danger) of excessive wealth.

We know that retreat communes often fail to build "enduring groups" because of their inability to institute commitment mechanisms, and because they establish "negative boundaries that tend to disperse whatever commitment members initially bring to the group."[81] Furthermore, groups without structure or a core organizing principle have often relied on one immovable and unchallengeable person or idea. Or they eliminate all boundaries, resulting in communities deemed unsanitary and financially bankrupt. Retreat communes become easily dichotomized, either adopting an inflexible dogma or rupturing boundary distinctions altogether. Both extremes have absolutely undermined the ability for this type of commune to continue.

JPUSA has survived since 1972 largely because of its collective commitment to following Jesus, but in a very particular way. A counternarrative to the conservative Jesus Movement, JPUSA's epoch evinces signposts that point to a new kind of evangelical. And these disciples differ from their baby boomer, evangelical forbearers. With little exception, JPUSA communards remain dedicated to their little slice of Heaven. And their survival depends on five fundamental things: mission businesses; plurality of leadership; individualism within collectivism; a divine calling that transcends work or ideological particulars; and external accountability to a denomination. For some, JPUSA's success is simply a result of divine favor. But examples of divine favor were made concrete in the community's firm dedication to a form of social activism wholly unlike Reagan- or Bush-era evangelicalism. Their mission had to be undergirded by a larger institutional force, if only in word. Not unlike other countercultural groups, JPUSA's decision to affiliate with a formalized structure feathered its cap. Nestling under a denominational umbrella helped it avoid cultural or social isolationism. Even better, the Evangelical Covenant Church's flagship university and seminary, North Park, is located within a mile of JPUSA. Thus the proximity of JPUSA's "parent" has helped the community remain committed to its own values and to the values of the larger church culture.

An analysis of JPUSA's organizational structure, its many social enterprises, and the stories of individual communards accounts for why it has survived since the 1972 genesis. But more than this, glimpsing the inner-life of the group illuminates a communal ethic that has extended beyond the original Jesus Movement. And this ethic, as encapsulated in JPUSA's earlier years, portended decline of the establishment version of Jesus Movement evangelicalism (its association with the Religious Right), creating a path for the continuance of the Evangelical Left in postmodern Christian expressions such as "emergent" Christianity. As an example of the Evangelical Left, JPUSA's social ethic bears similarities to the activism of the New Left. The next chapter will consider how the community's location has contributed to their position on social justice, continues to galvanize commitment from members, and inspires an ongoing ideological evolution.

4
BIG SHOULDERS, BIG HISTORY: WHY CHICAGO?

✳ ✳ ✳

It's not without historical precedent that Chicago would play a part in the development of a religious group or in radical activism. JPUSA is simply part of a larger story, one drenched with religion and politics. But initially Chicago wasn't a consideration for the group. After traveling throughout the Midwest, performing rock concerts and evangelizing, their decision to settle in one location allowed the community to grow in number and expand their concept of ministry. As an urban commune, JPUSA experienced a number of residential scenarios before securing its current site. Despite an initial capriciousness, it stabilized after purchasing its current residence, Friendly Towers. But the journey was arduous. Throughout the 1980s poverty in Uptown grew to the point of crisis. For JPUSA, the result was an early recognition of practical human need.

Chicago's history of radicalism and reform efforts provides a unique and welcoming context for experimental groups. Moreover, the significant Catholic presence in the city offers sympathy for collectivist groups seeking to live based on models of shared living and social justice. This history set the stage for a place marked by a legacy of social activism, religious fervor, and political progressivism.

REVIVALISM, SOCIAL REFORM, AND EVANGELICALISM: HISTORICAL CONTEXT

The American Midwest has a history of various forms of radical activism, not the least of which is religious populism. Geographical location and situational scenarios often play a role when political and religious differences are considered, particularly the great denominational divide between mainline and conservative Protestants.[1] But if conservative evangelicalism tends to be more concentrated in the Midwest and the South, what is it about Chicago that provides a good home for JPUSA, a group that essentially embraces an evangelical theological position but is wholly different from the politics of establishment evangelicalism? Does the group see the city as a mission field or simply a welcoming environment to live out its own ethos, while also serving the poor? Although Chicago is home to a number of conservative evangelical institutions (Moody Bible Institute, Willow Creek, etc.), does the community enjoy favor with their evangelical neighbors, or are they viewed as merely another socialist commune that has added the evangelical distinguisher? Members such as Jon Trott tend to avoid the evangelical moniker, but perhaps one reason JPUSA has gained acceptance has to do with a larger history of struggle layered over years of midwestern radicalism and populism.

The Midwest has often been viewed as fertile ground for Protestant revivalists, Catholic relief movements, and populists both right and left.[2] But earlier attempts to make American life better were often inconsequential, despite attempts to organize. Citing evangelists such as William Jennings Bryan, George Marsden points to a pattern that emerged during the Progressive Era—that "both parties [Republican and Democrat] were preaching moral reform and each presented a vision of America as the land where God's will should be done." Thus the focus remained on political rhetoric more often than sociopolitical action.[3] These similarities (at least with conservative evangelicals) continued until the 1960s. Sociopolitical-economic problems continued as evangelicals disengaged from social measures rooted in pure humanitarianism. Indeed, throughout the nineteenth century evangelicals *were* engaged in social justice. But amid the rising anonymity of the individual (lost in a sea of industry and immigration), organizations such as the YMCA and the YWCA attempted to offer assistance. Some of the more conservative evangelicals, according to Randall Balmer, soon retreated from social matters, leaving a space to be filled by organizations such as the New Left, and they would not reengage until the rise of the Religious Right. The upper Midwest would soon become home to a number activist groups.

Chicago's history of radicalism and social activism is fitting for a study of communes, as well as urban poverty. It is little wonder, given the problems that beset the 46th Ward, let alone the greater Chicago area. In some ways there is no better place than Chicago for an urban religious commune. And in other ways, Chicago's dualistic soul calls for a community that splits the difference between radical populism and establishment evangelicalism, a dichotomy that might signify JPUSA's tightrope. A curious mix of business, politics, and religion became characteristic of Chicago's ideological landscape. George Marsden cleverly demonstrates how John D. Rockefeller and D. L. Moody (the Charles Finney of his day) each contributed to a mythology that cast the city of big shoulders in a mold that defined it based on struggle.

Although Christians in Chicago's earlier years sought to Christianize (read Americanize) society, the goal of making life better simply for its own sake ended with new theological positions intended to counter the Social Gospel. Social reformers such as Moody (a dispensational premillennialist) believed the world would decline before the Rapture of Christians and the millennial reign of Christ.[4] Held in high regard by many evangelicals, this theoretical anchor held firm the doctrine of the Rapture, a theory of the Second Coming of Christ popularized by author Hal Lindsey's *The Late Great Planet Earth* (1970) and reenergized by Tim LaHaye and Jerry Jenkins's *Left Behind* series (1990s). JPUSA's activism distinguished its members from other evangelicals, particularly throughout the 1980s. And while they freely embraced a high view of scripture during the 1980s (a position that endeared them to evangelical apologists such as Norman L. Geisler), the community's political philosophy and emerging skepticism (cautious optimism?) about the end of time slowly distinguished them from the conservative "establishment" evangelicalism that has come to define Chicago.

CONSERVATIVE EVANGELICALISM IN CHICAGO

Between October 26 and 28, 1978, Chicago became ground zero for the planks of conservative, evangelical Christianity. Founded in 1977, the International Council on Biblical Inerrancy (ICBI) began a series of summits intended to clarify various theological matters. Three hundred members met in Chicago to discuss and adopt the *Chicago Statement on Biblical Inerrancy*. The papers delivered at the conference were edited and published by Norman L. Geisler (Grand Rapids: Zondervan, 1981). Jay Grimstead, founder and director of the Coalition on Revival, stated that the document was a "landmark church document." It represented the "largest, broadest group of evangelical protestant scholars that ever came together to create a common, theological document in the 20th century. It is probably the first systematically comprehensive, broadly based, scholarly, creed–like statement on the inspiration and authority of Scripture in the history of the church."[5]

Figures such as D. L. Moody have had an enormous influence on evangelical Christianity. But this particular event continued the heritage and in many ways connected institutional (establishment) evangelicalism to Chicago. Summit II met in Chicago between November 10 and 13, 1982, "to discuss guidelines for principles of interpreting the Bible." Those in attendance adopted the *Chicago Statement on Biblical Hermeneutics*. Summit III met between December 10 and 13, 1986, when the *Chicago Statement on Biblical Application* was adopted.[6]

While apologist Norman Geisler's participation in these historical documents is noteworthy, he also remains an important figure when considering JPUSA's community and their place in Chicago's history. Geisler was involved with Cornerstone for a number of years, where he offered lectures on Christian apologetics. And he also sided with the community during the Enroth controversy. Along with Geisler, JPUSA's collective affirmation of the *Chicago Statement on Biblical Inerrancy* helped solidify the group's position with other evangelicals. But the community's location continued to inspire a different political trajectory from those of other evangelical believers. And this political thread is important, given Chicago's ghosts.

DALEY AND CONFLICT

Chicago is known for its history of religious reform and relief efforts. But these waned as new models of Christian activism (salvation of the soul) replaced progressive understandings of evangelical social justice. As a result, government agencies and radical movements were left to fill the gap. After World War I and World War II, Chicago's social need intensified, but any sense of resolve was distant. Postwar Chicago experienced a massive influx of southern immigrants, many settling in Uptown. Between 1945 and 1959, 77 percent of the homes built in Chicago were outside the city limits. Immigrant workers and other minorities remained in the inner city, which became the backyard of Chicago's elegant Lake Shore Drive façade. "Uptown ranked second among Chicago neighborhoods in population density," writes historian Roger Biles. Twenty-seven percent of the area's dwellings, according to the Census Bureau, lacked sufficient plumbing, and 38 percent were considered deteriorated, making Uptown "one of Chicago's most abominable slums."[7] To complicate the matter, years of tension over racial inequity and poverty resulted in riots and attempts to escape the ghettos as the 1960s wore on.

A city besieged by income disparity (and noted for its multicultural population), Chicago grew to national notoriety as an urban nexus of poverty and prosperity, heavy-handed governance, and political malfeasance. An acclaimed big city boss, Mayor Richard J. Daley saw his rise to power during the 1950s both solidified and questioned during the 1960s. While his form of government quelled the unseemly elements of Chicago's underworld (at least in perception), Daley's tenure in office was both celebrated and ridiculed. Unable (or unwilling) to resolve the crisis of poverty and racial inequity, Daley's administration exacerbated racial tensions, ending with the failed public attempts of Dr. Martin Luther King, Jr., to resolve mounting problems and subsequent riots. Despite Daley's projected liberalism, conservatives welcomed his policies. Then he outraged New Left "yippies," who viewed his continued affirmation of middle-class values and support of U.S. foreign policy as indicative of the hypocrisy they sought to battle.

Insurmountable problems concerning race and poverty were not fully addressed by Daley's democratic machine. Consequently, Chicago's public image contributed to civil disobedience, which grew on a national scale. Civil unrest ensued at the 1968 Democratic National Convention, where yippie protestors brought national attention to the New Left, ending with the indictment of the Chicago 8 (later the Chicago 7), a group found guilty of violating the Anti-Riot Act of 1968. The preceding events culminated in the Days of Rage, riots launched by the New Left's "Weatherman" in 1969.

SOCIAL JUSTICE AND NEW LEFT SIMILARITIES

Throughout the 1970s and 1980s, evangelical activism was to a large extent confined to a war over family values. The idea of radical evangelical activism of the leftist variety was fleeting at best. In fact, when one considers an "evangelical activist," it's worth musing over it a bit: what sort of activism? Uniquely positioned as a scholar, evangelical minister, and Jesus Movement insider, historian Malcolm Magee, director of the Institute for the Study of Christianity and Culture, has shed light on what is often a pesky history of how Jesus freaks and Republicans actually formed their inimitable coalition. Writes Magee:

> In the 70s and 80s you could still find moderate and left-leaning Democrats who focused on these issues. Harold Hughes from Iowa could be used as an example. But more and more it became a battle between what was perceived as a "Christian" right and a "secular" left. The Jesus people and the musicians were not politically savvy enough nor historically aware enough to recognize that they were being co-opted. The idea that there was a place for a religious left with both personal moral concerns as well as a progressive economic policies was lost in the simplistic sound bites of the elections

of the late 70s and 80s. They were focused on trying to raise young families and live personally godly lives. Pseudo-histories like Francis Schaeffer's *How Should We Then Live* were widely circulated in churches and at house meetings. Little by little the intellectual transformation took place until it seemed like irrefutable common sense.[8]

Indeed, as the 1980s wore on, any sort of "religious left" became increasingly uncommon. And this is precisely what makes JPUSA so significant. In spite of the glacial-like movement of Christian hippies toward Ronald Reagan's brave new world (a confluence of religious and political conservatives), this community was able to maintain political autonomy while remaining thoroughly evangelical. In the aftermath of decades of inner-city turmoil, JPUSA offered Uptown a vibrant combination of radical activism, outreach measures reminiscent of the Catholic Worker, and the evangelicalism of D. L. Moody. The failure of the New Left made new forms of activism necessary. Todd Gitlin writes, "The New Left, like its predecessors, failed to create lasting political forms; when SDS [Students for a Democratic Party] was torn apart, so was the chance for continuity." Consequently, "the New Left failed to produce the political leaders one might have expected of a movement so vast." "The millennial, all-or-nothing moods of the Sixties," Gitlin contends, "proved to be poor training grounds for practical politics."[9] Similarly, a great number of Jesus freaks were ill prepared to organize any sort of sustained activist effort. After all, the end was near!

But the 1980s proved pivotal for post–Jesus Movement evangelicals, many still licking their wounds in the aftermath of the Jesus-freak exodus from culture. Activism was then recast for something wholly different, namely, to serve the Religious Right throughout the Reagan years, which was a near-tacit approval of everything progressive evangelicals stood against.[10] Put simply, cultural activism took on new meanings. Evangelicals, says Magee, "continued to focus on the larger economic social issues."[11] But to what end?

The Republicans aligned themselves with personal moral issues that they felt coincided with their political program. *Personal morality and responsibility was juxtaposed against government sponsored social irresponsibility in their rhetoric.* Concern over abortion, drugs and other issues that the Jesus people were concerned with were also by Republicans and in exchange they got support for the larger Republican economic program.[12]

Social and cultural activism was used to serve the rising tide of neoliberal agendas, to which Reagan-era policies are often connected. In short, the Republican Party attracted a very significant ally in the Jesus Movement—and the glacial tide of unfettered individualism would soon take on a religious smell. To complicate matters, the apocalyptic fears of Jesus freaks had to fade into the backdrop of globalization and Reagan's New World Order. But what about the power of local community? What of the once evangelical aversion to industrial capitalism? And doesn't unrestrained global capitalism contradict everything the Jesus freak stood for? These peculiarities have for years complicated our understanding of how the evangelical Christian views society and culture. It is within this liminality that JPUSA's ongoing experiment bridges a curious gap. It has occupied an interstitial space, one informed by New Left ideals and a Christian understanding of justice, not dissimilar to the Catholic Left or nineteenth-century progressivism.

JPUSA leadership began to view their divine calling as one that required a fierce commitment to those living (and surviving) in Uptown. Their vision can be traced to other luminaries, but they were not all evangelical. In Chicago, Catholic Worker and Social Gospel organizations certainly offered their fair share of relief efforts. But despite a rich history of evangelical outreach, historian Randall Balmer maintains that their efforts were not entirely seated within the time-honored tradition of liberal social justice. Throughout much of the nineteenth century, those who adopted dispensational premillennialism tended to "withdraw from campaigns of social reform . . . to devote their full attention to preparations for the Second Coming of Jesus, which entailed cultivating inner-piety and trying to convert others to the faith." Balmer goes on to highlight the exodus of evangelicals from public life and service, stating, "In the face of mounting social ills, evangelicals shifted their attentions from the long term to the short term—because the time was so brief, they believed, until the return of Jesus." D. L.

Moody viewed the world as wrecked, and he abandoned social reform for its own sake, focusing instead on "individual regeneration"—salvation of the human soul.[13]

Balmer's argument notwithstanding, there are examples of evangelical involvement with religious social work in Chicago. The Temperance Movement, the Salvation Army, and evangelical "rescue" work in the Pacific Garden Mission and the Moody Mission (later the Sunshine Gospel Mission) are evidence that evangelicals were socially attuned in ways that exceeded what may be commonly attributed to evangelicalism. Still, the critique offered by Balmer, at least as it concerns evangelicals and not liberal Protestants, highlights a paradigm that continues to define many conservative evangelicals today, or at least the public perception of evangelical Christians. Moody was involved in social outreach. The Pacific Garden Mission offered solace and "deliverance" to the downtrodden. But for what purpose? To a certain extent, there is a qualitative difference between activist approaches offered by evangelicals like Moody and organizations such as the Pacific Garden Mission, if compared to the liberal (evangelical) mainline. And this is certainly evident in their historical accounts. For Moody, salvation for the human soul was paramount. For the Pacific Garden Mission, offering wayfaring strangers an alternative to the devilish temptations of Chicago met the biblical mandate to share the gospel and make disciples. Meeting physical need was merely part of a larger thrust to rescue would-be converts from sin and Hell. But for liberals, justice was far more connected to the social gospel.

In contradistinction to a man considered the quintessential evangelical (Moody), JPUSA adopted what one could consider an unabridged version of the gospel, one broadly conceived, treating salvation of individuals in a holistic manner. But its antecedents prepared the way for a social consciousness long absent within evangelical circles. Viewing the social reform efforts of the Old Left as flawed, those within the New Left focused on individual persons, taking up what Todd Gitlin refers to as "practical moralisms."[14] These activists viewed their forerunners as outdated, overly focused on the economics of the proletariat. For them, the American middle class "seemed impersonal, bureaucratic, and inhumane," says historian James J. Farrell. A pacifist, Marxist, and Christian Socialist, Dorothy Day (1898–1980) was a significant figure in American Catholic social justice. Farrell points to the revolutionary publication of both Day and the French peasant intellectual Peter Maurin: "The *Catholic Worker* decried the assumption of American capitalism (and of American labor) that work could be understood mainly as a commodity rather than as a means of fulfilling people's spiritual and material needs." Maurin underscores Pope Pius XI's argument that raw materials leave the factory "ennobled" while workers come out "degraded."[15] Their teaching provided a model for hospitality houses, Christian communal living, and ethics based on the teachings of Gandhi. Among other social outreach measures, Day founded the Chicago House, which provided shelter for over three hundred individuals nightly. In many ways, the New Left drew inspiration from both Day and Maurin.

Although the Left seemed largely divorced from evangelicalism during the 1960s, many of the forerunners were grounded in the same impulse that continues to inspire JPUSA. Alive and well at the YMCA, University of Texas, a leftist faction grew. Inspired by the writings of Paul Tillich, Albert Camus, Reinhold Niebuhr, H. Richard Niebuhr, and Martin Luther King, Jr., the Students for a Democratic Society hoped to alleviate existential anxiety through finding a purpose in life, hoping to realize what the Old Left could not. Marx and Camus influenced the SDS community, but they also provided a sort of theoretical anchor for the members of the Christian Faith-and-Life Community at the University of Texas, embracing the "humanist ethos" as compatible with Christian doctrine, according to historian Doug Rossinow.

Chicago's homeless population benefited from social philosophies that originated with the New Left and the Catholic Left. And the problems associated with Chicago's Uptown have warranted action on the part of social outreach groups such as JPUSA.[16] The SDS established models for collective activism that were indeed *collectivist*, but they were not totalitarian. Rossinow notes how during the formative years of the New Left, both the Student Nonviolent Coordinating Committee (SNCC) and the SDS encouraged the concept of a "redemptive community." In their search for authentic examples of humanitarianism, New Left radicals believed the search for human authenticity occurred "in a communal context."[17] When the options were examined (the isolationism of a free-market system and the conformity indicative of collectivism), a middle way was considered—one that would ameliorate the crisis of meaning by providing a sense of community, but without totalitarian control. JPUSA's attempt to locate a balance between the individual and the community, while often falling short, has, to an extent, translated the philosophy of New Left radicalism in service to the evangelical worldview. This balancing act has helped the group develop a measure of integrity (often modeled through their music groups) that seeks to shed light on social inequities. And this bleeds into the neighborhood, humanizing all caught in the path.

Depersonalization of the individual often accompanies urban poverty, and it defines the landscape of Uptown. Through the 1960s and 1970s youth sought to pool their resources, hoping to counter a climate that came to define parts of Chicago and American society.[18] Sociologist Noreen Cornfield considers how during the counterculture, Chicago's communes attracted dedicated adherents to what amounted to ephemeral experiments. She writes: "During the 1970s, hundreds of young adults in the Chicago area sought to demonstrate their moral convictions by living in secular, urban communal households. Few of these communes survived after the end of the Vietnam War and the decline of the protest movements of the 1960s. Although the communes were temporary, their histories broaden our vision of social possibilities."[19]

These "moral convictions" recaptured many of the same impulses that defined the New Left. Moreover, the temporality of the communes and the exodus of urban churches as they retreated to the suburbs created a space for evangelicals to experiment with left-wing ideas, but within an evangelical framework. Thus Chicago has contributed to a context that warranted evangelical outreach that was to a large extent left wing. In considering JPUSA's activism and political affiliations as related to problems associated with Uptown, it is possible to trace some elements of the New Left to JPUSA. Although JPUSA adopted a theological statement that placed it firmly within the ranks of conservative evangelicalism, its focus (even when it looked for the Second Coming of Christ) had been on feeding its neighbor, spiritually and physically. JPUSA chose to adopt a more holistic model of the gospel.

There have been various attempts at resolving the problems created by poverty in Uptown, but few have succeeded. Gentrification, states one

JPUSA communard, has been the cause of relocation for a number of homeless persons. *Cornerstone* magazine offered JPUSA's perception of the housing crisis in Uptown that warranted immediate action:

> As "Reaganomics" took hold in the early 1980s, homelessness suddenly became one of Uptown's most noticeable features. Entire families had nowhere to go. The total number of those we provided dinner for grew (to between two hundred and three hundred a day), and the complexion of those eating with us changed as well, from predominantly single men to entire families. The vast government cuts in housing programs also created a tremendous demand for temporary shelter of any kind. It was obvious that housing had become Uptown's most pressing problem, and we were compelled toward finding solutions.[20]

These government cuts were part of a larger initiative by President Reagan to reduce corporate taxes. Reduction of the welfare state was paramount for conservatives. After Reagan assumed office in 1981, his administration advanced this initiative, going on to set a course that would become more business friendly in a labor-sensitive economy, notes sociologist Alexandar R. Thomas.[21] Reagan appointed antiunion officials to the National Labor Relations Board, who then outsourced production and hired permanent replacements for striking workers. Writes Thomas:

> Reagan himself pursued such a policy when he fired eleven thousand striking air traffic controllers in 1981. Regulations designed to protect the environment, worker safety, and consumer rights were summarily decried as unnecessary government meddling in the marketplace. Programs designed to help the poor were also characterized as "big government," and the people who utilized such programs were often stigmatized as lazy or even criminal. With the help of both political parties, the administration drastically cut social welfare spending and the budgets of many regulatory agencies.[22]

JPUSA felt the sting of these cuts, and the crisis (in the estimation of JPUSA communards) was a direct result of Reagan-era policies.

Chicago groups such as Hull House, JOIN, and Heart of Uptown have attempted to solve the crisis, as have pietistic denominations such as the Salvation Army. But JPUSA's mixture of evangelical spiritualism and leftist activism informed how the commune related to other city activists of the secular persuasion. JPUSA's direct response en masse to the problem of homelessness in Uptown occurred in the 1980s. Trott's recollection reinforces Todd Gitlin's 1970 account of Uptown, demonstrating how Gitlin's analysis is applicable to subsequent years. Trott recalls that by "the mid-eighties, homelessness had become not only a neighborhood but a national problem. This was glaringly obvious in Uptown, where in the best of times homeless men and women are easily visible, wandering down Wilson or Broadway streets. In the wake of budget cuts, homelessness became epidemic."[23]

And this was no surprise. For Reagan's administration, social policy was, according to Thomas, simply of lower priority than fiscal policy.[24] While JPUSA recognized the need for action, its affiliation with other radical groups came slowly. Trott recalls the urgency that marked Uptown:

> Between the years of 1970 and 1985, nearly fifteen thousand units of low-income housing vanished in Uptown. Then-radical Todd Gitlin . . . wrote in 1970 of his group's efforts to stop gentrification in Uptown. He thought they had succeeded in halting the construction of a community college which would have required the leveling of much of Uptown's core low-income housing. Heart of Uptown picked up the fight that Gitlin's group (JOIN) left behind, but by 1980, Truman College was a reality and 1,500 apartments were history.[25]

The connection to such groups came later. JPUSA's initial perception of Heart of Uptown created distance between the two groups. JPUSA was misguided, according to Trott:

> We believed the worst about Heart of Uptown without once sitting down and talking to them, grappling with their zealous rage at what was happening to Uptown's poor. Perhaps, like many "good" Christians, we tended to equate conservative politics with conservative morals. And we couldn't

help but react to Heart's adversarial approach to politics. We also—and this hurts to admit— reacted to their harsh exteriors, their unpolished language and angry tone. But if we had listened, we would have learned.[26]

JPUSA learned to cooperate with different organizations that held a common goal. Over the years the sociopolitical climate of Uptown has been the primary reason for JPUSA's willingness to join forces with various activist organizations. Groups like JOIN and Heart of Uptown began to respond to a growing crisis, locally and nationally. "Uptown's history" writes Trott, "was not unique. Both in Chicago and elsewhere, the one-sided struggle between the poor and building speculators has gone on for decades. Low-income neighborhoods fell into the hands of landlords who milked poor renters but didn't keep up the buildings."[27]

JPUSA's mission in Chicago is synonymous with that of others who sought social justice over any eagerness to see the Second Coming. Founder John Herrin recalls how the commune viewed outreach in the early days and why they chose Chicago: "It was just a big town and it was [a] really different environment . . . and most of the churches in the inner city (at least on the north side here) were really struggling to stay alive then."[28] As the population changed it became more diverse. Parishioners who had become mainstays either aged and passed away or moved to the suburbs. Churches once peopled by a couple thousand grew sparse, later attracting a mere forty on Sundays. For these Jesus freaks, Uptown's charm was its need. "And it was a different mission field, you know? We weren't . . . necessarily talking to high school kids. We were talking to all kind of folks with a lot of different problems. But we began to feel that maybe, maybe God wanted us to stay in Chicago, maybe that's why we came here."[29]

Groups like JPUSA continue to offer aid to the residents of urban America. However, JPUSA's vision is very different from suburban, evangelical Christianity—particularly baby boomers. Although the Evangelical Left is not a new movement, progressive Christians continue to embrace a leftist ethos, sweltering under a perception that the American pursuit of wealth is a destructive force, adversely affecting communities such as the 46th Ward. And the sentiment (the outrage) migrated from the New Left, giving rise to evangelical leftists such as author-activist Jim Wallis. But why do such diverging views continue? Todd Gitlin's account of the 1968 Democratic National Convention in Chicago includes an assessment of how the event still affected American culture in 1987 (the year of the book's publication). He writes: "Two decades later, the polarizations etched into the common consciousness that week [August 25–30, 1968] are still working their way through American politics."[30] Gitlin's account reveals an impulse that grew and continues to inspire social activists on the left.

The trajectory established by the New Left galvanized those who sympathized with both left-wing activism and evangelical Christianity. Jim Wallis decided to combine an evangelical theological orientation with a social position commonly associated with the Left. As one who felt the impact of the earlier movement, Wallis was able to enter the evangelical conversation pertaining to social justice with a sense of authenticity. Early in his life, Wallis became disenchanted with how Christianity was presented—a personal belief with little social relevance. After returning to his faith, he resolved, "God is personal, but never private."[31] In *God's Politics*, he writes: "The religious and political Right gets the meaning of religion mostly wrong—preferring to focus only on sexual and cultural issues while ignoring the weightier matters of justice. And the secular Left doesn't seem to get the meaning and promise of faith for politics at all—mistakenly dismissing spirituality as irrelevant to social change."[32]

The progressive-tinged suspicion for both Right and Left characterizes JPUSA. And like Wallis, *this* form of progressivism continues to populate the Democratic Party with Christians, finally bringing the United States its first African American president. The position of Wallis and JPUSA, however, still bears more resemblance to the Left than to contemporary liberalism. "It is precisely because religion takes the problem of evil so seriously," writes Wallis, "that it must always be suspicious of too much concentrated power—politically *and* economically—either in totalitarian regimes or in huge multinational corporations that now have more wealth and power than many governments." But he remains equally suspicious of religious claims, particularly when "claims of inspiration and success invoke theology and the name of God."[33]

While many in the New Left were not religious, like Wallis, their lack of faith in institutions led to an increased faith in radical activism as they took matters into their own hands. And in the case of JPUSA, this extended beyond soup kitchens and shelters. For leaders like Trott, it has become necessary to align with left-wing forces in Chicago. And it has also become quite necessary to challenge the Religious Right. During the 2004 presidential election, the Christian Coalition's Pat Robertson (the 700 Club) stated, "I think George Bush is going to win in a walk. I really believe I'm hearing from the Lord it's going to be like a blowout election in 2004. The Lord has just blessed him. . . . It doesn't make any difference what he does, good or bad."[34] Doesn't make a difference? Trott hopes to inform Christians and non-Christians of the "alternative" to the Religious Right, the Secular Left, and mainline, liberal Christianity. What's more, Pat Robertson's endorsement of Mitt Romney for the 2012 presidential election crystalized what leftists had thought all along: the Religious Right is more concerned with fiscal conservatism than with theological difference.

As if the gulf between the Christian Right and Left was not broad enough, JPUSA's activism bears similarity to revolutionaries demonized by conservatives in the not-too-distant past. JPUSA has protested American arms dealers who gathered at O'Hare Airport for an "Arms Bazaar" where third-world nations showed up to buy. Its members have engaged in peaceful protests outside abortion clinics. They have marched against Bush's "illegal war in Iraq." They have held counterdemonstrations against hard-right Baptist minister Fred Phelps, founder of the "God Hates Fags" website. And they have been connected to political involvement with Helen Shiller, once aligned with the Black Panthers and SDS.[35] A progressive alderwomen in Chicago, Shiller has been noted for her activism in the 46th Ward. Votes cast by JPUSA communards were "the difference in her first being elected in 1987."[36] Moreover, the community's affiliation with Shiller has served to further distinguish them from political conservatives. For most, all this would be ample fodder for conservatives who would sever the community's reputation as "evangelical." More to the point, members of a growing movement within evangelical Christianity would find their affiliations perfectly in line with Jesus's call for love. In this spirit, they worked with Organization of the North East, a group made up of every progressive and ethnic group in the Uptown/Rogers Park area, and they have remained actively involved in issues concerning housing, jobs, race, class, and gender. The New Left responded to a set of crises while challenging the methods of the Old Left. In like manner, JPUSA challenged the theoretical approach of the Religious Right and establishment evangelicalism.

The combined forces of urban poverty, free-market capitalism, and multiculturalism tend to exacerbate economic tension. In considering the landscape of mid-twentieth-century American religion and politics, historian George Marsden has emphasized the importance of the liberal/conservative divide, clarifying differences that have theological and political implications:

> On the liberal side of the divide were those Americans who placed their strongest emphasis on the values of openness, pluralism, diversity, and mutual tolerance of differences. If these Americans were religious, they typically subordinated theology to *ethical concerns*. Various resurgent conservatives, on the other hand, tended to talk more of finding ethical absolutes, which reflected long-standing Christian and Jewish teachings concerning the family, sexuality, discipline, and the importance of moral law.[37]

This divide was later exacerbated with the rise of the Moral Majority and the Christian Coalition. Still often unwilling to cede ground to any so-called liberal agenda for multinationalism, multiculturalism, or religious pluralism, conservatives have continued to nurse a long-standing objection to anyone who challenges their version of American exceptionalism. Thus we are left with "the Religious Right's shopworn narrative of the supposed Christian origins of the United States," writes Randall Balmer, "and its subsequent lapse into moral decay," a narrative that reinforces a uniquely American form of Christian individualism while also demonizing any form of collectivism.[38]

Marsden's and Balmer's quotes emphasize a strict dichotomy that is often characteristic of this period of U.S. history. And it is interesting to note that two champions of this divide (Moody the conservative and Day the liberal) have had an impact on influential students and practitioners of evangelism and social justice in Chicago. JPUSA's emphasis on balancing the needs of the individual and the community bridges a gap, its workers attempting to achieve the "greater good" (funding for the community and its social outreach programs) and, in so doing, finding nonmonetary value in the goods produced.

According to historian James Farrell, the *Port Huron Statement* was the first manifesto of the SDS, which (among many things) "called for the end of the depersonalization that reduces human beings to the status of things." Furthermore, it called for "human independence" while warning against "egotistic individualism." This imbued a sense of humanism into the SDS.[39] JPUSA's valuation of humanity exceeds the monetary payoff often sought in mainstream society. Moreover, communards such as Trott consistently note that American capitalism is one cause for the poverty and depersonalization often associated with postindustrial society. And while the Bible mostly informs the community's sense of humanitarianism, it is JPUSA's location that has continued to inspire its activism.

CHICAGO'S BACKYARD CELLAR

Chicago's history of radical politics, evangelical Christianity, and Catholic sympathy toward social activism has influenced the way JPUSA operates. Through its music and the Cornerstone Festival, this radicalism bled into other expressions of evangelical Christianity. Uptown's history of poverty, violence, cultural and racial diversity, class struggle, and deep religious faith created an environment largely defined by a sense of urgency. Thus JPUSA's choice to adopt a life of voluntary poverty places it in better standing with the local homeless population. *Cornerstone* magazine underscored the urgency that characterizes Uptown Chicago: "Who is Uptown? Uptown is alcoholic. Uptown is dope addict. Uptown is walking down the streets with your hands in your pockets. Uptown is gangs of all shapes and sizes. Uptown is old people . . . living all alone. Uptown spells divorce, and trying to get work at the 'daily pay' places."[40]

The neighborhood has changed over the years, but the basic problems associated with poverty remain: Uptown remains entrenched in a way of life that is a result of poverty. Amid the workaday world of Uptown there is 920 West Wilson Avenue. JPUSA's Friendly Towers is a relatively unassuming structure, when one considers its cultural reach throughout the years. My own visits have been relatively uneventful, though on arrival I understood that the culture is very different from my native suburbia. Sitting in my rental car, I caught the attention of a group of men standing on the sidewalk. I was clearly an outsider. Waiting for them to properly analyze both my car and me, I pretended to check messages on my cell phone, hoping to avoid exiting the vehicle. What did they want? After they lost interest, I set about my way, only to be greeted by others who needed spare change; most of my visits have included individuals seeking whatever assistance I could offer.

Streets in the neighborhood are peppered with apartments and stores, including a number of ethnic restaurants and food markets. Storefront signs are mostly in the native language of the merchant. Block after block is a mixture of storefronts, old gated houses, and alleys. The visual elements of just one street (which goes on for miles) are complemented by the mixed smells of fresh food and dumpsters. Motorists invite pedestrians into their sonic worlds of oversized stereo speakers, only to be outdone by the inevitable siren of a rescue vehicle. And pedestrians threaten motorists who are not driving with caution.

This scene indicates urbanity, not poverty. However, the dilapidation is clear when one looks at various buildings and the unending supply of metal trusses used for building repair, measures that never quite appear to be complete. And the ever-present population of seemingly troubled pedestrians indicates that mental illness is fairly ubiquitous throughout this part of the city. As some pass by, speaking to themselves or mumbling incoherently, others are clearer in their intentions, albeit startling. In one case a man and a woman were (it appeared) waiting for the bus. The cries of their child, who was no more than five, were met with boisterous threats from the father: "Be quiet!"

For a suburbanite it's difficult to find any sense of equanimity. And perhaps years of exposure to inner-city poverty does little to quell anxiety or to emotionally callus those who live here. The needs of this population—the tensions endemic to overcrowding and poverty—have been in place since well before postwar migrations northward. Nevertheless, this crisis scenario is unique in that it continues in the wake of the Daley years. As with any third-world scenario, the neighborhood attracts those on a mission. The ever-present notion of crisis necessitates JPUSA's service-based nature as a collective group. And for Kanter, the service-based commune seeks to serve "a special population; they have a mission."[41]

Cultural accommodation indeed accounts for why most communities survive and remain sustainable. This band of believers are able to nurture long-standing convictions while still holding those convictions under the microscope of public opinion, always reexamining their assumptions, unlike other groups associated with the Jesus Movement. Jon Trott recalls how others never fully flourished:

> Nationally, the Jesus movement was less and less visible. The Children of God, the Way International, and others had made inroads into the Jesus People's [the larger movement] ranks, yet regarding attempts at communal living, the number one result was not cultism but *eventual disintegration*. The widespread disappearance of nearly all the Jesus communes was a sign hard to interpret, many commentators suggesting that such communes—along with the movement overall—had merely been a "fad."[42]

The Children of God did not entirely disintegrate. However, controversies[43] that drew media attention forced the group to relocate its efforts abroad. While they continue as The Family International, the group exhibits meager cultural influence.[44] But why were such communes viewed as a fad? Why did they disintegrate?

The power of commitment is significant when applied to particular locations, each representing different sociocultural needs, warranting different forms and levels of commitment. Success, particularly when considering the context of Uptown, is achieved when high intercommunal expectations (and the erasure of competing commitments unrelated to the commune) are coupled with the affirmative boundary-distinction of the service-oriented commune. JPUSA's urban location makes necessary this sort of Kantnerian distinction. For example, historian Timothy Miller's account of rural communes portrays those who seek detachment from society, each group committed to constructing and maintaining a life defined against a postindustrial, mechanistic, materialistic world. In so doing, the main struggle for purpose involved fulfillment (and thus sustainability), primarily for communards.

In the case of urban, inner-city communes, the struggle for purpose (the sacrifice of one's personal agenda and privacy) surpasses therapeutic experiments for self-actualization or attempts to realize the ideal community, an impulse often characteristic of rural collectives. Inner-city communes such as JPUSA find fulfillment and purpose by extending their sense of struggle and purpose toward helping those living in the neighborhood. Undeniably the significance for how any community defines purpose is indelibly linked to a relationship to a specific location. Not surprising, there are two processes to healthy, sustained commitment: disassociation and association. The process of dissociation involves an individual's detachment from other competing obligations and responsibilities. The process of association attaches an individual (and, by implication, his or her identity) to communards and to the overall objectives of the community, thus solidifying a symbiotic relationship—the communard needs the community and the community needs the communard. Without this relationship, the communard might not find a sense of satisfaction (at least as he or she has defined satisfaction), and the businesses and outreach programs would simply not function. Ultimately, the problems associated with Uptown and JPUSA's mission to handle those problems are precisely the attraction for newcomers.

New members often join hoping to find emotional healing or a sense of purpose. Communard Raye Clemente notes her desire to serve Jesus and the homeless while also maintaining a subcultural ethos, as well as a relatively liberal political position.[45] Joshua Davenport was "angry with organized religion."[46] Otto Jensen had been seeking a new model of church.[47] Each has a need that must be filled. As it turns out, longevity of communities may be a result of how they negotiate the particulars of both the individualism of the mainstream and the collectivism demonstrated in the Book of Acts.

In a 1976 issue of *Cornerstone* magazine, Jon Trott cites Dietrich Bonhoeffer, who argued that Christians have a duty to be citizens of two worlds. According to Bonhoeffer, "The disciples of Jesus must not fondly imagine that they can simply run away from the world and huddle together in a little band."[48] Of course, this community does not retreat in this manner. Their location makes active social engagement necessary, if not wholly an element that defines their identity. For Trott, "the truth of the above quotation [by Bonhoeffer] is a constant burden of balance to us. The balance of not becoming a sheltered cloister of Christians blessing each other, or going the other way and getting into such a social gospel that there is no spiritual feeding or security within ourselves."[49]

Like so many other scenarios, negotiation and compromise become the hallmark for forward momentum. Although others have chosen to shirk the establishment by way of retreat, these believers have soundly avoided sociocultural isolation. But is the location of Uptown enough to sustain them? Can JPUSA, or any community for that matter, achieve a New Testament utopia? Communal enclaves of "warm, close, supportive relationships, writes Kanter, "[do] not always occur according to scenario. Reality modifies the dream." That is to say, although JPUSA's ideological position occasions an ongoing negotiation with the parent culture (one that allows ideological accommodation in the interest of relevance and sustainability), the group's choice of lifestyle might be in conflict with what is expected by establishment evangelicalism. Kantner writes that "the assumptions they [a community] make about what is possible and desirable in social life challenge the assumptions made by other sectors of American society."[50] But why would other sectors of society even care? Why does this particular group even matter?

JPUSA's lifestyle challenges the mainstream simply because its presence is inconvenient. Put another way, it problematizes the dominant narratives about American evangelical Christianity. First, the community's continuance as a visible, urban expression of the Jesus-freak movement serves as a reminder that the countercultural revival (thought faddish by sociologists) has had an impact that is far-reaching and incalculable. As a result of this miscalculation, there are relatively few studies on the larger movement. And these studies would have been quite useful for political analysts! Second, and more important, JPUSA's voluntary poverty, political position, left-wing activism, and dalliance, through the Cornerstone Festival, with new definitions of "sacred music" all form an image of a type of evangelical quite atypical of dominant narratives and mythologies often paramount to maintaining a "definable" base that can, for example, continue the hegemony of Republican Party–evangelical relations. JPUSA's version of the "Jesus-freak impulse" is actually structured as an alternative to the American Dream.

When the Cornerstone Festival was still in play, a symbiosis occurred that continued this curious mixture of evangelical mission and antiestablishment populism. The interplay between urban rescue mission and the festival placed JPUSA in a unique situation. But when one considers its alternative to the American Dream, radical as it may seem, one could draw a different conclusion. Isn't this yet another example of a faith-based relief organization, a largely conservative thrust? At first glance this indeed suggests that JPUSA's economic structure is actually more right-wing, if faith-based initiatives are any indication. But in considering George W. Bush's national push for faith-based initiatives, Jon Trott argues that to assume this initiative is right leaning is predicated on two assumptions. The first is that communes are primarily inspired by Marxist principles that question free-market capitalism. While Karl Marx had valid points concerning capitalist models of production and trade, JPUSA was actually inspired by the model of living established in the Book of Acts, not Marx. The second assumption is that the faith-based initiative, though inclusive in its language, is conservative by virtue of its affinity for *religion* as an answer to social problems, rather than nonsectarian governmental measures. Trott disagrees with the second assumption in two ways: First, he does not believe government-funded religious efforts undermine the separation of church and state. Second, he believes that measures become "conservative" only when they marginalize the efforts of other religious groups, noting President Obama's encouragement of faith-based social programs. Thus government, in the context of American society, actually serves a plurality of religious efforts. The matter becomes problematic only when Christianity is privileged for the purpose of government hegemony. Trott writes:

Where it would get dicey is if Evangelicals, or Catholics, or even Christians got the best seats at the table simply because of their identity religiously speaking. That said, I was deeply offended when, at an Evangelical Press Association convention a few years ago, the Bush White House sent a speaker to pitch us Evangelicals. His riff was disgustingly manipulative, consisting of a warning to us that if we didn't make sure the Republicans kept the White House (must have been in 2003 or 2004), all that Faith-based [money] would go the way of the Cuckoo Bird.[51]

Regardless of how faith-based relief efforts are positioned on the political spectrum, JPUSA's particular efforts are still inconsistent with how establishment evangelicalism perceives social aid, the allocation of wealth, and the American Dream generally. Furthermore, other inner-city rescue missions, such as Catholic agencies, do not necessarily challenge the American mainstream. In some regards, these agencies do the dirty work others are unwilling to engage in. But since JPUSA highlights what the American Dream fails to do, emphasizing poverty and free enterprise's inability to create jobs and wealth, it challenges the myth of the dream.

Throughout the late 1970s and 1980s, *Cornerstone* magazine emphasized how JPUSA perceived the American Dream. The following suggests that the United States had misguided priorities when considering the family: "And man said, 'Let the laborers under the leaders be gathered together in factories and let their children be raised in Day-Care-Centers'; and it was done."[52] The magazine also emphasized the ill attempts at resolving poverty:[53] "We expected the roaches, the rats and the mice. We expected the slum landlords offering poor plumbing and no heat, all for only $200 a month. Somehow we take it for granted. We, the fortunate, have learned the art of x-ing out entire sections, cities, and countries from our conscience. And Uptown is no exception."[54]

Uptown has sensitized JPUSA to poverty and mobilized its members to explore causal links (both real and assumed) between poverty and the sufferer. That is, JPUSA considers all potential factors when looking at urban poverty and homelessness: drug and alcohol abuse, mental illness, violence, cycles of inherited oppression, racism, unemployment, urban renewal, gentrification, and failed church and government social programs. Again, this reinforces the holistic interpretation of the gospel, one that considers human problems to be more about structural sin than individual sin. And if the problem is structural, the balance between individual and community, market and government, then operates as a counterweight to the cultural mainstream that appears married to political binaries and ideological gridlock. But how does JPUSA combine two opposing forces?

Location also plays a role in JPUSA's unique combination of socialism and capitalism. Yes, the community self-identifies as socialistic. But they also engage in free enterprise. However, this "agreement" with capitalism can be attributed to the way American society is already structured. Their choice to live in an urban area (rather than an agrarian setting) necessitates a relationship with industry. Moreover, their choice to fund social programs with private monies (though some government assistance can be accounted for) is necessitated by the government's inability to fully eradicate poverty. But regardless of the reasons for JPUSA's free-market agreement, how can it be considered socialist? It is possible to reconcile its socialism and capitalism by considering its economic structure on the micro level. Although the community must engage industry to generate income (since the government will not provide all needs), the common-purse arrangement places them in a different category. In essence, JPUSA's council (which decides how monies are distributed and to whom) acts as the government—at least when considering matters pertaining to daily life in JPUSA.[55] Yes, JPUSA's method of feeding and housing the poor amounts to a position that, in some sense, actually affirms the free market's right-leaning position; the community relies on self-initiative and private funding (their own) rather than state-based welfare provisions. But in this manner JPUSA also exhibits the anarchical (perhaps anarcho-syndicalism?) ideals of the New Left; the community distrusts both corporate *and* governmental powers and seeks to concentrate power and resources within their own local collective.

Any system of authority has to justify itself, since they are not, as Noam Chomsky aptly quips, self-authenticating. Howard Zinn's assertion that the New Left served "to create constellations of power outside the state" in the interest of "voluntary small groups" reaffirms the Left's tendency to disassociate with any version of totalitarian control.[56] In this manner, any form of collectivism that seeks dissociation from big business or big government casts its collective vote toward anarchy, or at the very least a micro version of a socialistic enclave. While this suggests that JPUSA offers little allegiance to the dominant political parties in the United States, most members continue to associate with liberal Democrats.

CONCLUSION

The Midwest has a strong history of evangelicalism, populist activism, and social reform. It is, according to the poet Allen Ginsberg, a vortex. And given Chicago's particular history, it comes as no surprise that a radical group would choose to call this city home. Impoverished neighborhoods still exist, warranting action from groups willing to serve. Uptown has been viewed as a port of entry for a variety of cultural and ethnic backgrounds. The migration of disparate ethnic groups and the massive influx of Appalachian "hillbillies" into Uptown created a multifaceted neighborhood, one that confirms why scholars envisage the causes of urban pluralism, poverty, and the impact of Chicago politics. However, to accept how the inhabitants (particularly the homeless) are often portrayed does a disservice to those who suffer and undermines any sustained effort to humanize them.

The structure of JPUSA remains influenced by the New Left's emphasis on the noble individual and the Catholic Worker model of community. Unable to ignore poverty, the core ethos of JPUSA is reinforced by location. The environment is such that cultural accommodation and engagement become natural results of a relationship between the group and the outside world. Put rather bluntly, JPUSA has successfully survived because Chicago's own backyard was in need of tending. Its ability to move with the flow of a neighborhood defined by pluralism and socioeconomic tension tested the metal of the group. And the result has been a level of activism largely absent within establishment evangelicalism. Still, JPUSA's ability to maintain its evangelical allegiance has, in many ways, endeared it to the more conservative strands of evangelical Christianity. But its decidedly radical approach to social justice and sympathies with the Evangelical Left remain a departure from mainstream establishment evangelicalism, raising the question: which form of evangelical Christianity will dominate the twenty-first century? Furthermore, does JPUSA's affiliation with New Left principles of activism portend newer, more radical versions of political and theological positions within the commune or within American evangelicalism? The next chapter will explore the evolving ethos of the JPUSA community and its possible implications for the greater evangelical subculture.

5
THEOLOGY, POLITICS, AND CULTURE
✶ ✶ ✶

Religious movements in the United States have often influenced how people of faith define and understand culture and social justice. Complicating the matter, communes (whether religious or secular) have often exhibited very limited social activism, or their levels of engagement have been structured as oppositional to mainstream society. JPUSA's choice to remain an activist group defies common understandings of communalism, particularly groups identified with varying strands of belief in the apocalypse. And it problematizes evangelical Christianity during a time when evangelicalism is largely bifurcated. In the case of JPUSA, one would think solidarity with the parent culture (evangelicalism) would serve to endear it to evangelicals who have historically attended the Cornerstone Festival. While its parent denomination continues to support in word, and conservative evangelicals continued to attend Cornerstone Festival until its retirement, it is clear that neither solidarity nor ideological consistency has played a significant role in JPUSA's longevity to date. In fact, the council's ability to reinvent its public image has kept the community fresh, if controversial.

As we have seen, studies on the sustainability and longevity of intentional communities have shown that in most cases, groups structured around a charismatic leader or an inflexible ideology were often short-lived. When ideology diverges from the dominant culture, a community either disbands or remains relatively sectarian. But JPUSA has managed to avoid this. Its activism is connected to a decision to place authority in multiple leaders, whose perennial goal is to nurture a cultural relevance that binds them to their surroundings.

This chapter will demonstrate how beliefs about salvation, the end of time, and political affiliation have defined evangelical social justice in the United States, surfaced in the Jesus Movement, and come to influence JPUSA's ideological evolution. The so-called millenarian impulse influenced evangelical activism between the 1970s and 1990s, causing widespread Christian fascination with Rapture theology, to the extent that a cottage industry of end-times publishing swept up churches sweltering under the impression that a demonic "one-world government" would either wholly eradicate spiritual freedom or arise as the arbiter of doomsday. The chapter demonstrates how this impulse was revitalized during the Jesus Movement, was celebrated in popular evangelical music, and is now losing force, as evangelicals begin to question religious certainty. The chapter concludes with the claim that theological and political adaptability has contributed to JPUSA's longevity and social impact, warranting a larger question: would a similar functional paradigm serve society as a whole?

PLACING JPUSA WITHIN EVANGELICALISM: MODERN TO POSTMODERN

Broadly speaking, the Jesus Movement included four different expressions. These have, in some fashion or another, contributed to remapping the landscape of American evangelicalism: evangelical, new paradigm churches such as Calvary Chapel and Vineyard; isolationist communes such as the Children of God and Tony and Susan Alamo's Christian Foundation; mainstream communes such as Shiloh houses; and groups such as Jesus People Army and JPUSA's parent group, Jesus People Milwaukee. Despite this spotted history, JPUSA cannot be counted among the post–Jesus Movement, new paradigm evangelical mainstream. Nor can it be counted among communes associated with doomsday isolationism. While isolationists constructed enclaves attempting to question a culture bereft of moral values before the advent of the apocalypse, JPUSA (though moderately millenarian in earlier years) was more interested in practical matters of justice. And although David Gordon argued that during the 1970s JPUSA exhibited the same millenarian tendencies as other Jesus freaks, the community has changed to one that is now somewhat interstitial, one that remains simultaneously antiestablishment and connected to the wider culture.[1] Unimpressed by the evangelical marketing machine, JPUSA views isolationism as dangerous to both the individual and the larger church culture. Simply put, its members are best understood as *practical contemplatives*.[2]

Always seeking to put faith into practice, their service to the poor is tempered by a thorough examination of the Right, the Left, and their own community. Consequently they enjoy some freedom to discuss ideas openly. Both leaders and rank-and-file members often form opinions based on a combination of spiritual experience, biblical exegesis, and recollections of their own religious past. Wearing an Obama shirt, jokingly referring to himself as an "Obamagelical," the outspoken politically liberal Jon Trott recalled an inability to resolve an existential crisis in his youth. And in a mainline liberal fashion, Trott's pastor suggested, "There are many roads to Rome . . . what matters is your sincerity," whatever your belief. Trott's response was measured and probing: "So, when you say God, you don't know what you mean." His pastor did not resolve the matter. "He [the pastor] did not live on the planet of anxiety that I lived on."[3]

Many JPUSA communards have attempted to find a space somewhere between the ambiguity of theological liberalism and the certainty of theological conservatism. But despite his need for clarity, for Trott, conservative responses to the world also indicate a near-flawed theology. For him, early Jesus Movement converts were sold a bill of goods. The initial humanitarianism of the Jesus Movement was eclipsed by theo-political powers (read Religious Right) that championed visions of empire (a Christian one), fears of a New World Order, and a sense of immediacy concerning personal salvation as the Rapture approached. As the Religious Right came to power, Jesus freaks were converted to a different Jesus—one that was patriotic, individualistic, and Republican. But JPUSA was able to avoid entanglement with the Right while simultaneously maintaining a relatively conservative theological position, at least for a while. Given its historical evolution, how can we classify it? And does its propensity to evolve preclude any evangelical orientation?

Even at its most conservative, evangelical Christianity is too complex to categorize. The various expressions (fundamentalist, nondenominational, Pentecostal, charismatic, orthodox, emergent) remain porous and conflicted, in part due to the forces of pluralism. Given the multiple political and theological beliefs that make up those who claim any or all of these classifications, understanding what qualifies as "membership" within each tradition remains to be seen. Alex Schaefer considers the fiscal conservatism of the post-1960s evangelical culture and the rise of liberal evangelicals, suggesting that the New Right "tapp[ed] into the anti-liberal sentiment and moral concerns of Evangelicals" and that "its embrace of *laissez-faire* is one of its weakest planks, because capitalism itself helped undermine 'traditional values.'"[4] As a result, the *language* of liberalism was used to co-opt Jesus freaks. In fact, the language of the counterculture was not entirely separate from the language of conservatives who sought limited government. After all, says historian Malcolm Magee, "the 1960s were characterized by a distrust of the government. It was not seen as too big a jump to go from an anti-Vietnam version of anti-government to a Ronald Reagan version of anti-government. Many of the rallies and concerts in which musicians were present and performed were focused on moral issues."[5] Its embrace of conservative theology and rejection of a materialism (largely associated with laissez-faire capitalism) initially defined baby boom evangelicalism. But the antimaterialism often associated with Jesus freaks faded with the rise of Reagan-era conservatism and the Jesus Movement's more significant cultural legacy, contemporary Christian music. And it's this sense of internal conflict that makes the category of evangelicalism so nebulous.

Religious and social historian D. G. Hart has argued that evangelicalism does not truly exist as a movement precisely because of its amorphous nature. While the evangelical spirit of the nineteenth century is not dismissed, Hart argues that evangelicalism is merely another form of fundamentalism. The difference is that this form of fundamentalism (conservative

Protestantism) is culturally engaged, lacks collective agreement, has no central authority, and is driven by popular opinion. For Hart, the qualifier "evangelical" is simply an adjective used to describe the zeal of a particular kind of Protestant Christian.[6] But Nathan Hatch maintains that the ability to reach decisions by popular opinion (without central authority) is, in fact, precisely what has strengthened evangelical Christianity and qualifies it as a movement.[7]

For JPUSA, the signifier "evangelical" was paramount to its communal identity throughout the 1980s. Without it the group would have remained on the fringe, with little hope of attracting large numbers to the Cornerstone Festival. In the 1980s Cornerstone offered lectures and workshops designed to train Christians in biblical apologetics (a distinction for both evangelicals and fundamentalists), using the works of C. S. Lewis, N. T. Wright, Flannery O'Conner, Francis Schaeffer, Norman Geisler, and Josh McDowell. During this era of Cornerstone, JPUSA remained unflinchingly evangelical and theologically conservative. But the dogma of conservative theology has often obscured praxis (at least for JPUSA). Engaged in critical theory to the point of allowing a certain measure of epistemological doubt, JPUSA's activism went on to distinguish it as uniquely positioned to challenge the dominant paradigm, even in the 1980s.

With the exception of minor musings over how God metes out salvation, communards (especially the council) have historically been theologically conservative, thus complicating our ability to locate them within a fully left-leaning ideology. Arguments from Hart and Hatch notwithstanding, in the 1990s there arose an upsurge of self-identified evangelicals who parted ways with ideas traditionally (if stereotypically) associated with evangelical Christianity. Then later in the decade, progressive forms of evangelicalism began to find popular acceptance, reaching a groundswell at the turn of the twenty-first century. Postmodern Christians "emerged" to enter conversations about faith, doubt, and literary criticism. So JPUSA's quest for faith simply represents one of many attempts to wrestle with the deep-seated questions associated with modernity and postmodernity, without drowning in the process.

Emergent Christianity represents an ongoing "conversation" concerning philosophical topics such as modernism, postmodernism, poststructuralism, and pluralism. Given the collapse of absolute truth-claims and the increasing fragmentation of the individual within the global economy, emergent Christians often find solace in public iterations such as www.emergentvillage.com and in progressive "postmodern" evangelical leaders such as Tony Jones, Brian McLaren, Phyllis Tickle, Doug Pagitt, Shane Claiborne, Rob Bell, and a host of "new monastics."[8] In many ways both emergent Christianity and the Evangelical Left are similar with respect to their counterrightist activism. And despite the growth of rightist allegiances, groups affiliated with the Evangelical Left and emergent Christianity have delineated the evangelical approach to culture in such a way as to allow those who adhere to various beliefs a certain margin of error, inspiring humanitarianism within those who would otherwise maintain an upward gaze colored by an imminent doomsday.

Although Christian humanitarianism was quite present in denominations such as the Salvation Army, certain nineteenth-century evangelicals, and liberal Protestants up through the 1930s, the Evangelical Left uniquely defines itself *against* mid-twentieth-century forms of evangelical Christianity that in many ways never fully realized any full-throated response to structural or systemic injustice. Now uncertain about ideological particulars, these evangelicals live with theological ambiguity, but they also apply a softer version of the social gospel, one still firmly wedded to evangelical belief. Regardless of the zeitgeist that defined JPUSA theologically, its *impulse* remained rooted in faith, one that encouraged members to live in the way of Jesus, a way that, for them, was in contradistinction to both American evangelicalism and the Religious Right. But given JPUSA's emphasis on practical human need—and attendant beliefs that both the state *and* JPUSA businesses should finance the general welfare in service of morality—how can we determine where an evangelical impulse ends and the social gospel begins? Put another way, can we consider them evangelical in the traditional sense of the term?

Historian David W. Bebbington's classic method of defining evangelical Christianity is a useful model for analyzing JPUSA's theological position. For Bebbington, the essentials of evangelical belief include a dedication to Christian conversion, biblicism (a high view of scripture), crucicentrism (the belief that the crucifixion of Christ atoned for the sins of humanity), and activism.[9] In the 1980s JPUSA exemplified all four. But was the community truly a part of evangelicalism?[10] As members of the Evangelical Covenant denomination, JPUSA has enjoyed a certain ecclesial respectability necessary for survival. Although evangelicalism may lack collective agreement (according to Hart), the movement, if we can call it that, has gained significant cultural traction that now extends into the cultural mainstream. This can be seen if one considers how evangelicals throughout the 1960s and 1970s viewed the more radical Jesus-freak communes that peppered the United States. Traditional evangelicals measured the viability of these groups based on ideological expectations common among self-defining evangelicals. As a result, many groups found themselves affiliating with the larger parent culture, hoping for evangelical acceptance.

In the interest of evangelical solidarity, the Cornerstone Festival once gave JPUSA a chance to muster a public image for the evangelical community, annually reintegrating the commune into the parent movement. But in the wake of the festival's closing, how will JPUSA fare? Without Cornerstone it may be a stretch for the group to attract travelers to their low-income operation. Furthermore, will they lose public affirmation and larger sociocultural influence? Put another way, to continue under the umbrella of evangelicalism, JPUSA must please an evangelical constituency, which is at the very least moderately conservative. But what accounts for the disparity between JPUSA and its more conservative affiliates?

RECONNECTING YOUTH TO . . . SOMETHING

Preston Shires has argued that both Christian fundamentalism and liberal Christianity alienated youth throughout the 1960s.[11] Fundamentalism was anachronistic, judgmental, and, according to historian George Marsden, culturally isolated.[12] On the other hand, liberal Christianity did not provide answers to existential anxiety, often failing to deliver on promises to aid the needy. Shires explores the collective effort to combine the best of two worlds, writing, "The eventual unity and common purpose shared between countercultural Christianity and evangelicalism surpassed that shared by the Beats and the Old Left . . . so much so that whereas the Old Left and the New Left disagreed on the means and purpose of reaching a non-capitalistic manner of life, countercultural Christianity and evangelicalism eventually became unified both in goal and practice." The "common purpose" shared by countercultural and establishment evangelicals extended into the 1970s, climaxing to form what would later become a new movement. Shires reasons that the inability for the Old and New Left to agree on strategy worked to evangelical advantage, particularly as the right came to new power during the 1980s. He continues: "And even though historians speak of evangelicalism in the latter 1970s without reference to the Jesus movement, it is the melding of these two initially somewhat distinct movements that explains why the 'evangelicalism' of 1980 was radically different from the 'evangelicalism' of 1965."[13]

Adherents to New Evangelicalism and Bill Bright's para-church organization, Campus Crusade for Christ, actively sought to recruit youth who were (in the estimation of conservatives) equally dissatisfied with watered-down liberalism and the culturally obscure, recalcitrance of fundamentalism.[14] In response, evangelical Christianity was given an intellectual boost. Then Christian apologists such as Francis Schaeffer attempted to provide polemics rooted in Scottish Common Sense Realism, while remaining unrestricted by the fundamentalist bogeyman of anti-intellectualism or a politic of separation. Schaeffer's God, according to Shires, was one who was identifiable by those disenchanted with all other human constructs, one that "middle-class youth could both have a feeling for and be intellectually proud of; and, not least in importance, he was a God who opened up infinite possibilities for human creativity by liberating the individual from naturalistic philosophy and the technocratic lifestyle naturalistic philosophy had imposed on society." Speaking the language of the counterculture, Schaeffer tapped a rhetorical strategy that resonated with Jesus freaks. "Freed from the machine and connected to the infinite," writes Shires, "the human experience became a never-ending adventure. This was full-fledged expressive individualism."[15] JPUSA embraced this early on. Schaefferian apologetics served JPUSA communards who, throughout the 1980s and part of the

1990s, sought intellectual reasons in support of faith—though, as we shall see, this would later be jettisoned.

The ability to freely experience and express God in multivalent ways became emblematic of the early Jesus freak. This distinguished the Jesus Movement from conservative, Calvinist-based evangelicalism and mainline liberalism. But unlike JPUSA, many early Jesus freaks were unconcerned with the need to intellectualize God. Embracing the Pentecostalism that attracted youth disenchanted with empty theorizing, Jesus freaks on the West Coast quickly became quintessential examples of baby boom, Jesus Movement evangelicalism. With the exception of JPUSA and the burgeoning Evangelical Left, Jesus-freak conservatism (at least the West Coast version) became the staid mythology of Jesus Movement lore.

PRACTICAL DIFFERENCES

While JPUSA reengaged Christian apologetics in the 1980s, other believers continued to find truth in spiritual experience. New paradigm, post–Jesus Movement churches provided a middle ground between liberal Christianity and fundamentalism. But this middle ground is different from Schaeffer's version. Most groups classified as "new paradigm" offered answers to existential crises while also encouraging Pentecostal expression. As such, these groups were therapeutic, individualistic, and antiestablishment. Furthermore, the emphasis on experience created a situation where the post–Jesus Movement church could be classified as both primitive and (ironically) postmodern. Historian Donald Miller has compared baby boom evangelicalism to enlightenment-based philosophical models that have traditionally dominated Western Christianity since the eighteenth century. The result, he argues, has been that "religious debates have been relegated to discussing the truth or falsity of *beliefs*, making religion 'disembodied,' cerebral matter."[16] He goes on to highlight how new paradigm Christianity has reacted to this, arguing that

> many assumptions of Enlightenment thought have been challenged. The clay feet of rationality have been revealed, and postmodern philosophy is

questioning the authoritarian character of any claim to a universal epistemology, or theory of knowledge. Given this philosophical context, new paradigm churches can be viewed as cultural pioneers of sorts. They are attempting to reintegrate bodily experience into religious life.[17]

These claims appear to establish the presence of a postmodern, evangelical criticism that actually antedates expressions of emergent Christianity. But while Miller reasons that new paradigm churches have somehow pioneered the now common acceptance of the so-called crisis of representation (a semiotic development that recognizes the problems with language), they were not so willing to dispense with a biblicist position on divine authority or encounters with the Holy Spirit. The Jesus Movement emphasized hyperspiritual experientialism. Thus a kind of "course correction" was needed, according to Jon Trott. Unlike its progenitors, JPUSA attempted to balance a moderate Pentecostalism (emblematic of Jesus Movement congregations) with Reformed apologetics. In so doing, its members embraced the teachings of a number of authors, apologists, and philosophers such as Schaeffer, C. S. Lewis, Blaise Pascal, A. W. Tozer, Søren Kierkegaard, Dietrich Bonhoeffer, Walker Percy, and G. K. Chesterton. But like most churches, the rank-and-file remain disinterested in theology or high theory, though JPUSA pastors have used "foundationalist" apologetics to offer a sense of ideological security to seekers within the commune. Still, literary rootedness did not dissuade early JPUSA communards from their skyward gaze.

JESUS FREAKS: THE WAITING

The Students for a Democratic Society were politically active, but many hippies remained (for the most part) anti-intellectual and apolitical. Thus the hippie ethic was consistent with fledgling Jesus Movement converts who sought experience over intellect, body over mind (or at least a collapse of mind-body dualism), and a soon-to-come messianic figure. For many who would have once affiliated with the New Left, concerns about social change were redirected to otherworldly matters: transformation of the self, ecstatic religious experience, and the end of time. This millennial urgency informed Jesus freaks' aversion to the "wisdom of man," inspiring an exodus from mainstream culture. Recalling H. Richard Niebuhr's *Christ and Culture*, sociologist Ronald Enroth has argued that Jesus freaks were "casebook examples of Christ-against-culture."[18]

This anticultural position allowed a focus on "ultimate concern" and personal encounters with Jesus through the Holy Spirit. And while many were only moderately Pentecostal (particularly those associated Calvary Chapel), converts and communes inherited two distinct impulses: the hippie movement's intrigue with mysticism (which translated into Pentecostal emphasis on direct encounter with the divine) and the countercultural quest for a new age, often exemplified in the belief in a secret rapture of Christians. The former influenced the latter. Disenchanted with staid denominationalism, early Jesus freaks were drawn to an experience-driven form of Christianity. Thus the Pentecostal connection (and apoliticism) should not be taken lightly. Historian Grant Wacker argues that "pentecostals were ahistorical, first, in their lack of interest in the history, and second in their conceptualization of the relation between Scripture and the cultural context in which it arose. There was, however, still another form of ahistoricism that helped sustain and insulate pentecostals from outside criticism. They were ardent millenarians."[19] Jesus freaks were similar to Pentecostals and can be located within the larger tradition of experience-based millenarianism. Even the moderately "Pentecostal" Calvary Chapel emphasized direct contact with the Holy Spirit and an inevitable climax to human history, a belief common to many forms of Protestantism.

As the charismatic movement rose to significance with churches like Vineyard (offshoots of Calvary Chapel), the larger Jesus Movement placed greater importance on the doctrine of the Rapture as new converts awaited the second coming of Christ. The result was a focus on evangelism, relegating social justice to subaltern status. But the precedent had been set earlier. Wacker writes: "It is indisputable that pentecostals were strongly influenced by an apocalyptic eschatology drawn indirectly from Adventist and directly from Plymouth Brethren traditions. They looked for the imminent rapture of the saints, followed by the return of the Lord and the events described in Daniel, Ezekiel, and Revelation."[20] And at times, heavenly signs took the form of human messengers.

MUSIC OF THE END: EARLY CHRISTIAN ROCK

Lonnie Frisbee was a hippie who converted to Christianity at the beginning of the Jesus Movement. After Pastor Chuck Smith hired Frisbee to act as a countercultural outreach pastor for Calvary Chapel (ground zero for the Jesus Movement), Frisbee quickly became iconic of the West Coast Jesus freak, his hair, beard, and public utterances likening him to an Old Testament prophet. Frisbee encouraged a skyward gaze, preaching a combination of Christian spiritualism (portents and futurism), the revolutionary hippie aesthetic, and evangelical millennialism.

Dispensational premillennialism, a doctrine fleshed out by nineteenth-century minister John Nelson Darby, found a growing audience in post-1960s Jesus Movement mythology and doctrine. Darby's doctrine reached beyond the nineteenth century into the twentieth as author Hal Lindsey's *The Late Great Planet Earth* influenced both the Jesus Movement and the emerging "Jesus music" (later, Christian rock). Although Jesus freaks practiced an altered version of Christianity to fit the vernacular of the counterculture, they retained the primitivism of ecstatic, embodied religion, as well as a view of global events often intertwined with a dispensational premillennialist interpretation of the end of time. Early Jesus freaks were concerned with immediate conversion of souls as they prepared for the Rapture. Looking for signs of the end, Frisbee viewed the Six-Day War between Israel and the surrounding Arab nations as evidence for the imminent return of Christ. Fascination with apocalyptic literature and global events, while not new, developed at a rapid pace as books, movies, and music affiliated with the Jesus Movement told the same story: the end was near.

Authors and musicians joined the foray, each offering a warning of impending doom, as well as clues intended to help consumers decipher global events. Throughout the 1970s Jesus rockers such as Larry Norman sang about the Rapture while author Hal Lindsey encouraged unconditional support of Israel, believing that Americans were expected to play a role in unfolding prophetic events, ushering in the return of Christ, the reign of the anti-Christ, and the battle of Armageddon. Historian Preston Shires notes Lindsey's preoccupation with the Middle East's role in divine plan. For Lindsey, "The affairs in the Middle East had foreordained roles to play out: Israel, the Arab nations, the Soviet Union, Europe, and China were spirito-politico entities." Moreover, "God allowed for Arab antipathy toward the Jews to escalate so that in the near future an Arab-African confederacy headed by Egypt would attack Israel." Lindsey maintained that "biblically grounded Christians stood against Arab nations." For him, this alliance would end in a battle involving Russia. The anti-Christ would promise peace, only to later bring deception. "Part of the reason countercultural Christians would move rightward in their political orientation," argues Shires, had little to do with domestic policies, but "a great deal to do with world affairs." For early Jesus freaks, unconditional support for Israel was, according to Shires, "perhaps the first shepherding of Jesus Freaks *toward a political position*."[21]

Songs influenced by politics of the end were grounded in a deeper, populist response to a chaotic world. But they also represented a particular interpretation of historic events related to biblical prophecy. Historian David W. Stowe has argued that through the teachings of Hal Lindsey and Calvary Chapel's Pastor Chuck Smith, "the theology of Rapture and Armageddon [became] one of the *central threads* in the music and belief of Baby Boom Christians, touching the music of everyone from [Jesus rockers] Larry Norman and Keith Green to Bob Dylan."[22] Norman's classic "I Wish We'd All Been Ready" (part of the track to the film series that mirrored Lindsey's work) highlighted the sense of urgency with which evangelicals dealt; it was the anthem of the Jesus Movement's Rapture theology and became the earworm for fundamentalists and evangelicals during the 1970s.

Stowe has observed how a sense of urgency defined musicians during the 1970s and influenced various Jesus rockers, noting Lindsey's *The Late Great Planet Earth* as a significant influence on apocalyptically minded Jesus freaks. Having sold twenty-eight million copies by 1998, Lindsey's novel, writes Stowe, "popularized and condensed a body of thought about the end of the world that reached back over a century."[23] Stowe reminds us that the attraction of Lindsey's book was in its attempt to connect global events to one interpretation of biblical apocalyptic literature. Considering the events that, for many, reified pre–Jesus Movement millenarianism, Stowe notes a series of events that inspired a generation to continue their skyward gaze: "All that remained to complete prophecy was a rebuilding of the Temple on its original site in Jerusalem, where the Muslim Dome of the Rock currently stands." Events intended to set into motion history's end "seemed imaginable in the late Sixties." He continues: "The rise of an Antichrist promising to bring world peace; the bodily ascent of Christians to heaven, called the Rapture; seven years of persecution and disaster, the tribulation, presided over by the Antichrist; a final show down between Israel and her enemies, Armageddon, in which Jesus would return to lead Israel to final victory. Then the millennium, a thousand years of peace. Lindsey's book was colored by his experiences with the Jesus People."[24] The greatest impact of this teaching can be seen in Christian media. And the influence on grassroots efforts to *missionize* can be seen in Jesus Movement communes and the street proselytizing of Jesus freaks, prevalent throughout the 1970s and early 1980s.

It is within this milieu that JPUSA evolved from a skyward-looking group of Jesus freaks to a community eager to plumb the depths of biblical foundationalism, a reaction to hyperspiritualism. But while they were influenced by millenarianism throughout the 1970s, they adopted a more nuanced approach to the doctrine of the Rapture as the 1980s wore on. For founding member Glenn Kaiser, JPUSA has always sought to meet the "real on-the-ground needs of people . . . not mere thought and theory."[25] Although he insists the community has kept their feet on the ground, historian David Frederic Gordon's research on the community suggests that early JPUSA communards exhibited the same dualism adopted by Jesus freaks on the West Coast (the world was evil and retreat was necessary), and they believed the Rapture was quite imminent. In 1978 he observed that JPUSA

> routinely made comments indicating the imminence of this end of the world. . . . Planning for the future on both the group and individual levels is kept at a minimum. No one in this group whom I questioned on the matter

had any personal plans for the future. The group as a whole did little to support itself financially and made plans for housing new members only when they became hopelessly overcrowded.[26]

Kaiser is partially accurate that the community has always wedded a sense of practicality to what is otherwise a skyward gaze. But Gordon's work complicates this, demonstrating a similarity between JPUSA and the Jesus-freak ethos of the 1970s. Still, the community has undergone a number of theological changes since the 1990s. Their ability to engage the wider culture in grassroots fashion is evidence of this. And this can be seen in their commitment to the shelter program, annual planning for the once significant Cornerstone Festival, and dedication to community-owned and -operated mission businesses, for which self-sufficiency is a prime mover. Although it once embraced the extreme spiritualism so prevalent in the early days of the Jesus Movement, JPUSA recognized the need for a grassroots activism inspired by theological depth.

MORE SHIFTS TOWARD THE PRACTICAL

Although the community began during a revival largely associated with conservative evangelicalism, the leaders went on to experience a number of changes, which eventually affected their own self-definition. While they have always remained sympathetic toward the doctrine of the Rapture, the conservative leanings of Hal Lindsey and Campus Crusade for Christ leader Bill Bright clearly delineated between JPUSA and baby boom evangelicals throughout the 1970s and 1980s. Still, JPUSA communards continue to believe in the Second Coming. But the way spiritual "immediacy" is defined, and how levels of social engagement (activism) are understood, differentiate them from other rapture-minded Christians. Like other evangelicals, JPUSA's expectations about the end of the world (date setting) changed. The following demonstrates how early JPUSA adopted a position of eschatological immediacy, later becoming more flexible as communards accepted teleological ambiguity. Glenn Kaiser writes:

In the very early years we were more leaning towards classic Calvary Chapel/Jesus Movement pre-trib[ulation][27] rapture. And over some years, simply came to think that He will come when He comes and we needn't fret nor accent much more in terms of detail which seem more mystery than crystal-clear in the Bible. We're happy to discuss various positions among the churches but it's not a major issue to us, just that He is indeed returning at some point and that day "is closer than when we first believed."[28]

JPUSA's response to anti-intellectual, Jesus-freak experientialism influenced its views on culture and eschatology. As the group sought a muscular intellectual world rooted in modern, Enlightenment-based apologetics, the community deemphasized the hypereschatological foci held by the followers of Hal Lindsey. But while they remained cautious of forerunners who held (in their estimation) unbalanced biblical views, the community never fully dismissed Pentecostal theology or the doctrine of the Rapture. Still, their attempts to engage apologetics in defense of orthodox faith continued to distinguish them from other baby boom evangelicals who focused on the apocalypse.

As the 1990s approached, JPUSA began to define spiritual urgency and human need in terrestrial rather than celestial terms, though it has never discounted the importance of Christian conversion for the individual. But when compared to the larger Jesus Movement—or the zeitgeist that defined much of conservative evangelicalism throughout much of the 1970s and 1980s—JPUSA diverged, emphasizing that eschatological *ambiguity* necessitates moral and social *responsibility*. Thus, this band of believers can be understood as pilgrims striving to connect two worldviews, remaining both socially and apocalyptically minded. They attempt to find a middle ground between an ethos of social engagement for its own sake (the homeless need to eat) and apocalyptic hope of God's kingdom to be established on Earth. Otto Jensen and his family joined the community in January 2008. Ironically, a seminar at JPUSA's Cornerstone Festival challenged his views about the end of time—that social justice trumps any theory about the apocalypse. Musings about the Rapture in relation to practical matters of justice now relegate the doctrine of the Rapture to a secondary nonessential for JPUSA leaders. Many of them have shifted focus from an apocalyptically inspired model of outreach to a humanitarian (even if biblically inspired) model of social justice.[29]

THE POWER OF PLURALISM

A quintessential Jesus Movement church, Calvary Chapel is similar to JPUSA on the basic doctrines of Christianity. But the stark differences can be seen in how the two groups have historically related to culture and society; the former evolved alongside New Evangelicalism's cultural crusade while the latter chose to distance itself from the sociocultural machine created by the evangelical subculture. Whether JPUSA is truly new paradigm or emergent remains a matter of perspective. But one thing is clear: post–Jesus Movement evangelicalism is changing. Some groups are reacting to and some are operating in concert with American culture.

The turn of the twenty-first century marked a shift as JPUSA began to question the validity of Christian apologetics. Seeds had already been planted during the 1990s as JPUSA leaders (including Trott) became disenchanted with what they viewed as flawed enlightenment models of propositional truth. For leaders like Trott (who, incidentally, serves as a researcher for the commune), arguments about foundational truth were no longer applicable within a world now defined by postmodern rupture and literary deconstruction. Despite Trott's earlier propensity *toward* Christian apologetics, he has become forthright with his own ideological struggle, well aware of the problems commonly associated with religious certitude. While he still laments the ambiguity of liberal Christianity, he remains biblically progressive, explaining his position as an attempt to "remove my own cultural bias, unexamined assumptions (by examining them), and so on."[30] This view was certainly evident at the Cornerstone Festival, where seminars shifted toward emergent theology during the final years.[31] None of this is to say that members of JPUSA have leapt headlong into theological liberalism. Trott fully affirms the Apostle's Creed. But as with emergent Christians, he entertains a postmodern understanding of the faith, stating:

> My biggest struggle was and in some ways still is the hiddenness of God . . . living communally, I think we were tapping into elements that evangelicals at that point weren't tapping into . . . now I think even emergent is getting passé . . . but obviously the church is undergoing a shaking along with everything else under this new kind of poly-cultural reality that we're all having to embrace, whether we like it or not. I like it.[32]

At twentieth century's close, Cornerstone seminars became more reflective of the postmodern fascination held by a growing number of evangelicals. This proved positive for JPUSA and Cornerstone, ensuring a continued evangelical orientation (without the restrictive baggage of conservative evangelicalism) as emergent Christianity grew. And as it turned out, Trott was not alone in his departure from apologetics; but this did not sit well with some. Various countercult groups and the apologetics community felt JPUSA had "drifted."[33] And JPUSA's fellow evangelicals have also made this observation.

The *Phantom Tollbooth* is an online magazine that publishes a variety of music, books, and movie reviews, as well as various interviews and resource links. The magazine was involved with the Cornerstone Festival for a number of years. Shari Lloyd and Linda LaFianza, editors for the magazine, note that while JPUSA has always been politically democratic, its theology changed. Before the advent of emergent, JPUSA bore positions similar to those of an "evangelical Baptist," according to the *Tollbooth* editors, a perspective reinforced by JPUSA's then choice of lecturers. Then in February 2010 Lloyd and LaFianza stated, "In the last three or four years, there's been a swing into emergent church beliefs and the seminar speakers are more theologically liberal." Although this approach to Christian belief has consistently grown in influence, "nothing too formal was ever announced or stated."[34] The festival's original slogan was once "Cornerstone: Raw Truth." While Trott admits the "modernistic," ring of the aphorism, he still believes the phrase once captured the festival's core ethos—"provocateurs," forcing people to "reexamine or examine for the first time your unexamined assumptions."[35]

It is tempting to write these changes off as anomalies connected to communal life. But remember, JPUSA is part of a larger evangelical denomination. On the surface JPUSA's evolution may appear to be something specific to its tattered history. Doesn't its story merely relate to its own situation? But this is part of a larger historic struggle involving Christianity and social activism. Furthermore, its changes (resultant reactions to and in concert with pluralism) parallel how those within establishment evangelicalism continue to wrestle with fundamental beliefs about culture, identity, Christian exclusivism, mission work, nationalism, imperialism, the family, peace, war, the environment, sexuality, gender roles, immigration, pacifism, individualism, collectivism, the private sector, the public sector, and truth. These questions were raised in the 1960s as Christian SDSers sought ways to put faith into practice and as Jesus freaks waited for the Rapture. Then something happened. As the Jesus Movement ended, many chose to affiliate with right-wing consensus.[36]

A DIVINE CALL TO CULTURE: RIGHT OR LEFT?

Evangelical Christianity has largely been considered a conservative cultural force, despite the rise of the Evangelical Left. Although historians such as Randall Balmer have aptly noted the problems associated with reducing evangelicalism to political coalitions,[37] the Religious Right (particularly evangelicals) nevertheless accounts for a great number of those who supported Republican presidential candidate George W. Bush. Certainly the more controversial social issues that have defined the right have been abortion and gay marriage. And with the addition of gun control and immigration reform, this has continued even through the Obama administration. Oddly, the hot-button issues that have mobilized the Republican base still ring true with JPUSA, but the issues remain merely systemic.[38]

Communes are often noted for either excessive dedication to rules or to anarchy. But in the end, communal resilience is still linked to formative values revealed in the lives of members (keeping them engaged in the ethos of the community) and to an ability to shift appropriately with culture, even when that shift signals a differentiation from a conservative consensus on social issues. Many in JPUSA have drifted, particularly when considering their position on feminism. Trott recalls how some reacted to changes in JPUSA that were made public at Cornerstone:

> I know for a fact that big chunks of the counter-cult community and the old apologetics community think we drifted. And probably where I've seen that again is with the women's issue. I have been fairly vilified by some people for my ideas about women, which to me is like, ya know, I guess if anything it probably feeds my pride. It makes me happy to be disliked by people that believe that way.[39]

JPUSA ordains women and holds that gender roles are not absolute. Both men and women share an equal voice. But it took time for a true egalitarian position to emerge. Regarding roles in ministry, Trott writes:

> We, I think, were influenced more by the charismatic movement . . . folks such as Katherine Kuhlman . . . and Catherine Booth . . . not that we were always crystal clear on this stuff. Things early on were often foggy. Carl Parks of Spokane's Jesus movement, for instance, had done a book with his wife that was horrendously male-centric . . . and though we didn't buy it, neither did we react as I would . . . today. Keeping in mind that our movement was only a few years old.

JPUSA's views on marriage have also changed over the years. For the group, messages preached in the early days were often mixed. Around 1978 the standard teaching involved male headship—wives were to submit to husbands. Tapes by Bible teacher Bob Mumford affirmed this position, calling for submission to husbands "even if the husband was asking them [wives] to do something contrary to scripture." The sin would fall on the husband. "The reaction from JPUSA," writes Trott, "was immediate and harshly negative." Communards noted the teaching as "off the wall" and countered that Christians "must never violate his or her conscience, no matter who was telling them to do this or that." Trott considers how JPUSA's views on gender have changed: "I think these seeds helped move us inexorably toward rejecting 'gender role' teachings in marriage as well as in the pulpit. Then by the mid-80s," notes Trott, "I was consciously aware of Christian feminism, and starting to seriously interact with it. I think my own journey helped, but wasn't definitive, in other persons' journeys here [in JPUSA]." In the 1980s *Cornerstone* published an article on the ERA, moving the community moderately leftward. They "recognized the validity of the feminist critique of history and the social structures of inequality to which history had contributed." But they did not support the ERA, though they stopped demonizing it, which was a significant move for evangelicals.

JPUSA offered seminars on gender egalitarianism and sexuality at its festival and partnered with Christians for Biblical Equality, an organization that encourages the equality of all women, men, ethnic groups, economic classes, and age-groups. Moreover, its activism extended to civil rights as it annually invited Dr. John Perkins, an African American minister and activist for racial reconciliation, to lecture at the festival.[40] But the move to the right or the left remains a nebulous dichotomy, a complexity JPUSA recognizes as inexhaustible. For example, some members believe that resolving poverty and adopting a holistic view of life (which includes valuing single mothers) will help limit abortions. Unlike arch-antiabortionists, some of the leaders contend there are incidents (such as rape or the safety of the mother) that may warrant abortion. The rank-and-file, however, remain conflicted. They seek to wed a moderate theological position to a socially liberal conscience, a position negotiated by those within the Evangelical Left. Issues such as abortion have kept the community from complete alignment with any thoroughgoing liberalism. And this is precisely why JPUSA has often been difficult to classify, says Trott, noting that any "historical snapshot" of the commune would yield conflicting assumptions about their political allegiance. Unwilling to align fully with either major political party or philosophy, they remain, in many ways, politically enigmatic. Still, Trott recalls that as evangelicalism moved "very consciously to the right" as a whole "we found ourselves moving left," though abortion "was one [issue] that probably held us from moving more rapidly to the left."[41] Then the community began to change yet again, as second-generation communards began to entertain different views on abortion.

THEOLOGY, POLITICS, AND CULTURE

While many second-generation communards challenge staid understandings of cultural issues, older members continue to combine left-wing ideals of social justice with a relatively conservative cultural ethic. Colleen Davick joined JPUSA in 1992. She was raised in a conservative Christian home and attended a Bible college in Texas but sought something deeper than a suburban life defined by work and home. Inspired at the Cornerstone Festival to consider a different way of life, Davick shed a world where "if you're a Christian, you're a Republican." While she agrees with the overall Democratic position of the community, Davick argues that Jesus did not seek to change people politically. To a certain extent, this reasserts the Jesus-freak dichotomy of the spiritual and the practical and highlights specifics that have influenced and differentiated post–Jesus Movement "new evangelicals" and communities such as JPUSA.[42] In this manner, Davick's position is not unlike that of veteran members who seek to maintain the revivalistic element of the Jesus Movement while simultaneously evincing a quasi–social gospel ethic.

Both the Jesus Movement and evangelicalism have wrestled with the extent to which Christians should engage society, and to what extent the spiritual and the practical can be appropriately balanced, though many recognize the practical *is* spiritual. But establishment evangelicalism (at least during the 1970s and 1980s) continued to vilify activism related to the Left. Any vestige of an evangelical social conscience actually served as jeremiads, calling the nation back to its mythical roots. That is, for many conservatives, social action meant sharing the gospel and bolstering Christian nationalism, often connected to religious imperialism and belief in the Rapture.[43] But while the doctrine of the Rapture influenced the social conscience of early Jesus freaks (as well as their megachurch offspring),[44] JPUSA's conscience was and is pragmatically driven. Glenn Kaiser's mission-field—his account of a "gospel calling"—avoids polar extremes, seeking to feed both body and the soul. In the end, he errs on the practical:

> JPUSA was and is about people before a particular doctrine—the core issue that Bible doctrine guides us to [is] LOVE in ACTION and that means

meeting real on-the-ground needs of people around us, not mere thought and theory. . . . today persons in our midst need love and practical help. . . . yes, the Gospel, but it's a seamless garment for Jesus . . . so must be for us.[45]

WHAT SORT OF ACTIVISM?

The 1970s and 1980s were paradoxical for evangelicals. To a certain extent they were culturally engaged. The Christian Coalition and Moral Majority rose to power, marshaling sociocultural capital to empower the Religious Right. In so doing, conservative evangelicals engaged culture on social issues. Gay rights, abortion, feminism, and school prayer all galvanized believers who took their marching orders from Pat Robertson, Jerry Falwell, D. James Kennedy, and Focus on the Family's James Dobson. But many on the right still remained disengaged in the area of social justice, at least as defined by the Left. Instead of emphasizing humanitarianism (with exceptions such as Compassion International and World Vision), evangelicals offered what they believed to be the answer to existential crises—the gospel of personal salvation from individual sin, for them the primary cause of social ill. This has, arguably, kept evangelical denominations relevant. Baby boom, new paradigm churches are growing, while the more socially conscious, mainline liberal congregations still struggle to retain parishioners; it's no surprise that megachurches and "hipster" Christianity have been the dominant evangelical forces throughout the last decade.

JPUSA (and various burgeoning house groups of emergents) offer a counternarrative. In considering the power of the right, JPUSA's greatest divergence from the original Jesus Movement and establishment evangelicalism involves its levels of and reasons for cultural engagement. For Jon Trott, the Right was incongruous with what he viewed as biblical living:

> It was sort of a watershed moment for me. And I wish I could tell you the year. . . . It was one of the early years of the Moral Majority. The Moral Majority had just formed in the early eighties. . . . And we were at a meeting with the Christian Legal Society which was really an interesting mix

of lawyers . . . there was a significant presence by the Moral Majority that year and Cal Thomas actually got up and spoke . . . all four planks of the platform that he said they were . . . these were the biblical planks of what the Moral Majority is about.[46]

Trott was surprised by what amounted to a forthright admission by the Right on matters he considers anti-Christian. The first "biblical planks" asserted involved a strong military. His response to this reaffirms both his and JPUSA's departure from official articulations of what defines much of the right's core:

> Now I'm not necessarily a pacifist. I'm a philosophical pacifist. But operatively, I understand the possibility anyway, or the cerebral possibility anyway, of just war. You know, a concept of a just war. . . . I've never seen one. . . . that said, as he [Cal Thomas] unpacked what he meant by that (which basically indicated that America needed to be armed to the teeth so that we could be the policemen for the world and keep evil at bay). I felt every atom of my being going, "This is so unbiblical, this is so unrooted in any Christian understanding of what reality is." I check out of this. I reject this.

Trott recalls the community's vituperative denunciation of the Reagan administration, maintaining that JPUSA "began to see a number of very troubling trends among the right wing. . . . The right wing has traditionally been . . . a nationalistic movement. It's a movement for empire . . . we intuited that. We felt there was something amiss." It has been well established that nationalism often leads to forms of imperialism, resulting in either "soft power" (cultural hegemony) or "hard power" (military). As a central plank, "just war" continues to define those on the right and continues to inspire leftwing activism from progressives.

Although various Protestants and Catholics contend that there is a biblical basis for war, Trott considers historical context, rejecting arguments that apply ancient political models to contemporary U.S. society. "In the Old Testament, Israel was a theocracy. America is not a theocracy. It never has been a theocracy. It's a modern democracy . . . yes the Puritans were in on it early in the game. But that concept very early on went by the wayside." However, despite JPUSA's left-leaning position, the Jesus-freak connection to the Right remained strong; historians continually reiterate the Jesus Movement's connection to Christian nationalism. In subcultural fashion, JPUSA has worked to differentiate from the socioeconomic position of the Right as related to U.S. foreign and domestic policy. Along with its aversion to policies of empire, JPUSA's primary quibble with the right amounts to how poverty has been handled. President Reagan's policies affected low-income families.[47] Reagan's "draconian" policies (welfare cuts) were contributing factors to Chicago's homeless population, necessitating the community to expand their shelter as a result of urban renewal. Founding member John Herrin's account is not unlike Trott's:

> To be honest with you, the Reagan era was not good for us or Chicago. There was a lot of you know this whole trickle down . . . boy we weren't seeing any trickles here. A lot of funding was cut for social services in this city, and we were not firm believers you know . . . to us the Reagan [policies] . . . looked like . . . it looked like big business to us. And it really kind of stunk. And really didn't relate to the people we dealt with. I'm sure Reagan, and of course George W. Bush, probably had more to do with this community being predominately democratic today than anything.[48]

The connection among Ronald Reagan, George W. Bush, and poverty is a reoccurring sentiment JPUSA leaders continue to express. Furthermore, their suspicion of the conservative Christian connection to American "empire" is not without precedent. Put simply, they are not alone in their assessment. Pauline Lipman aptly traces how the US evolved from a New Deal system that provided a safety net for the working class to a system that rewarded corporations and the wealthy. State powers worked to offer salve to the more privileged parts of organized labor, which would quell any potential revolt. Then, as labor unions received fair pay, fair hours, and benefits, consumer activity was boosted, creating the need for outsourced labor.[49]

JPUSA's storied account of activism amounts to what was actually a larger response to events that unfolded throughout the 1970s and 1980s.

During this time, notes Lipman, "the UK and U.S. governments audaciously attacked key sectors of the labor movement, dismantled aspects of the welfare state, and deregulated the economy so capital could flow freely to new arenas for profitable investment." The result was an unfolding paradigm that pushed progressive agendas backward. "In the United States," writes Lipman, "a hegemonic alliance of neoliberals, neoconservatives, and other sectors of the population congealed to promote an agenda that allowed the rich to accumulate enormous wealth at the expense of the majority."[50] In her research on urban education and poverty Lipman focuses on Chicago as a prime case study for understanding how this city was dramatically affected by policies (particularly the restructuring of school programs) established during the 1970s and 1980s. Chicago is, she argues, "a prominent case of the transformation of the industrial, Keynesian, racially segregated city to the entrepreneurial post welfare city."[51] Renewed entrepreneurial efforts inspired industrialists to remake urban centers, displacing low-income residents through "slum clearance," public housing, and spatial restructuring around new freeway systems.[52] Industrialists continued to brandish their wares in the face of the have-nots but did so to the tune of urban betterment. Nowhere is this more apparent than in the strategies of gentrification. Lipman captures the problems quite well:

> Social control has always been a function of urban government to control labor organizing, social movements, and urban rebellions, and to enforce racial segregation, defend private property, and diffuse social conflict and resistance. But aggressive policing and racialized containment are specific features of the neoliberal state's management of potential resistance and social disintegration due to cuts in social welfare and magnified urban inequalities. It is part of a strategy to "return" the city to the (White) middle and upper middle class.[53]

This strategy, she writes,

> was pioneered by New York Mayor Giuliani's aggressive "stop and frisk," "zero tolerance" policing, tactics used to increase the "quality of life" by

targeting immigrants, gays, people of color, and the homeless. These policies were then adopted by cities throughout the United States, each location reveling in an Eden of the Haves, crystalized in the granite enclaves of "gated communities, corporate plazas, and high-end shopping malls," which operated as zones spatialized around citizenship deemed both exclusive and exclusionary.[54]

Further complicating the matter, schools were targeted in an effort to clear neighborhoods of "undesirables." "Schools are community anchors," writes Lipman, "in the face of gentrification, loss of affordable housing, lack of jobs and public services, and overall disinvestment. Policies that destabilize schools and displace children or their teachers undermine this important role." These initiatives trickled down to urban centers of primary and secondary education. In Chicago and other cities, "policies to close schools and replace them with schools targeted to the middle class are integral to production and consumption of gentrification." Closing schools pushed existing residents out of neighborhoods primed for gentrification, leaving space for a new class of homebuyer. New development, she reasons, is built on "the debris of disinvestment, deindustrialization, and decline of public housing in the urban core of the past 25 years." The 1980s and 1990s became seminal in this development. Massive public housing projects became home to large communities of African Americans who were not counted among those who benefited from the city's new economy. But then these residents were "abandoned by urban and federal social programs, disinvested of public infrastructure, racially segregated, and pathologized by corporate media, conservative think tanks, and academic scholarship." In yet another development, the Chicago Housing Authority (CHA) failed in its responsibility of maintaining these buildings, which later justified their demolition. The demolished area became quite valuable for investors. Residents were displaced.[55]

JPUSA's calling is simply a response to a larger development in Chicago, one that has controversially exacerbated divisions of class and race. As a progressive group, JPUSA fits into a continuum that exists as a distinctly different expression of coreligionists who have nursed their appetites in the shadow of affluence. Over the years JPUSA has continued to diverge on matters associated with its own parent culture. And in so doing it has aligned with a number of positions on the political spectrum. Locating the community's identity still remains problematic. Here is what we do know: the shifting sands of pluralism notwithstanding, the core ethos remains contrary to that of the evangelical mainstream.

COMMUNAL IDENTITY AND THE POLITICAL

In many ways social and cultural isolation serves the endeavors of communes seeking to avoid materialism and nationalism, though this has often led to communal demise or social isolation. For example, the Children of God drew quick media attention as it established ubiquitous cells. Members wore sackcloth and ashes, held prayer vigils in public spaces, and called the nation to repent while spouting jeremiads involving proclamations of doom. COG began to recruit new members via the controversial practice of "flirty fishing," a method of proselytizing that incorporated sanctified prostitution into missionizing, a tactic that also secured financial support from wealthy individuals targeted by what was essentially COG's escort service. But flirty fishing was only part of the story. The practice of "sharing" (plural marriage) marked the group as heretical within the larger Jesus Movement.[56] Then, after allegations of child abuse, COG relocated to other countries, continuing its ministry under the name "The Family International." COG's nomadic existence (families frequently relocate) keeps the group relatively isolated and, more to the point, culturally irrelevant.[57]

Responding to a growing materialism within evangelical circles, groups such as COG became retreat-based, distancing their respective communities from official expressions of both the Right and the Left, carving out a very different space within the Jesus Movement epoch. Understandably, JPUSA has had to work for evangelical trust in the wake of groups such as COG, perhaps a moot task in light of JPUSA's recent scandals. But the community's high view of scripture and moderate sympathies with the Right on abortion and homosexuality endeared them to the larger evangelical subculture though lines have remained thin.[58] These core issues no longer provide traction needed for any long-standing affinity with the Right. And allegations of excessive authoritarianism may undermine what they have sought to accomplish. Moreover, populist evangelical affinities (an attractive element for JPUSA) have not inured the communal council, as with other evangelical Christians who quickly aligned their respective churches with social issues that were (quite frankly) in vogue.[59] But for JPUSA, the stakes are simply too high. Contrary to isolationists, fundamentalists, and baby boom evangelicals, leaders in JPUSA have made eradicating poverty and homelessness a priority. Despite David Gordon's assertion that the community is relatively isolationist—that they do not encounter pluralism in the same way as suburban, post–Jesus Movement communes—they have evolved since initial observations were conducted during the late 1970s.[60] This is quite evident, since the community showed up on the White House's radar.

In 2004 the George W. Bush administration contacted the Cornerstone Festival office and requested an audience for either President Bush or Colin Powell. Uninterested in "mixing politics and faith,"[61] JPUSA and Cornerstone declined an offer to host the president.[62] Disinterest in blending the religious and the political notwithstanding, JPUSA made evident its political sensibilities at Cornerstone. Furthermore, its position on the war in the Middle East informed its feelings about President Bush, providing confirmation of its general discontent with Republican-inspired evangelical Christianity. As a result, JPUSA continues to remain informed about global events, hoping to educate those who visit the commune. And until Cornerstone closed its doors, JPUSA's politically based seminars reflected multiple perspectives on the complex interplay between the global and the local, war and peace, the conflating of God and country, and the delicate line separating Christian missions from cultural imperialism.

NATIONALISM, IDENTITY, AND THE WORLD

For many evangelical Christians, efforts to avoid (or at the very least minimize) social justice have often been linked to millenarian expectancy or

Christian nationalism. Evangelicals (particularly fundamentalists) have sought either to convert people before the end of time or to reestablish a Christian nation before the end, advocating a "Puritan heritage that America was a new Israel," according to George Marsden.[63] They have often been paradoxical and deeply alienated—at once militantly antisociety (America is Babylon) and pro-America (America is a chosen nation). These evangelicals sought to retreat from a corrupt, unchangeable world while also voting on legislation intended to create policies meant to bolster a myth of the "Christian nation."[64]

This conflict of national and spiritual identity is a tension that spiders its way throughout American culture, tapping the shoulders of those whose gaze is leftward: you must leave! Debates about the environment are irrevocably tethered to the myth. As I have written previously, according to Frank Schaeffer (son of Christian apologist Francis Schaeffer), "Richard Cizik, former vice president of the National Association of Evangelicals, had almost been forced out . . . when James Dobson [Focus on the Family] wrote to the NAE [National Association of Evangelicals] board demanding Cizik's dismissal for saying that he thought global warming was real."[65]

There are certainly those who oppose this issue based on a perceived lack of scientific evidence or the fiscal affects of environmental activism and industrial overhaul—the loss of jobs. However, Dobson represents a continuum of evangelicals (which includes baby boom, Jesus Movement veterans) who affirm the doctrine of human depravity and view as suspect any attempt to "engineer" divine plan. The moratorium placed on environmentalism has been cloaked (at least in the past) in a shroud of religious determinism. Put another way, while conservative evangelicals have often opposed government regulations on economic grounds, the specter of eschatology, I would argue, fuels economic theory, at least for those who have maintained a commitment to theologies associated with the Rapture and the Middle East.

This brand of evangelicalism has often characterized social justice as a mere bandage on a wound that yields to divine plan, healed only after a quite specific cosmic story unfolds. If this were otherwise—if Dobson's call for Cizik's resignation were merely a difference of opinion on matters of science or fiscal responsibility—he would not have called for the resignation of a position that represents spiritual leadership. Was Dobson's problem theological? Although James Dobson also represents a tradition of evangelicals who seek to (ironically) Christianize society, the millenarian impulse remains a powerful influence over biblical literalists. But this impulse does not negate the need to Christianize society. On the contrary. The apocalyptic tradition has many facets, two of which have thoroughly defined conservative, American evangelicals since the nineteenth century.[66]

As evangelical Christianity was revived among America's youth in the 1960s and 1970s, two competing forces defined how evangelicals would engage society. For early Jesus freaks, social action involved rigorous evangelism as the faithful sought to convert souls before the Rapture. For the burgeoning Religious Right, action often involved restoring America to a "Christian nation." But what sort of action did JPUSA embrace? Although Colleen Davick stated Jesus did not come to engage politics, like others in JPUSA she remains committed to social justice. Her agenda, though, is not to create a Christian nation or to hasten the second coming. Like others in the community, her vision of social justice is nuanced—in contradistinction to the aforementioned Jesus freaks and religious rightists—valuing practical outreach for its own sake: people need food and shelter.

JPUSA's agenda has never been to create a "lighthouse group" that defines itself as some quintessential Christian expression or the ultimate model for living.[67] Moreover, the leaders view Christianity and the concept of national identity as incompatible. Throughout the years, the Cornerstone Festival offered workshops intended to challenge Christian nationalism, calling evangelicals to understand the complexities of foreign relations and the convoluted nature of ferreting out decisions concerning landownership within tribal societies. In other words, JPUSA does not attach the same cosmic imperative to theologically driven battles over land, as do evangelicals whose gaze remains fixed on Jerusalem. Left-leaning evangelicals such as Jon Trott work to bridge the gap, hoping to demonstrate the complexity of evangelical Christianity—that not all evangelicals resonate with the political agenda of rightist nationalism. Noting Manifest Destiny, Trott connects the Right's thirst for empire to what he maintains is a privileging of big business over environmentalism, reinforcing Marsden's analysis of the paradoxical nature of the Right's desire to avoid society while simultaneously engineering it.

While most groups affected by evangelical beliefs about the end of time or Christian nationalism are not violent in any concrete sense, their positions concerning war and ecology may hint at a different sort of violence—environmental destruction through *inaction*. Violence can arise to serve what some believe to be a correct course of action, a phenomenon that historian Jon Pahl refers to as "innocent domination."[68] A journalist with deep environmental convictions, Trott works to protest what he believes to be destructive environmental policies held by the Religious Right, instituted by big business. Leaders within the Evangelical Left such as Brian McLaren and Shane Claiborne (both of whom have lectured at Cornerstone) reason that the "kingdom of God" is both spiritual and physical. And McLaren highlights the consequences of unregulated business:

> I saw the devastation unleashed by insufficiently-regulated corporations, denuding and flattening once-majestic mountains, poisoning springs and creeks, sickening people, laying off workers, and making a few executives rich. Then a few months later I went fly fishing in Yellowstone, awed by the powerful presence of bison and elk, the fresh scent of grassy meadows in summer green, the shine of snowy peaks in the distance. Those two landscapes linger in my memory—one sold short for a fast profit, one conserved for posterity.[69]

Like McLaren, Trott and other JPUSA leaders believe that environmental responsibly is part of a more holistic understanding of the Christian gospel. Attempting to alert their evangelical constituents to the dangers of not nurturing this holistic viewpoint, the Cornerstone Festival worked to highlight the specious claims advanced by big business and big religion. While the culture war was a thrust to reestablish the civilities of puritan America and the attendant "rugged individualism," subcultural expressions like Cornerstone have attempted to gesture toward the nebulous connections between Christian faith and ideas nurtured by the establishment. That these connections have often resulted in compressing big religion and big business is not surprising.

In response to conservative policies on the environment and social justice (hoping to reconcile evangelical Christianity with pluralism), a number of emergent Christians have come to the fore. Since the increase of emergent Christianity in the 1990s and the subsequent rise of new leaders such as Shane Claiborne (following ideas previously established by evangelical leftists such as Jim Wallis), there has been a concerted effort by those affiliated with the Evangelical Left (as well as some on the right) to question environmental and foreign policies held by Republican evangelicals. Still, these remain merely fringe expressions of evangelical radicalism, though the climate is changing. The Evangelical Left works to change the oft-held assumption that Christianity and nationalism are part of some sort of divine plan. Through the years Cornerstone seminars hosted speakers who questioned the war in the Middle East, and it encouraged an evangelical presence that might combat right-wing positions on environmentalism, foreign policy, war, health care, and feminism. But JPUSA is not the norm. And the Evangelical Left still enjoys scant representation on the national level. Despite any perceived deaf ear offered by evangelicalism proper, JPUSA's leadership carried a torch, hoping to exemplify a different version of Christianity, one difficult to categorize: antinationalist, anti–capital punishment, pro-life (with provisions), fiscally leftist, feminist, womanist, christocentric, inclusive, biblicist, deconstructivist, environmentalist, rapture-hopeful, yet eschatologically cautious. In this sense JPUSA does exhibit a lighthouse mentality of sorts, but only insofar as it hopes to inspire other evangelicals to think critically about persons and policies so readily lionized by Republican evangelicals.

When considering the apparent ubiquity of Christians who voice a patriotism that is quite frankly a form of Christian nationalism, JPUSA and others in the Evangelical Left remain actively opposed to rightist nationalism on grounds that nationalistic politics amount to an anti-Christian ethic. Founding member Wendi Kaiser is distressed over how so many tend to confuse patriotism with Christianity, noting her distaste for misplaced patriotic forms of Manifest Destiny. Although the veneer of single issues sensationalized by media and the culture war maintains its slim connection to the Right, the fact that JPUSA remains orthodox in its Christianity tilts it toward the evangelical signifier. However, its moderate inclusiveness might undermine what is historically exclusive about conservative evangelicalism.

While the leaders allow for ambiguity on matters of Christian salvation and have adopted most social causes typically affiliated with the Left, their position on abortion and homosexuality (though tempered with nuances) still reestablishes a conservative connection socially.[70] The community cannot be counted among mainline liberals. But, as we shall see, members from the second generation come closer than the founders to this position.

CULTURE AND SOCIETY: THE BIGGER PICTURE

Baby boomers in the evangelical mainstream have often been confronted with the tensions endemic to Christianity and culture. Are they to engage or disengage? Are they to create a Christian nation or simply await the end of time? As we have seen, some Jesus freaks retreated to isolationist communes. Others returned to an altered version of postmillennialism.[71] But far more became part of the Religious Right.[72]

In the midst of cultural fragmentation among evangelicals, JPUSA attempted to locate a space best suited to its vision of biblical living. Its members rejected Christian nationalism, remained active in social reform, and waxed hopeful that there would be a Rapture of some sort. There is a historical continuity in JPUSA's position on culture. Put another way, a precedent for its version of Christian living was established well before the Jesus Movement. Consider the underlying impulse behind nineteenth-century reform efforts: liberal Christianity's move toward the social gospel; the progressive populism and social measures of William Jennings Bryan; the apoliticism of conservative evangelicals who followed in the tradition of evangelists D. L. Moody and Billy Sunday. Though JPUSA's philosophy does not fully resonate with any of these, each informs what the council believes to be a holistic understating of Christian commitment. But the motive is not restorationist. The group does not seek to reconstruct society or create a Christian nation. Nor do they allegorize or relativize biblical passages (for fear of robbing the text of supernatural authority) or literalize biblical passages that deal with gender constructs or end-time cosmology. Noting Jesus's command to help children and the less fortunate, JPUSA's leaders maintain this: theirs is simply a mission to offer aid to "the least of these."

These Christian hippies and punkers allow for a certain amount of subjective biblical interpretations about culture, as we have seen, amounting to a mixture of communal agreement and individual conscience. In this sense, big religion bows to the individual, and the individual negotiates with the collective. For example, founding member Glenn Kaiser reconciles positions on culture by adopting a practical expression of Jesus's call to activism. For him, "JPUSA simply responded to those coming to us each day for help, help of all kinds be it spiritual, food, clothing, shelter, whatever. I would say we rather rapidly realized the Mt. 25 [Matthew, chapter 25] list of responding to people's needs that Jesus spoke of what was central and not merely incidental to sharing a verbally credible Gospel."[73] In the end, Kaiser collapses the Right-Left continuum, arguing that the love of God usurps other political or theological particulars. This should not be read, however, as an anti-intellectual position. First, he arrived at this position via textual analysis. Second, in grassroots fashion, Kaiser (and many other JPUSA communards) is more concerned with feeding the hungry than with ivory-tower musings about theory. And this amounts to an ironic return to the grassroots activism of the New Left and Jesus-freak revolutionaries, who were frustrated with the "merely theoretical," though quite grounded in it.

JPUSA's outer mission never fully takes it beyond the first level of Maslow's pyramid, although those living *within* the community certainly move to higher levels. And while many communards remain intellectually engaged, Kaiser has pointed out that those whom they serve (the homeless and the traveler) could care less about high theory or theological particulars. Thus while Kaiser and Trott fully engage political and theological theory, in the end their greater concern (which defines the community) is social activism. But does this define JPUSA's gospel message? And does it square with the evangelical position on salvation?

Nineteenth-century reformers embraced a different understanding of the Christian gospel, one that prioritized humanitarianism and, in many cases, preached a practical, service-based message, lessening previously established imperatives for individual conversion of the soul. Advocates for the social gospel deemphasized focus on eternal salvation, arguing that the message of Jesus was to save the individual physically, morality merely a positive consequence, eternal life an incidental plus. Applying Christian ethics to social problems, advocates for the social gospel adopted postmillennialism, believing Jesus would return after the Earth had been socially engineered via Christian teaching. Controversially these advocates maintained that the state (which was ostensibly Christian) had a responsibility to create legislation, regulating programs in service of the greater good, thus realizing Christian morality by ameliorating social ills and vice.

Aversion to the social gospel within some post–Jesus Movement churches is palpable. Indeed, many evangelicals (regardless of their positions on the Rapture) are fully engaged in social justice. Parachurch organizations such as Compassion International and World Vision continue relief efforts to feed the poor. But even new paradigm churches argue against government-funded relief efforts. For them, that responsibility is reserved for the church. Big religion (so it seems) bears more responsibility than big government, or even big business. For these churches, any attempt to relativize scripture (toward a social gospel end) robs the text of classical atonement theology. For conservatives, then, the social gospel incorrectly dismisses (or at least undervalues) what they maintain is the real problem: human depravity, a condition solved only when individuals accept personal responsibility for sin and accept Jesus as savior. This rather wobbly proposition (poverty is ameliorated through belief) is further exacerbated by the proposition that the epidemic of global poverty must primarily (if not solely) rely on the efforts of big religion, a sketchy proposition in an age of terrorism. But even conservatives continue to lobby Congress in hopes of gaining legislation, albeit for different purposes, right? And this is where the Evangelical Left enters, hoping to smooth over the rickety soup kitchen with roads fully funded, serving the common good.

And so evangelicalism is riddled with a tattered history, one involving debates about who is most responsible for financing social programs. Whose responsibility is it? A bit of context: liberals who embraced the Social Gospel Movement, notes James Davison Hunter, "became simultaneously sensitized to the appalling social conditions and needs generated by industrial capitalism and aware of the church's failings in ameliorating those needs. Born in response was the Social Gospel."[74] Of course reactions to the Social

Gospel Movement were legion, and thus emerged New Evangelicalism. This aversion to government-funded social aid was also present in churches spawned by the Jesus Movement. Jesus freaks retained the antigovernment leanings of hippie anarchists, all the while hoping to meet the deep-seated needs of U.S. society by preaching Jesus to the masses.[75] Ironically, the Religious Right has continued to produce special interest groups, each seeking to Christianize U.S. society through government-mandated programs.[76]

There is a lack of social justice initiatives within some post–Jesus Movement churches, but the landscape is changing. Although conservative churches continue to grow, evangelicals are evolving into a different kind of social force, one that maintains some similarities to the Social Gospel Movement but couches activism in millennial terms. For example, emergent Christians and some Jesus-freak veterans often engage social justice not because they dismiss the doctrine of the Rapture but because they are uncertain about *when* the end will come. This development is relatively new, considering the number of Jesus Movement converts who followed the teachings of Hal Lindsey. Furthermore, this level of uncertainty can also be found in conservatives who maintain that while the Rapture will happen (often noted "in their lifetime"), one does not know the hour. Thus responsible Christian living now dictates that the faithful remain good caretakers of the planet and fellow human beings.

Now often eschatologically ambiguous, a growing number of evangelicals note the importance (even urgency) of demonstrating Christian faith by working to better society. Jon Trott believes that some sort of temporal, terrestrial grand finale will occur. And yet, while he holds that humanity is on a downward spiral, his Wesleyan theology compels him to remain a social activist, as he and other members continue to offer aid to the homeless, protest the sale of firearms, remain an active voice for feminism, and protest the war in the Middle East.

A NEW POLITICS OF THE END: IMPLICATIONS

Theories about doomsday and the apocalypse press on nerve centers that inform the way religionists perceive the universe and its destiny—and it often has practical consequences. In the words of David W. Stowe, "Belief in the apocalypse tends to work against active politics."[77] But this belief has grown diverse, complex, and often reflective (if only incrementally) of pluralism. For example, new emerging expressions of Christianity often do not support war in the Middle East, recognizing the irony of engineering any potential end of time. Left-leaning evangelicals such as Brian McLaren, Jim Wallis, and Shane Claiborne continue to challenge evangelicals who maintain that our actions have bearing on cosmic events. For Wallis, "Many American Christians are simply more loyal to a version of American nationalism than they are to the body of Christ."[78] McLaren is equally forthcoming about how apocalyptic belief can affect evangelical political ethics. In an effort to demonstrate how an overly deterministic eschatology can negatively impact activism, he writes, "If the world is about to end . . . why care for the environment? Why worry about global climate change or peak oil? Who gives a rip for endangered species or sustainable economies or global poverty if God is planning to incinerate the whole planet soon anyway?"[79] McLaren's questions tap the core of an evangelical belief that has influenced social activism for many years. Hoping to emphasize an obvious disconnect, he asks a series of questions:

> If the Bible predicts the rebuilding of the Jewish temple (or requires that rebuilding for its prophecies to work in a dispensationalist framework), why care about Muslim claims on the Temple Mount real estate? Why care about justice for non-Jews in Israel at all—after all, isn't it their own fault for being on land God predicts will be returned in full to the Jews in the last days? If God has predetermined that the world will get worse and worse until it ends in a cosmic megaconflict between the forces of Light (epitomized most often in the United States) and the forces of Darkness (previously centered in communism, but now, that devil having been vanquished, in Islam), why waste energy on peacemaking, diplomacy, and interreligious dialogue?[80]

Positions held by McLaren, Wallis, and others on the left indicate a growing trend among evangelicals. Still, conservative Christianity has a significant impact on American politics. But even when JPUSA fully embraced the eschatology associated with the Right, its members' sense of social activism remained unfettered when so many others exuded heaven-mindedness as they read the works of Hal Lindsey and Tim LaHaye.

Despite the fact that there exists a near recidivistic quality to American millennialism (one ever set on doomsday scenarios), there is a growing ecumenical effort, a collaboration to join with other persons of faith in hopes of realizing the end of war, hunger, AIDS, and the dangers of climate change. And while there was a concerted effort in the past to demonize global humanitarian efforts as being futile at best or anti-Christ at worst,[81] some premillennial evangelicals admit (unlike their evangelical forerunners) that they simply do not know when the end will come. But as McLaren intimated, the power of Rapture theology remains strong for many. And it influences (if only subconsciously) political decision or indecision.

SAVED?

In tracking changes in JPUSA, I have focused on belief in the Rapture, largely because it was so prevalent during the Jesus Movement, and it intensely affected how various communes chose to engage the world around them. Further, both Jesus Movement and evangelical positions on the second coming of Christ have been directly linked with the belief in salvation through Jesus. Despite intrigue with otherworldly concerns, even the most isolationist communities have tended to fall within the evangelical continuum when considering eternal salvation. Research on the most radical of Jesus Movement communes (such as the Children of God) demonstrates how groups whose organizing premise (separation from tradition) did not alter what was viewed as essential to their faith—salvation through Jesus.

From 1972 until the 1990s, JPUSA's position on eternal salvation for the individual (atonement of sin through Jesus' death and resurrection) was clear. From 1984 until the mid- to late 1990s, lectures at the Cornerstone Festival were designed to argue for biblical absolutism and a strict model of evangelical-based exclusive truth-claims: Jesus was the only way to God. While JPUSA leaders still believe Jesus is the only mediator between hu-

THEOLOGY, POLITICS, AND CULTURE

manity and God, since the turn of the twenty-first century Cornerstone seminars revealed an increasing tolerance of nuanced opinions about Heaven, Hell, and who qualifies as "saved." Recognizing the fluidity of religious belief, founder John Herrin admits, "Christians can interpret [the Bible] a thousand ways if not a million."[82] When interviewing Jon Trott, I recalled author Brian McLaren's position on divine judgment, an argument comparing Mahatma Gandhi to the controversial right-wing Baptist minister Fred Phelps. McLaren ventures that although Gandhi was not a Christian, God would likely accept him, but not Fred Phelps. Trott agreed. The significance of this is in the relationship between McLaren (an inclusivist) and JPUSA/Cornerstone. McLaren has spoken at the festival and, for the most part, exemplifies JPUSA's position on social justice, but he takes emergent philosophy well beyond itself, now exuding a wider brand of ecumenism, often to the chagrin of others within the emergent community.

Although JPUSA leaders such as Glenn Kaiser do not fully align with McLaren's personal edicts, there is a closer affiliation with his form of inclusivism than is widely espoused within establishment evangelicalism. What is more telling is Trott's own concept of salvation. He disagrees with liberal theology's inability to provide clear answers, on the grounds that its ambiguity offers a nebulous view of God (a largely useless idea for one who needs certainty), if only in modest amounts. Unwilling to cede ground to either liberalism or conservatism, Trott equally affirms a possible wide net of salvation, admitting that he does not know who God deems worthy. Others in the community share this sentiment. While they see Jesus as unique and fully embrace a classical understanding of the atonement, they reserve judgment of the spiritual Other, recognizing (ironically in classic liberal form!) that "spirit-regeneration" may occur in individuals regardless of their religious affiliation or belief. It is this ability to navigate both *orthodoxy* and *pluralism* that keeps the community intellectually engaged, unlike previous Christian communes and, to a certain extent, unlike both liberal and conservative Christianity.

This sense of ideological negotiation has been transferred to younger communards, who in many ways have taken flexibility to greater lengths. For many of them, ideas are more complex than realized, and thus negotiable.

Like the founders, Joshua Davenport (a newer communard) notes that the sanctity of life (as one example) should include problems associated with war and human need, seeking to avoid political orientations based on single-issue topics such as abortion or gay marriage. But his true divergence from orthodoxy concerns his doctrine of salvation. As with others in his generation, Davenport does not claim the title "evangelical," arguing, "The gospels are too big to know." For him, evangelicals are too quick to systematize faith, often ignoring historic struggles concerning the question of what constitutes a follower of Christ. Following the lead of fellow communards and other evangelicals, Davenport believes that only Christians go to Heaven. No surprise. But he goes on to recognize the complexity of what actually makes someone a Christian, arguing that one simply cannot know a person's heart. For him, the possibility of a Christian who is simultaneously Muslim or Hindu is quite possible. Valuing the *path* of Christ over belief, Davenport holds that conversion is merely a matter of whether the light has gone on.[83]

For many in JPUSA, this light inspires a level of activism that strips the self in service to the Other. This is part their strength and, in some ways, forecasts the hopes and dreams of those who continue to champion the ethos of the Evangelical Left. Put simply, immediacy trumps ideas. Their ability to sacrifice personal comfort becomes easier if the stakes of human physical need remain high. And the pressures of pluralism (recognized inconsistencies between specific belief and universal humanity) are incrementally adjudicated, measured against the truer and more immediate threat—poverty. Put another way, pure humanitarianism (even when inspired by the teachings of Jesus) makes personal sacrifice easier when one realizes that more immediate needs are pressing in. And this is the heart of the Left.

While JPUSA in no way dismisses the practice of Christian missions designed to convert the individual soul, the premium placed on human physical need also meets the needs of communards who feel compelled toward human service, regardless of ideological particulars.[84] Given the evolution of JPUSA's positions on eschatology and human salvation (the nuances), it is necessary to consider where its members fall within the evangelical continuum, if they do at all. JPUSA is changing along with other expressions of evangelicalism, but not all. The question is whether those evangelicals who attended Cornerstone for years, many of whom remain committed to JPUSA's many music groups, have changed enough to stomach the ideological shifts that have occurred in JPUSA. If not, the community's success (if defined in terms of cultural engagement now through Grrr Records) may rely solely on its sustained effort to aid Chicago's homeless. And if it is unable to sustain amicable discourse with evangelicalism proper, JPUSA may run the risk of urban isolation. No longer connected to a larger outlet such as the Cornerstone Festival (which for years kept JPUSA linked to the pulse of the world), the community may become redefined via a model of self-referencing, without having to deal with the shifting sands of pluralism in the outside world.

CONCLUSION

As with many religious communities operating in a democratic, pluralistic society, JPUSA's political and theological affiliations are a result of a myriad of social forces. The commune managed to break from the Jesus freak mold cast by historians of American religion who have written about the counterculture and the Jesus Movement. Although its early years were marked by the same apocalyptic urgency as the greater Jesus Movement, JPUSA refocused efforts toward practical matters of social justice. The community remained hopeful of the Rapture but avoided extremes prevalent in doomsday groups, as well as establishment evangelicals who took their cues from Hal Lindsey.

Without question, the Jesus Movement became an arm of the Religious Right, either broadcasting scenarios of divine wrath or encouraging Christian nationalism via popular evangelical media. However, JPUSA engaged the muscular intellectual world of biblical apologetics in the 1980s (a reaction to Jesus-freak experientialism), then later adopted more nuanced understandings of Christian belief. As such, the influence of pluralism was quite unavoidable. And this can also be seen in the wider evangelical world.

As will become evident, JPUSA's involvement with mainstream culture was apparent at the Cornerstone Festival. Although they might carry what sociologist Christian Smith calls "sacred umbrellas,"[85] the community cannot be easily categorized. While they enjoy a certain level of intergroup accountability and spiritual safety, members remain connected to society in a way unlike former Jesus Movement communes.[86] Thus JPUSA's ability to connect—navigating issues commonly associated with both the Right and the Left—has contributed to their viability. But merely remaining connected is not enough to warrant a distinct place within evangelicalism proper. And it does not validate any sense of uniqueness when considering larger studies on communities or popular media. When we compare its members' identity and ethos to those of other evangelicals, it becomes clear that JPUSA can best be understood as a radical example of the Evangelical Left. As such, it is a product of pluralism and postmodern Christianity, a development that makes it necessary for the group to straddle two very different approaches to the evangelical worldview.

The changes in JPUSA and Cornerstone placed them at odds with many who once attended the festival, as long-held paradigms were often challenged. But while many who attended indeed represented establishment evangelicalism, others (particularly those in their early twenties) became disenchanted with new paradigm Christianity, noting its historical connection to baby boom evangelicalism and the Religious Right. As JPUSA's theology continues to mirror postmodern Christianity, one wonders how the community will fare in the future. While I argue that JPUSA's ability to engage social justice and evolve ideologically has kept it alive and relevant, its success largely depends on what evangelicalism will look like in the coming years. If projections are accurate, JPUSA's complexion portends a new kind of evangelical—socially conscious and comfortable with ambiguity. And this new kind of evangelical has its own rock stars.

6

THE CHRISTIAN WOODSTOCK: VERNACULAR RELIGION, INFLUENCE, AND CONFLICTING WORLDS

✶ ✶ ✶

The American counterculture of the 1960s served as a cultural flash point, a strange (even naïve) storm that changed how we perceive youth, process ideas, and express art. The Jesus Movement radically redefined evangelical Christianity. And the new order promised young people a new way to understand Jesus, as they prepared for the coming Rapture of believers. The urgency that drove Jesus freaks (as well as parachurch organizations) required of them a solid nod to the teenage pop-culture vernacular. Although this movement has faded into a rather odd obscurity, the spirit continues to surface in various forms, redefining boundaries and reorienting the faithful to new, emerging ways of signifying the sacred. From 1984 until 2012, thousands of mainstream and subcultural Christians attended JPUSA's Cornerstone Festival, an event intended to celebrate the edgy qualities associated with the counterculture. Despite Cornerstone's evangelical orientation, the event challenged fundamental musical and ideological assumptions. This chapter will explore the origin and cultural impact of the multivalent Cornerstone Festival, JPUSA's contribution to countercultural expressions of evangelical Christianity, and JPUSA's role in remapping the boundaries that have historically oriented the Christian music industry to a traditional dichotomy of sacred and secular. Through Cornerstone, JPUSA challenged establishment evangelicalism and mainline contemporary Christian music (CCM).

EVANGELICALS AND POPULAR CULTURE

The Jesus Movement challenged mainline, liberal Protestant positions on theological certainty, as well as commonly held evangelical positions on religious (Pentecostal) experience. In so doing, Jesus freaks reaffirmed absolute commitment to literal interpretations of the Bible while also bringing the "primitivism" of Pentecostal Christianity into the mainstream. But the movement's greatest contribution to U.S society was cultural: hair, clothing, music, visual art, publishing, film, television, and festivals. Initially a cottage industry, evangelical popular media contributed to the growth of both mega and new paradigm churches.

As the Jesus Movement began to dissolve, the Religious Right absorbed evangelical pop culture, furthering its own agenda. Post–Jesus Movement Christian conservatives used music, books, and film to engage the culture war, arguing that social issues such as abortion, feminism, gay rights, and secular humanism were all signs of a declining Christian nation. Tapping the work of Colleen McDannell, Eileen Luhr has argued that popular culture helped young Jesus freaks learn values associated with conservative Christian belief. According to her findings, the impact of the movement increased as "independent Christian bookstores grew from 725 to 1,850 between 1965 and 1975."[1] While the use of the cultural vernacular was nothing new for evangelicals, the Jesus Movement provided a template for cultural engagement that elevated evangelicals to new status. Like early evangelicals and fundamentalists who hoped for a glorious end of time (marked by a secret rapture of born again believers), Jesus freaks were accused of retreating from society. Young converts were depicted as dour agents of doomsday religion, while they interpreted international events through a theological grid popularized by apocalyptic author Hal Lindsey. But this changed as Presidents Jimmy Carter and Ronald Reagan carried evangelical rhetoric to the fore. Jesus freaks followed and were absorbed into the evangelical mainstream.

Although it would be unfair to assume Jesus freaks were automatically co-opted by the Right, it is safe to assume that the new "evangelical base" was a growing youth culture whose cultural products (popularized by the counterculture) were employed in service of newfound faith. And this is nothing new. Culturally relevant missionary work can be traced back to the Great Awakening. George Marsden notes that "Charles Finney was, in fact, one of the progenitors of modern advertising technique.... His pioneering work paved the way for later twentieth-century radio and TV evangelists to master mass communication techniques."[2] Moreover, evangelist Aimee Semple McPherson's ability to combine the gospel message with modern theatrics carried Finney's technique into the twentieth century.

Early revivalists such as Billy Sunday (1862–1935) "turned to the techniques of modern show business as a means of drumming up support," writes Marsden.[3] Political scientist Duane Oldfield also iterates the ongoing connections between pop culture and evangelicalism, emphasizing the "populist, democratic character of American popular religion." Key players have often used whatever is necessary or available. Oldfield states that American evangelists have often been willing to "speak the language of the people, crude and sensationalistic though it may be. The enthusiasm of the backwoods camp meeting, the theatrics of turn-of-the-century baseball player/evangelist Billy Sunday, and the antics of televangelists Jim and Tammy Bakker [Jimmy Swaggart and Ted Haggard are current examples] have shocked the respectable but demonstrated a continuing ability to connect with a mass audience."[4]

As an outflow of this post-hippie revival, the Jesus Movement's message was artistically communicated through multiple mediums. Contemporary Christian music emerged out of the spirited "Jesus music" of the late 1960s and 1970s as music groups like Children of the Day, Love Song, Andrae Crouch, Randy Stonehill, Barry McGuire, and Larry Norman laid the foundation for artists who would play a role in the creation of a new industry—the parallel universe of popular evangelical music. Then, a new kind of

Christian artist emerged during the 1980s, contributing to a new way evangelical youth would engage the faith. Keith Green, Amy Grant, Michael W. Smith, Petra, Stryper, Whitecross, dc Talk, DeGarmo & Key, and Jars of Clay would all become the standard-bearers in the lexicon of Christian pop. Eileen Luhr's analysis of this American cultural moment is quite apt, as reiterated below from my previous work.

Throughout the 1980s, argues Luhr, parents "aggressively sought to reclaim the category of youth," hoping to restore meaning, purpose, and "'traditional' authority in both public and private spaces."[5] The perception of cultural threat warranted new ways of viewing culture, thus continuing the evangelical heritage of cultural activism. Contrary to the Old Right, these families believed they could co-opt converts to "'restore' Christianity to the dominant spaces of suburbia."[6] For conservatives, young people represented a new hope to challenge issues considered detrimental to traditional values. The elimination of school prayer and the legalization of abortion mobilized a new generation of culture-savvy evangelicals. Couched in the rhetoric of war, these issues were presented (via Christian rock) in a way that tapped youth rebellion, thus serving the purposes of conservative organizations such as the Moral Majority and the Christian Coalition. Moreover, Christian metal bands, writes Luhr, were "an integral part of the cultural work of the Christian Right "which comment[ed] on contemporary society."[7] This new form of sociocultural activism also served "Middle America" by exploring "suburban revivalism," a development Luhr links to baby boom evangelicals and the various cultural possibilities established during the Jesus Movement.[8]

As a journalist for the *Washington Post*, the *Washington City Paper*, and *Spin* magazine, Andrew Beaujon curtails the typical academic approach to cultural theory or history as he offers an on-the-ground account of a complicated (and at times controversial) Christian music industry. In *Body Piercing Saved My Life*, Beaujon considers the current status of this industry and includes an interview with one the most successful executives in Christian music. Bill Hearn, president and CEO of EMI Christian Music Group (a branch of the mammoth EMI), argued that SoundScan reporting technology "showed that a lot more Christian music was being sold than the secular music industry wanted to admit," writes Beaujon. In 2006 EMI Christian Music Group accounted for "40 percent of the resulting $700 million business" and proved to be "one of the most profitable companies in the EMI system around the world."[9]

The social influence of CCM is far-reaching. It has become "a major component of the financial underpinnings of American evangelicalism's mass media and bookstore infrastructure," observes Larry Eskridge, "as well as a significant aspect of everyday life and devotion in the evangelical subculture, spawning radio station formats, summer festivals, websites and the like."[10] The genre was once relatively inconsequential. But in the past twenty-five years, Christian pop groups (and, more generally, musicians of faith) have come into their own, despite proclamations of evangelical faith. In 1985 Amy Grant released *Unguarded*, which became a commercial breakthrough on the *Billboard* albums charts. Then, "Find a Way" became Grant's first Top 40 single, after which her duet with Peter Cetera, ex-singer of the group Chicago, thrust Grant into the limelight. "The Next Time I Fall" rose to number one on the charts, making Grant a star to believers and unbelievers alike. The world of Christian music "had long awaited such general-market validation," writes Beaujon.[11] Grant now enjoys "six Grammys, numerous Dove Awards, [and] a star on the Hollywood Walk of Fame."[12]

Despite this apparent success, there has been an ongoing struggle between Christian musicians, the general market, and the local church. One of the earlier Jesus rockers, Larry Norman, was accused of being too Christian for the general market and too rock 'n' roll for the church. Then, when JPUSA's Rez Band attempted to engage the market, their topics did not endear them to either world. Much like Norman, Rez was, according to Beaujon's analysis, considered "too hard for the Christian market and too Christian for the general market."[13] Nevertheless, StarSong Records signed Rez and released what became a "classic of Christian rock." *Awaiting Your Reply* was, in the words of Beaujon,

> one of the few albums from the movement's early days that was as good as anything in the general market. But because of Rez's subject matter, the group remained a cult band in the Christian scene, foreshadowing the way

THE CHRISTIAN WOODSTOCK

Christian music would treat its square pegs in the future. . . . And so began a subculture within a subculture, that of artists ignored by "mainstream" Christian music, itself barely noticed by the larger pop culture.[14]

Indeed, Rez functioned on the margins of both the general market and the world of Christian music. But their influence reached beyond their own album sales. *Awaiting Your Reply* created a template for the emergence of new types of Christian rock, such as the general market groups P.O.D. and Jars of Clay. Reacting to the banality of commercially driven

FIGURE 6.1 Resurrection Band's "Awaiting Your Reply" (1978)

CCM, there emerged emancipated evangelical musicians hoping to push the cultural envelope. As a result, the classifier "CCM" would later fade into obscurity.

Much of the debate about CCM has been due to disagreements about how Christian musicians should interact with the world around them. Jay R. Howard and John M. Streck offer three different approaches to CCM that categorize the genre based on how the Christian music industry has historically dealt with tensions between faith, art, business, entertainment, and culture. "Separational CCM" is fundamentally dualistic, exemplifies H. Richard Niebuhr's concept of "Christ against culture," and is used to glorify God and evangelize the lost. Until recently the Gospel Music Association (GMA) modeled this in its strictest sense as it guarded the now shopworn understanding of "Christian" or "gospel" music.[15] In response, "integrational" CCM musicians view the separational approach as culturally irrelevant. An example of Niebuhr's "Christ of Culture," integrational musicians work to cross over into the general market, defining themselves as Christian entertainers. And though they remain vocal about religious faith, the primary purpose is not to evangelize.

But this approach can be reconciled with the GMA's definition of Christian music. At first blush the categories of separational and integrational are different in their perspectives on *how* to define Christian music. Despite this difference, both are utilitarian. And despite the way CCM is understood, musicians in both categories tend to view the world in binaries, striving to remain Christian witnesses through entertainment. In reaction to this dualism, "transformational" Christian musicians view art as a valuable means to enter the world as agents of God. The arts are enjoyed for the pleasure they bring. Any consequential Christian witness is merely incidental to what they believe is a result of God's presence within all creation. This approach can be connected to three of Niebuhr's categories: "Christ above culture," "Christ and culture in paradox," and "Christ the transformer of culture." Howard and Streck's three categories of CCM offers a useful model—one that provides frames of reference from which to draw when exploring the meaning and functions associated with the Cornerstone Festival. Furthermore, they are valuable when considering how groups like Rez have been perceived, and how they have contributed to a fundamental paradigm shift in evangelical pop music.

That music groups have often tapped the political goes without saying. The Grateful Dead, the MC5, Public Enemy, and U2 all evidence the power wielded by musicians and their followers who have sought to change an anemic culture. A group influenced by the music of Jimi Hendrix, Led Zeppelin, Jefferson Airplane, and Cream, the Rez Band charted a new path for CCM.

CHRISTIAN FESTIVALS: FROM CASH TO KORN

Rock concerts and sock hops have for years offered youth something of an outlet. Then when these gatherings moved to the outdoors, a truly communal activity emerged. Stretching back in time to the 1960s, the most seminal events have served as iconic reminders of a bygone era, now immortalized in Woodstock, Altamont, and the Monterey International Pop Festival. The emergence of a rock festival culture was simply the counterculture writ large. The rock festival was, according to writer and activist Bill Mankin, "a cornucopia of artistic and personal expression and experimentation that permitted each individual to dramatically accelerate their personal countercultural learning-curve with a single, concentrated dose." He continues:

> Within two years the multi-day outdoor rock festival had spread across the country, giving vastly larger numbers of Americans a chance to venture much more deeply into the heart of the counterculture itself, and to personally sample some of the trappings and elixirs it had to offer. In those early years, each festival was unique, dynamic and experimental, and they evolved fast. A few rose to mythic status after films documenting their wonders appeared in theaters nationwide, rapidly swelling the ranks of would-be festival-goers looking for the next festival, and inspiring new entrepreneurs to stage even more of them. In one form or another (depending on how the term "rock festival" is defined), dozens of these events occurred in America between 1967 and the mid-1970s.[16]

Indeed, rock festivals have always served as a rally cry for youth. Collectively, they could realize who they were in the grand scheme of things—or at least the counterculture. And more poignantly, they could explore new ways of living and being. Continues Mankin:

> For those who were relative virgins to such things, a rock festival could provide them with an initiation or a jump-start. If they'd already learned a thing or two elsewhere, a rock festival could broaden and intensify their awareness and experience, or let them push their own boundaries a bit further. One thing about rock festivals: because each attendee was surrounded by such a large crowd, so many of whom seemed to be "doing it" (no matter what "it" was), whatever personal inhibitions they may have had when they arrived tended to loosen up pretty quickly. But whether or not they were inclined to personally sample the various exotic fruits on offer, or to engage in any extreme or risky behaviors themselves, they could readily observe others who did, giving them an even broader set of experiences and benchmarks by which to re-examine or redesign their own life if they were so disposed. For many young people, in the midst of their most impressionable and formative years, a rock festival could represent a significant rite-of-passage. Some found they could leap from relative innocence to full immersion in a single weekend.

Evangelicals have often puzzled over how to appropriately accommodate culture. After all, if it is not done properly, ministers of the Christian message risk harming their ability to properly shepherd the faithful. But the Jesus Movement created a new way to engage. Then with the rise of Christian rock concerts and enigmatic Jesus music festivals, young people were finally able to experience community events with other like-minded fans of rock 'n' roll, something yet-to-be added to the Sunday morning gathering. One of the first major "Jesus festivals," Explo '72, was a cultural milestone that led to other gatherings of hip, young evangelicals who hoped to enjoy sanctified versions of pop music. In no small fashion, the event went a long way in solidifying the connection between conservative evangelicalism and pop music stars, allowing even young Republicans a space to encounter two separate dichotomies. "It was the perfect trip for a young, conservative Christian like [Mike] Huckabee," says John G. Turner, "as Explo '72 foreshadowed the subsequent emergence of evangelicals as a powerful voting bloc."[17]

Indeed, Explo '72 was nothing like the Cornerstone Festival. Sponsored by Campus Crusade for Christ and led by conservative Bill Bright, Explo '72 assuaged the fears of evangelical parents by placing the Reverend Billy Graham on the same billing as Kris Kristofferson and Johnny Cash. It was the perfect blend of pop culture and conservative sensibilities, which would serve to create a template, allowing evangelicals to enter the cultural mainstream in force. Writes Turner: "The organization's embrace of rock music at Explo '72 went a long way toward revolutionizing evangelicalism's relationship with popular culture. Only a few fundamentalists seriously swim against the cultural tide today. Explo may not have changed the world, but it changed American evangelicalism."[18]

In fact this was a calculated move on the part of Campus Crusade for Christ's International Student Congress on Evangelism. The festival became what news editor Edward Plowman referred to as "the largest youth training conference in church history."[19]

Explo '72 set the stage for a cultural explosion that would come to define evangelical youth for the next three decades. In some ways early Jesus festivals were simply Christianized attempts at "countercultural" forays, such as the original Woodstock Festival. Founded in 1970 by Asbury Seminary professor Paul Lyons, Ichthus was to become "an alternative to Woodstock." Self-described as the "longest-running Christian music festival in the nation," Ichthus is now under the Creation Festival umbrella, and it has become the only Christian music festival held in the fall rather than summer. Henry Thomas and Tim Landis cofounded Creation Northeast in 1979, which is now considered to be the largest Christian festival in the United States (averaging 50,000 in attendance) and includes offshoots such as Creation Northwest and Sonshine in the United States and abroad.[20]

In other ways these did not come close to mimicking the edgy thrust often associated with Woodstock's history, a now tired mythology that surrounds the original event. AGAPE, Ichthus, Godstock, Atlanta Fest, Jesus-

Fest, Creation, Sonshine, Fishnet, and Purple Door all serve similar purposes. And it is tempting to suggest that the Cornerstone Festival diverged from all these in its choice of bands and guest speakers. But the truth is, they all recognize the power of indie music. What differs the most boils down to how each festival operates in relation to the record industry. Most tend to stick with the time-honored top-down approach, where corporate sponsorship and executive gatekeepers ensure that profit and value remain ever connected with "product." Not surprising, the primary focus is mainstream music. Even the side stages (though often designed to cater to fans of indie music) still retain the general smell of corporate music. Only recently has Creation Festival begun to offer more edgy groups once primarily associated with Cornerstone—a smart move, given the decline of Cornerstone and the displacement of its demographic. Still, despite attempts to offer indie bands on the "fringe" stage, Creation's primary thrust is clearly commercial music, whereas the landscape of Cornerstone (its geographical layout) dedicated the lion's share of its real estate to fringe stages. Distinctly different, Cornerstone tended to emphasize the bottom-up model. In this fashion, the democratizing impulse of grassroots music works to challenge the hegemonic stronghold of corporate gatekeeping. While all these festivals in some fashion showcase artists who have survived the gauntlet of public scrutiny, Cornerstone's charm was clearly in its generator stages. For these festivalgoers, music was a democratic utterance, something that swelled from the ground, catching on by word-of-mouth.

Given the rapid changes now occurring in the music industry, this newborn emphasis on "liveness" should not shock. Revenue streams generated by recorded music tend to be minimal, with the exception of synchronization licenses, assuming an artist is fortunate enough to strike a deal with producers of film, television, or video games. And so it goes without saying that there is now more money to be made in live performance. "The music business has been turned upside down in the last 10 years. Live music is more important," says promoter and festival entrepreneur Vince Power. "Festivals are a big part of that because of the amount of money an artist can earn in one show." However, large events tend to be risky business. In recent years there has been a greater shift toward smaller events. "There will always be small festivals," notes Power, "with between 1,000 and 5,000 people, that are built on the basis of being more like a community festival."[21] And this is good news for indie groups and record labels, since the market appears to be flooded by too many big players. According to Power, "signing up bands is a big problem at the moment because there are too many bands going out too often."[22] This means that festivals like Cornerstone model a new industry paradigm, one that values local community, grassroots activism, and bottom-up expressions of art. And this radically distinguished Cornerstone from other CCM-based events.

As thoroughly middle-class expressions of solidarity, music festivals (Christian or otherwise) help us to name and categorize tensions common to a dichotomy of the high and the low, the corporate and the individual. Widely celebrated throughout the 1970s, Jesus festivals went on to develop commercial relationships with theme parks throughout the 1980s and 1990s. In some fashion this departure from the antiestablishment thrust of earlier rock festivals typifies what we have long suspected: a deep connection between evangelicals and industry, now a forlorn relationship owing to the rise of the Evangelical Left. Still, slick corporate-fueled festivals like Creation remain wildly popular, but none has had the sociocultural impact that Cornerstone had. CNN.com reported that Cornerstone "spawned a revolution in Christian rock, which is now selling around fifty million discs a year . . . ahead of jazz, new age, classical—with the creative chaos of Cornerstone right in the middle."[23] But it did more than this.

To the staff of Cornerstone, their festival was an alternative to other Christian music events, a contrast to "safe" music.[24] Put another way, the JPUSA community felt the need to offer a venue where Christian musicians felt free to perform music typically *not* accepted by the Christian mainstream (whether due to style or to lyrical content), and where discussions on politics, religion, and art mirrored to some extent what they believed to be both biblical and holistic. While other Christian festivals continue their appeal to fans of mainstream Christian rock (what is considered normative to the parent culture), members of JPUSA argue that Cornerstone highlighted a subcultural aesthetic often absent from gatherings sponsored by the gatekeepers of establishment evangelicalism. "As we conceived it," writes Jon Trott, "Cornerstone Festival would be to Jesus festivals what Seven-Up© was to cola: the *unfestival*." He continues:

> No Jesus festival existed in the Midwest, and by the early eighties we began to dream about doing one, with a distinct "JPUSA" flavor, ourselves. We knew and respected the promoters of other Jesus festivals, but due to tremendous church resistance to rock music and other cultural forms of expression, the promoters favored "safe," middle-of-the-road CCM performers over the increasing number of innovative Christian rock bands. In addition, festival teachers sometimes seemed to be chosen more for their drawing power than their power to minister from the Word of God.[25]

At its best, Cornerstone connected JPUSA to the wider evangelical subculture. Then, with the news of newly saved member of the band Korn, Cornerstone gladly included Brian "Head" Welch on the billing, endearing itself to nonbelievers. Welch continues to perform with Korn but openly professes his newfound faith. In some sense this returns us to the days of Johnny Cash, a time when the record industry boasted a number of faith-based artists but saw no need to create a separate industry. The dividing line between secular and Christian music as an industry construct is in part a development that was necessary with the birth of CCM. But Cornerstone has to a certain extent ruptured those boundaries. Its very public evolution signaled a noticeable differentiation between JPUSA and establishment evangelicalism—and it mirrored the changes that would come with the rise of new forms of evangelical Christianity and its music.

IN THE BEGINNING

By the 1980s CCM was ubiquitous. But despite Chicago's deep connection to evangelical Christianity, it did not offer any sort of massive Christian rock event—at least on the level of the rock festival. Cornerstone began at the Chicago County Fairgrounds in Grayslake, Illinois, in 1984, a seminal year in the rise of Reagan-era evangelicalism. Influenced by the European-based Greenbelt Festival, JPUSA member Henry Wong served as Cornerstone's director for the first sixteen years, after which John Herrin assumed the directorship. The festival was later relocated in 1991 to the six-hundred-acre Cornerstone Farm outside of Bushnell, Illinois. JPUSA purchased the property after Chicago zoning regulations forced festival staffers to either cease activities early in the evening because of noise ordinances or relocate the event. From 1991 until 2012 the sleepy Midwestern, agrarian Bushnell rose to notoriety, and it benefited from the annual influx of festivalgoers. This rural community, seemingly stuck in time, once welcomed thousands of radical Christian rockers, many sporting the hard-core, punk rock, or goth aesthetic. And now it's all a memory. After a few years mulling over the finances, JPUSA staff decided 2012 would mark the festival's swan song.

IMPRESSIONS

Cornerstone was the public face of JPUSA. And this gathering of sweaty, head-banging, faith-driven fans offered a relatively uncommon experience, at least for the evangelical mainstream. The Cornerstone Farm was nestled in the midst of a vast field of corn, unsuspectingly tethered to the underworld of punk, goth, emo, and metal. But then there was the curious addition of church youth groups with all the attending qualities of wide-eyed youth, hopeful youth pastors, and camping gear in tow. The arrival of church buses, vans, and cars sporting the "Cornerstone or bust" statement hinted at a certain expectancy, one that validates a subcultural experience once relegated to either curious voyeurs or jeremiads offered up by preachers seeking to unmask the heresies of rock 'n' roll. New arrivals were easily spotted: their cars were still dust-free. When stopping to get gas, one could not help but notice that the gas station and fast-food store had been overrun not by farmers but by newcomers: "Cornerstoners," often tattooed, pierced, blasting hard-core music from cars and vans. Festival director John Herrin notes the sense of youthful disorganization Cornerstone once conveyed: "I think if you go to the typical Christian music festival, as soon as you walk in the door, you know the adults are in charge. When you walked through the gate at Cornerstone, I hoped the first thought was maybe nobody's in charge."[26] The line of vehicles that waited to enter the farm hinted at the possible size of the event. Festivalgoers were always greeted by ticket-takers (either volunteers or members of JPUSA) often wearing the festival uniform: shorts, sandals, and the possible message-oriented T-shirt or tattoos and clothing advertising for various subcultures or "indie" bands, causing the newcomer to ask, "What is this place?"

When one drove along the dusty road attempting to find a space to set up camp, the senses were overcome. Golf carts carrying "straights" and "freaks" were used as quick transportation around the farm. Generator stages every few feet showcased hard-core punk rock bands. People shouted at vehicles while using their bodies and wooden signs to advertise music groups and movements. If one dared to roll the car windows down (the temptation was too great not to), flyers were shoved in. The aroma of waste trucks and portable toilets would often waft over, only to be outdone by the smell of the shower building, mixed with the sweat of hundreds of unshowered head bangers and the ever-present fragrance of vendor food, reminiscent of carnival life.

Cornerstone operated on the evangelical fringe, and it attracted everyone from the typical evangelical youth group to the disenchanted 1960s leftover seeking to recapture the magic of the hippie and Jesus Movement. At its best, the festival attempted a sort of multicultural approach to "manyness." But its pluralism was limited.

In many ways the festival captured the "old-time religion" of its evangelical forefathers. But it is important to recognize that Cornerstone (like JPUSA) was replete with both meaning and ambiguity, as the leadership has acknowledged the fluidity of theology while still affirming certain fundamentals of the Christian faith. These fundamentals were evident, though the politics of JPUSA were not quite as visible to fans. For example, during an election year the George W. Bush administration contacted the Cornerstone office and requested an audience. JPUSA and Cornerstone declined, a decision not broadcast to the general consumer.[27]

Festivalgoers tended to be fairly conservative, even exacting in their attempts to prove their positions true. Oddly, while the Christian music industry and its fans are more than often to the right of center, Cornerstone

FIGURE 6.2 Images of Cornerstone festival-goers. © 2010 Cornerstone Press/Jesus People USA Evangelical Covenant Church; all rights reserved.

as an *event* was decidedly left wing, at least politically. Put simply, properly categorizing the festival has always been difficult, and it cannot be fully associated with the traditional models that characterize marketing Christian pop music. Thus, like JPUSA, Cornerstone was interstitial, though its influence was far-reaching.

Lasting for an average of five days, Cornerstone was organized around the weekend of July 4. Some of the official performance venues included Main Stage, the Underground Stage, the Decapolis Label Showcase, Rock for Life, the Impromptu Stage, the Rave building, the Maloca Tent, the Gallery Stage, Encore 1, Encore 2, the HM Magazine Stage, Late Night Worship at the Beach (a lake), and The Asylum (a Goth tent, complete with coffins and music ranging from eerie to "industrial"). Tooth & Nail Day showcased artists promoted by Tooth & Nail, a cutting-edge Christian record company. Groups such as P.O.D. (Payable on Death), MxPx, Saviour Machine, The 77s, Pedro the Lion, Sixpence None the Richer, Danielson, and the Galactic Cowboys either have obtained status of cult notoriety within the evangelical subculture or have risen to modest fame in the general market, often embracing a subtler approach to Christian evangelism. Other well-known groups within Christian music circles include The Choir, Vengeance Rising, The Chariot, Demon Hunter, Norma Jean, Underoath, Extol, One Bad Pig, MewithoutYou, Anberlin, The Crossing, Busker Kibbutznik, The Lost Dogs, Reliant K, Vigilantes of Love, Rez Band, Our Corpse Destroyed, and Brian "Head" Welch, formerly of Korn. As band names go, this list continues a tradition whereby evangelicals have always sought to encode band names and titles with meaning, even when designed to satiate consumers who crave methods of "signifying" that have been subsumed: attire, words, gestures, lyrics, musical style, language.

Although the festival was initially conceived as a music event with a few seminars and added art attractions, it grew over the years and offered a range of activities not typical to the average festival. Since its inception Cornerstone hosted a series of lectures at JPUSA's "cstoneXchange" (formerly "Cornerstone University"). Often led by noteworthy scholars, seminars included discussions on global affairs, sexuality, the music business, political theory, subcultural theory, Christian missions, communal living, philosophy, health care, and technology. And they offered a wide range of activities intended to meet a breadth of interests: art exhibits; hands-on arts and crafts; a film festival; a skateboard ramp; crafts for children; puppet shows and theater for children; the Cornerstone Games; water activities at the Cornerstone Farm Lake; native pow-wow tribal dances; theatrical productions; and workshops on writing and poetry. Unlike other events similar in scope and size, the methods of expressing religious faith were varied, if often complicated by conventional mores.

In some ways Cornerstone bore resemblance to vaudevillian antics: a singing rubber tree was backed by women dressed as nurses; groups gallivanted around, sporting pirate attire with boom box and "pirate music" in tow; parades formed spontaneously; makeshift stages arose with unique campgrounds (complete with homemade swimming pools and air-conditioned tents); and members of a Norwegian "black metal" music group resembled the crew of a Viking warship (complete with blood and spikes). At its core, Cornerstone offered heterodox expressions of an orthodox cosmology. But orthodoxy can take many forms, often changing to the tune of pluralism. This mixture of unlikely fans embraced a broad range of activities that (despite individual roles or positions within the evangelical community) existed as an alternative to mainstream, establishment evangelicalism.

IDEAS AND REPRESENTATION: INFLUENCE ON INDIVIDUALS AND CULTURE

To a certain extent, the fact that Cornerstone's genesis paralleled the heyday of Reagan-era evangelicalism should not be taken lightly. Certainly JPUSA's theology throughout the 1980s mirrored that of baby boom conservatives. But despite the conservative 1980s, JPUSA managed to blunt the efforts of evangelical cultural gatekeepers—at least within the world of Christian rock. The community's representation of a particular counterethos created what I contend was a ripple effect in the Christian music industry, beginning with differentiation, a social comparison Dick Hebdige refers to as "significant *difference*,"[28] As with JPUSA's commune, Cornerstone's location played a role in this differentiation. The isolation of the property contributed to inspiring festivalgoers to think differently about faith and music, if only for one week. Moreover (and ironically) this form of brief cultural isolation inspired creative forces that ultimately challenged CCM.

The power of mass agreement at the festival was evident as like-minded enthusiasts found themselves engaging in collective responses, often affirming an evangelical distinction (though at times with a twist). While Cornerstone offered a kind of musical and spiritual escapism, where fans were free to experiment with ideas, the concerts still carried the power of the performative. Through the mere power of celebrity, belief was simultaneously challenged and reinforced. Put another way, when music groups connected with fans of similar aesthetic taste (clothing, hairstyle, music, etc.), ideology was either relegated subaltern (rendered inconsequential) or realigned to fit what was thematic to the festival, a particular group, visual artist, or poet. And this poses a question: were fans caught up in yet another moment of collective affirmation, much like any gathering of pop culture enthusiasts?

For example, most groups at Cornerstone used the rhetoric of equality in performer-fan relationships. But the constructed nature of performance is always hierarchical, isn't it? The typical performance stage elevates the performer to a position higher than the audience, implying status above the fan. Then, technology amplifies messages and illuminates images (corporal, rhetorical, and visceral) privileging the rock star in the minds of fans.[29] The culture of fandom, says Daniel Cavicchi, is filled with those dedicated to the moment. And this is certainly nothing new. Stardom is often coded with a kind of divine status. But in this context the authority of the performer was authenticated by consent of the church and the gospel music industry; thus the message might have been accepted as truth—the power of the affective reaffirms belief. Lawrence Grossberg has suggested there is "significance" placed on fan *response*. Put simply, it is easy to collectively agree on the message when orators are positioned as divine vessels, albeit unintentionally.[30]

Symbols and performative structures have the ability to encapsulate in catchy phrases deeper ideas, often surpassing the surface meaning of symbols. For Victor Turner, "What is made sensorily perceptible, in the form of a symbol . . . is thereby made accessible to the purposive action of society, operating through its religious specialists."³¹ In some ways fans endow Christian musicians with the same religious authority as ministers; today's CCM artists are similar to yesteryear's televangelist. Thus sense perception is connected to action, particularly actions (in this case performance) carried out by evangelicals. Put another way, Christian bands often attempt to make clear (and, more important, culturally relevant) what ministers may fail to do; for example, the Christian heavy metal band Bloodgood's song "Crucify" portrays the *Passion* in heavy metal theatrical form. At Cornerstone there was often a critical tension between artistic intent, fan response, and festival vision. But can common language (when elevated by means of "pop" rhetoric) actually influence an audience? And if so, what does this say about religion, music, capitalism, and American culture?

Simon Frith has argued that pop music has the ability to form identity, particularly since product consumption often occurs within the context of community. We enjoy popular music, he writes, "because of its use in answering questions of identity: we use pop songs to create ourselves a particular sort of self-definition, a particular place in society. The pleasure that pop music brings is the pleasure of identification—with the music we like, with the performers of that music, with the other people who like it."³²

Young consumers, says Frith, are able to identify with values oriented around product—and there is, of course, an intense relationship between personal taste and self-definition. Thus "the social functions of popular music are in the creation of identity, in the management of feelings, in the organization of time. Each of these functions depends, in turn, on our experience of music as something which can be possessed."³³ Or as Sarah Thornton elegantly puts it, "Youth often seek independence from the 'tyranny of the home' through their management of time."³⁴ For evangelical youth, the possession of Christian pop icons (managed in time and space) signifies and reinforces social and spiritual identity. Indeed, there is a long history where mass affectivity has worked its magic to salve our spiritual malaise. If, as Larry Grossberg suggests, "popularity is less a matter of different cultural practices than a form of articulation and effectivity," then the power of fan-idol relationships is a result of structures able to influence. Consumers of pop culture are often influenced to adopt new fashions or new ideas, or they are attracted to lifestyle choices they may otherwise avoid. But when married to religious and political ideology, the stakes seem higher, don't they?[35]

Considering the transnational nature of evangelical missionary work, Melani McAlister explores how evangelical youth culture encourages global activism in service of both God and humanity. Using an analysis one could connect to Freud or Marx (or others who have questioned the validity of "true" free will), she considers how these young missionaries serve their own ends by carrying out moral duties expected by the established order, a construct that has been wholly entwined with an unswerving American imperialism. Hoping to connect with the needy and the unsaved, missionaries engage in what McAlister calls "enchanted internationalism," a sensuous perspective that envelops the missionary in a real-yet-safe experience and "binds affective community, public intimacy, and religious passion."[36] Put another way, these encounters (which are encouraged by many evangelical musicians) provide an imagined sense of community where one does one's duty, only to return to the comforts of the global North. The result, McAlister considers, is nothing less than a soft form of imperialism:

> For US Christians, however, "enchantment" inevitably indexes a complex form of compassion, one that carries the longing for genuine community as well as a haunted sense of othering. For Americans, the lives of global South Christians are narrated, almost inevitably, through stories of poverty, persecution and suffering . . . there is the very real possibility that displays of compassion are exactly that, performances enacted for the purpose of touting one's own political or moral virtue.[37]

McAlister's analysis is quite apt when applied to CCM musicians connected to establishment evangelicalism, a movement dedicated precisely to what McAlister suggests. But as we shall see, music groups that once frequented Cornerstone would often operate contrary to evangelical assumptions and in many ways challenged the very structural frame from which they arose.

Grossberg qualifies the notion of power relations, stating that recipients of the message are not (in all cases) culturally duped receptacles. "People are never merely passively subordinated," he argues, and are "never totally manipulated, never entirely incorporated. People are engaged in struggles with, within, and sometimes against real tendential forces and determinations in their efforts to appropriate what they are given."[38] Given innumerable sets of complex relations (some stable and some not), the ability to resist any dominant paradigm is possible. But then we have Antonio Gramsci's concept of "cultural hegemony," a sort of unseen power exerted by a dominant, powerful group. In this case, one's choice is quite illusory, while still effective, as long as one *believes* they are in control.

Whether this evangelical gathering created belief or reinforced existing beliefs, the power of messages (or messaging) was negotiable and provisional. Simply put, some were influenced while others were not. While there was the tendency for message-based music to influence, there remained the possibility for resistance—a self-evident conclusion. Many groups showcased at Cornerstone emphasized social unity, deemphasizing the "pop idol" model encouraged by the music industry, undermining the "divine receptacle" status of the elevated performer. In this sense, there was constant negotiation between how fans responded to the image of celebrity and how they responded to the message of evangelical piety. Contrary to the assumption that youth are largely passive consumers, many of these youth exhibited glimmers of individual choice, even as they took on the role of co-performer. Many joined spirited drum circles. Others were caught up in a community dance circle with the world music of Busker Kibbutznik or the Celtic-inspired group The Crossing. As fans danced with tambourines in hand, they blurred the lines between performers and spectators. Considering the styles and venues associated with traditional music, Alan P. Merriam wrote that "while it is true that our concert performers tend to be rather sharply differentiated from their audience, what of contemporary folk music situations in which the audience is encouraged to participate, or certain aspects of jazz in which the audience joins the musicians fully, perhaps by dancing?"[39] Along with Christopher Small,[40] Merriam attempts to value audience participation, considering how concertgoers contribute to making music and meaning. The result amounts to ongoing negotiations between cultural hegemony and individual agency (power and choice).

THE RESULT OF INFLUENCE

While it appears the fans of Cornerstone retained some form of choice in the midst of fiery rock 'n' roll preachers and the general milieu of multicultural expression, complete autonomy was still conditional. Fans remained alert to what might have signaled the dreaded specter of religious or political unorthodoxy.[41] This notwithstanding, the level of cultural influence was unparalleled. JPUSA's musical outreach offered a place where civil discourse certainly reinforced faith, but it also produced new ideas and thoroughly ruptured how we have traditionally understood and defined religious belief. The seminars, for example, challenged long-held theological paradigms and questioned the political darlings common to the evangelical identity. Was this an important space? "Opposition may be constituted by living, even momentarily," writes Grossberg, "*within alternative practices, structures, and spaces* [emphasis added], even though they may take no notice of their relationship to existing systems of power. In fact, when one wins some space within the social formation, it has to be filled with something, presumably something one cares for passionately." The "functionalism of the identity" that was constructed at Cornerstone "opened the possibilities of positive empowerment." It was this space and place that allowed evangelical youth to experiment within alternative practices, structures, and spaces while tempered by safe surroundings and Christian community. Youth and adults were indeed empowered through reaffirming belief in the midst of doubt, or through freely entertaining doubt to challenge belief.[42]

To the extent that festival frenzy can leak into the halls of the establishment, this event did so to the tune of rock music. CCM historian Mark Allan Powell maintains that JPUSA and Cornerstone may have been influential in what editor of *HM* magazine Doug Van Pelt considers to be a "paradigm shift in the mid-'90s . . . [a] renaissance . . . where believers started remembering that art was a valid vocation."[43] JPUSA's Rez Band "demonstrated that it was possible for Christians to play marketable hard rock music," writes Powell, "without 'crossing over' to the secular field or 'selling out' to Christian music industry," though Rez did establish a template whereby out-of-the-box artists could (and would) contribute to the so-called crossover phenomenon. Powell places the group at the fore of the shift, which occurred in the CCM industry throughout the 1990s:

> Rez Band's music never seemed contrived. It did not come off as contrived to sell in a way that followed fashions of the music scene or sought to fulfill the expectations of industry-sponsored focus groups. Perhaps even more to the point, however, their music never seemed contrived to minister: it did not come off as spiritually manipulative but as simply and faithfully expressive of what the band wanted to say. Rez Band was "an alternative Christian rock band" at least a decade before anyone knew that "alternative rock" (Christian or otherwise) existed. In the 1990s, many Christian artists (e.g., those associated with Tooth & Nail[44]) would try to do what Rez Band had done: carve out a niche where they could be true to themselves and to their audience in ways that circumvented expectations and prioritized both artistic and spiritual integrity.[45]

Rez's hard-rock approach was unlike others heard in the earlier years of CCM, and the band intoned lyrics that dealt with controversial topics (poverty, drug abuse, teen pregnancy, racism, suicide, violence), none of which made the cut for other, more "suitable" Christian pop groups. While others sang strictly about salvation and the second coming of Christ, members of Rez sang about a more holistic gospel, and they envisioned an outlet for exposure where nontraditional Christian bands of all styles could practice their craft within a safe zone. The result was the launching of a new model for faith-based music. And that model redefined cherished boundaries associated with evangelical music and performance.

Although Rez founder Glenn Kaiser values music that is not utilitarian, he still believes music should be message driven. But what message? Jay Howard argues that early Rez "successfully expanded the boundaries of musical styles within CCM" and addressed issues CCM tended to avoid, such as apartheid and disability. "Over time their music became too utilitarian," he notes, "as opposed to having value in its own right as reflection of the creative divine image of God." Despite this, Howard values the band's

THE CHRISTIAN WOODSTOCK

impact, stating that they were "important for the burgeoning of Christian hard rock." Perhaps the difference between Kaiser and those whom he has influenced can be attributed to historical baggage. Many Jesus Movement veterans still believe that music should demonstrate an obvious Christian message. Still, according to various fans and producers, the social messages nestled within the lyrics of "transformational" music (as well as some of Rez) exemplify the same Christian urgency as topics such as repentance or the Rapture.

Although Rez bears greater similarity to its Bible-thumping forerunners than to modern groups, whose messages are often hidden in metaphor, its cutting-edge approach to musical style (and its decision to discuss the taboo) places the band at the helm of a tidal wave—one that aided faith-based artists in the invasion of the general market. The magazine *Heaven's Metal* (now *HM* or *Hard Music*) was established in 1985. Like the magazine *CCM* (*Contemporary Christian Music*), *HM* is the *Rolling Stone* of Christian rock. Founder and editor Doug Van Pelt makes a strong connection between Cornerstone and the general market, pointing out that the Rez Band's 1978 release of *Awaiting Your Reply* was "decidedly harder than anything previously released in the small but germinating CCM industry at the time." Given this, the band's "utilitarian model," notes Van Pelt, "was quite necessary at the time, which built trust with parents and those of the older generation that were somewhat suspicious of this genre of music called 'rock.'"[46]

While it appears that Rez Band's "separational" approach to rock music—its mission-mindedness—undermined artistry, JPUSA's now defunct *Cornerstone* magazine (which antedates *CCM* magazine) played a significant role in marketing new, alternative Christian music before magazines such as *CCM* or *HM* made their attempts. Moreover, groups promoted in *Cornerstone* magazine actually included all three of Howard and Streck's models. Although JPUSA bands like Rez were initially separational, their groundbreaking approach to faith and art proved influential for evangelical pop musicians who sought general market distribution and distinction.

JPUSA's structure created a ripple effect, influencing culture through both the Cornerstone Festival and the Rez Band. The result was a music industry that evolved; record companies, producers, and media moguls grew more accepting of rock bands whose roots were decidedly evangelical. The now germinating world of *popularized* faith-influenced rock music continues to rupture traditional delineations between the sacred and the profane. And while other evangelical rock bands have enjoyed very little cultural traction, with scant hope of making a dent in the mainstream, Rez charted new territory largely because of its affiliation. In short, the cultural impact of Rez could not have occurred if not for JPUSA's left-leaning fiscal model. Linda LaFianza and Shari Lloyd, editors for the edgy, online evangelical magazine *The Phantom Tollbooth*, argue that JPUSA's communal structure allowed Rez to continue well beyond what is allowed by general market record labels. Counting on obsequious youngsters, these record labels establish strict contractual agreements, which ensure that investors will recoup as albums sell. If sales are poor, the artist is dropped. LaFianza and Lloyd point out that Rez "did not rely on their performances or record sales to pay the bills," a business model that is evermore important in an age of failing corporate labels and Internet piracy. As members of a left-leaning community, the band was afforded significantly more time than its free-market counterparts—time to hone the band's artistry and group chemistry and to develop a grassroots fan base.[47] Although Rez enjoyed distribution deals with Christian record labels outside of JPUSA, its communal approach to living allowed the band a greater measure of time and artistic freedom, often absent in corporate record labels. As a result, both Rez and Cornerstone eroded categories that had been relatively canonical for gospel music.

THE FUTURE OF EVANGELICAL MUSIC

Cornerstone defied how the cultural mainstream has traditionally understood and presented Christian pop music. But this tension has a backstory. There is a lengthy history involving debates (associated with the Gospel Music Association) over how Christian music should be defined, marketed, and consumed. Traditional definitions of what qualifies were once oriented around the use of particular words such as "Jesus" or strict signifiers connected to a Christian worldview. *The Billboard Guide to Contemporary Christian Music* is among many sources that have published the GMA's original definition of gospel music: "Gospel music is music in any style whose lyric is substantially based upon historically orthodox Christian truth in or derived from the Holy Bible; and/or an expression of worship of God or praise for his works; and/or testimony of relationship with God through Christ; and/or obviously prompted and informed by a Christian worldview."[48]

The GMA Dove Award is the Gospel Music Association's equivalent to the Grammy Awards. Songs that qualify must have distribution with SoundScan and must receive votes from official members of the GMA. In 2009 the GMA clarified the distinctions of "gospel music:"

> From time to time, screening judges may encounter product submissions in the Album and Song categories that raise questions about whether or not the product's lyrics are appropriate for the GMA Dove Awards. To assist the judges in their determination, the GMA Board has authorized the following lyric criteria for use in these instances: *For purposes of GMA Dove Award eligibility, the lyrics of all entries in the Album and Song categories will be: based upon the historically orthodox Christian faith contained in or derived from the Holy Bible; or apparently prompted and informed by a Christian worldview.*"[49]

Both of these definitions remain problematic. Does instrumental music qualify? How does one decide what constitutes a Christian worldview? And who decides? Does a song have to use lyrics from the Bible? Doesn't the Bible include a variety of topics about which to write? For many artists and scholars, the definition warranted further consideration.[50]

Powell suggests that definitions are (or should be) approached subjectively: "Genres of literature are audience-defined. Critics can talk about the typical characteristics of a 'tragedy' or a 'horror story' or whatever—but ultimately, tragedies are works that readers find tragic and horror stories are stories that readers find horrifying . . . and sometimes this defies or transcends the author's intention."[51] For Powell, CCM is "music that appeals to self-identified fans of contemporary Christian music on account of a perceived connection to what they regard as Christianity."[52] While not shared by all, this definition can be applied to many Cornerstone groups whose lyrics did not always indicate Christian belief. Thus the festival encouraged a sort of subjectivity within socially affirmed boundaries of Christian orthodoxy. Whether by accident or by design, Cornerstone modeled a broader view of faith-based music. Consider a few lyrics from the song "Woody" by the Cornerstone veteran group The 77s:

> I'm staring headlong
> into the jaws of death
> Big teeth, big mouth
> bad, bad breath.
> And I promised myself
> I'd never do this again
> and I don't understand it

The only reference to anything remotely Christian (or spiritual) is still ambiguous.

> Help me, I'm going down again
> Help me, I can't tell
> none of my friends
> 1 2 3, struck out again
> pull a sheet over me,
> but don't cover my head
> I wanted bliss, ended up like this
> betrayed myself with
> my own Judas kiss
> Momma never told me
> there would be days like this, no!

The song ends by implying that someone is seeking to be rescued.

> You get what you pay for, I guess. Can I pay for this?
> I been eaten up and swallowed
> by what I wanted and I wanted more, more than this
> Tell me, what's worth more. What you'll lie for or what you'll die for
> I follow my heart and it lies and it lies. And I don't understand it

Help me, I'm going down again. Help me, when will this ever end?
1 2 3, if I strike out again, do I lose?
Am I dead? Dead
Am I dead? Dead
Am I dead? Dead
Am I dead? Dead[53]

While this particular song is paradigmatic of how ideas were represented at Cornerstone, the group's anthemic "The Lust, The Flesh, The Eyes & The Pride of Life" revealed what was an ongoing trace at the festival, one that captured the "Christianity" of the event while simultaneously avoiding the more obvious lyrical trappings of the CCM mainstream. But even in songs such as this, there is a subtlety that merely hints at Christian belief:

Well, I feel
Like I have to feel
Something good all of the time
With most of life I cannot deal
But a good feeling I can feel
Even though it may not be real
And if a person, place or thing can deliver
I will quiver with delight
But will it last me for all my life
Or just one more lonely night
The lust, the flesh
The eyes
And the pride of life
Drain the life
Right out of me[54]

JPUSA's initial vision resulted in a unique expression of evangelical Christianity and new, emerging methods of how its music might be classified and performed in years to come. "Cornerstone had a partial impact on this emerging model of Christian music," writes Doug Van Pelt. The festival "probably helped educate and edify this new emerging model, simply by accepting artists on the fringe, like Tonio K, Vigilantes of Love, Sixpence [None the Richer], POD, Flyleaf, Mark Heard than other more 'mainstream' Christian fests, like Creation, who cater more towards the family-safe Christian radio and soccer mom audience."⁵⁵ The more significant groups on the list, in terms of mainstream distribution, include Sixpence None the Richer, P.O.D. (Payable on Death), and Switchfoot. A landmark achievement for evangelical popular music, Sixpence None the Richer appeared on the *David Letterman Show* and has enjoyed licensing deals with network television. And in scandalous form, P.O.D. shocked and inspired adoring fans by touring with Ozzy Osbourne's Ozz Fest, as well as other general market groups. But why the scandal and shock?

During the 1980s some styles of music (such as punk rock) were often unacceptable by standards established by mainstream CCM. Furthermore, the idea that a group of Christians could perform in anything other than an officially approved venue (church, coffee house, Christian festival, etc.) was anathema to the evangelical edict to be in the world but not of it. That Christian music groups found it difficult to find employment with "secular" venues only exacerbated the problem, making it difficult for subcultural, evangelically oriented music groups to gain mainstream exposure. In response, Cornerstone provided a venue where fringe groups were fully accepted, despite theological ambiguity, political orientation, or musical style. Glen van Alkemade is a member of JPUSA, managed a stage at Cornerstone for a number of years, and has been able to observe the impact of the festival from the inside. Recalling how the Christian music industry often accepts fringe styles of music only incrementally over time, van Alkemade notes that the early 1980s proved especially challenging for Christian punk bands. Unable to secure performance dates in bars or churches, Christian punkers looked to Cornerstone and they found an audience. Van Alkemade points out that Cornerstone contributed to a greater acceptance of styles such as punk. The result was a growing number of churches that were "accepted by more conservative or mainstream denominations as legitimate expressions of Christian faith. And these were rock 'n' roll churches that had punk bands playing in church."⁵⁶

Cornerstone's challenge to CCM, its marketing model, and conventional evangelical mores eventually inspired its festival progeny to make a mark on the popular mainstream. The general market success of groups like Switchfoot, Sixpence None the Richer, and P.O.D. demonstrates how the festival redefined the many ways a Christian band can sound, where it can perform, and what it can be. To be clear, the acceptance of fringe styles such as punk rock reveals how the festival remapped boundaries traditionally used to signify (and codify) the styles of popular evangelical music that have been accepted by the Church. And despite the growing number of evangelical musicians entering the general market, CCM industry executives have benefited from the success of crossover groups. Jars of Clay, Switchfoot, Sixpence None the Richer, and P.O.D. have all made CCM a sellable and acceptable subgenre for the secular mainstream. Andrew Beaujon recalls his own analysis of Cornerstone and the impact of groups such as P.O.D.:

> I knew the members of P.O.D. were born-again Christians, but their lyrics were so much background noise to me, just more chest-beating rap-metal. . . . I finally *listened* to P.O.D. Every song, and I mean every song, referred to the band's spirituality. And this was no niche act—P.O.D.'s last record had sold three million copies, and they played concerts with groups like Linkin Park and Korn. At the time I went out to meet them, they were the biggest-selling group on Atlantic Records not named Led Zeppelin.[57]

The fact that many of these groups choose to identify with the general market creates an interesting scenario with which CCM labels must contend. And the fact that many of the groups tend to deemphasize an obvious Christian message only underscores my argument: they can no longer be classified as "CCM." In short, at its best Cornerstone signaled the emergence of new forms of "message music." In response, the music industry will have to either do away with CCM as a niche genre or create new categories.

GRASSROOTS AND CHANGE: NEW PARADIGM FAITH-ROCK AND THE DEMOCRATIZATION OF MUSIC

Christian crossover success stories notwithstanding, CCM executives must deal with emerging marketing models that might prove challenging for establishment CCM, a genre once firmly ensconced within the world of Christian conservatism. In its ecumenical approach to faith and music, Cornerstone's influence has in many ways undermined the efforts of CCM gatekeepers, not to mention the Evangelical Right. A breeding ground for showcasing art with general market potential, Cornerstone provided hope for evangelical artists who sought mainstream acceptance and distribution. It was the populist spirit of the event that contributed to this development among musicians who, in previous years, would have been content with hawking the gospel using catchy "Christianized" lyrics within strictly Christian venues. For *HM* magazine's Doug Van Pelt, Cornerstone did not merely push artistic boundaries—it created a democratic venue where unknown artists could promote their creations to groups far larger than churches and Christian coffee houses. In 1984 (the year of Cornerstone's founding) CNN reported on the event. Even then the festival caught the attention of media outlets as fringe groups (often antithetical to establishment CCM) were celebrated. This provided a "platform for artists pushing the creative envelope, writes Van pelt, and created "exponential, or at least strong, healthy growth in the alternative, metal and punk tributaries of the CCM industry."[58]

The populist power of Cornerstone contributed significantly to shifts in CCM's evolution. Certainly the mainstream CCM industry has cajoled subcultural consumers by offering their own forms of edgy music. But the catalogs of gospel gatekeepers were challenged only after noncommercial groups were provided a space to develop a notable following. Since 1984 festival staffers advanced the cause and art of groups largely unrecognized by the Christian mainstream. From its genesis, Cornerstone offered a welcoming environment for those who would push the cultural envelope (musically and ideologically), structuring the event to allow anyone to perform and market their art. Musicians were even allowed to establish campsites and construct homemade stages (powered by generators) to perform their music for thousands who walked by the stage/campsite.

This approach to democratizing music and performance distinguished Cornerstone from other festivals. As a result, the festival was "probably the largest gathering of . . . [faith-based] indie bands anywhere in the country,"

THE CHRISTIAN WOODSTOCK

FIGURE 6.3 A generator stage. © 2010 Cornerstone Press/Jesus People USA Evangelical Covenant Church; all rights reserved.

according to festival director John Herrin.[59] The signifier "independent" is typically used when one makes a comparison to the corporate model of music marketing. In this case, independent music serves to empower musicians who cannot access, or care not to access, the secular or Christian mainstream. The result is growth among indie groups that compete with corporate labels in grassroots fashion. For Van Pelt, generator stages bolstered independent artists "far away from the controlling power of the 'gatekeepers' (labels) in the CCM industry."[60]

Much like JPUSA, Cornerstone allowed for individual expression and empowerment in the midst of what was a collective attempt to retain the spirit of the Jesus Movement, as well as the edge of the original Woodstock. Along with lectures about living "in community," this egalitarian approach to performance offered anyone a chance to market their own music and opinions. While mainstream CCM maintained a presence at the event (corporate record label bands widely showcased to pay the bills), the ethos that undergirds the corporate industry was *blunted* as indie music was honored and encouraged. Thus JPUSA successfully transplanted various "impulses" that still define its own inner-city community. "Change life! Change Society!" wrote sociologist and philosopher Henri Lefebvre. These, he argued, were ideas that lose meaning "without producing an appropriate space."[61] On some level, JPUSA created a space that once inspired new ways of considering both art and ethos.

ROCK BANDS WITH CHRISTIANS OR CHRISTIAN ROCK? NEW INDUSTRY MODELS AND INDEPENDENTS

Cornerstone did not enjoy the same commercial appeal and high attendance as festivals like Creation. But it didn't have to. Legendary Christian rock producer Steve Taylor hints at Cornerstone's social impact: "I don't think that you can overstate the importance of the Cornerstone Festival."[62] Doug Van Pelt agrees, applying Taylor's statement to the CCM industry: "While having a population of roughly 25,000 in attendance each year," he recalls, Cornerstone was "a rallying point for a worldwide scene," one that embraced "new and eclectic art forms." After writing about both the Christian and mainstream industry for a number of years, Van Pelt concluded that Cornerstone created "a synergy that helps the industry grow." For him, the way the CCM industry operates is "being changed and challenged by new business models and a drastic reduction in CD sales."[63]

While the event offered an eclectic mix and challenged the mainstream, it remained subcultural till the end but still retained something to which those in the mainstream often aspire—artistry largely divorced from the power centers of evangelical music, which often dictate what constitutes "Christian" music suitable for evangelical youth. Toby Mac, Christian music producer and former member of the CCM group dc Talk, has also intimated that the festival operated on a different level from others, stating that the event was "*the* serious art festival" of Christian music.[64] Serious indeed. And for staffers it was nothing less than a chance to show fans a new way to live and to think.

THE CHRISTIAN WOODSTOCK

Whether separational, integrational, or transformational, popular evangelical music ruptures our assumptions about religion and art. Although earlier forms of this particular music cannot be classified as pure entertainment (as it existed to evangelize the lost), current indie DIY forms have exceeded what was expected. These music groups combine many styles and genres, songwriters penning material that thoroughly explores social justice. And they seem to always exist outside of the corporate mainstream, though not always by choice. But even successful general market "Christian" bands often attempt to maintain an indie appeal. Independent music challenges the mainstream as the Internet increases exposure and as grassroots companies and concerts invert notions of music industry power. Although Cornerstone operated off the grid, it remained influential in that it "has absolutely challenged the CCM industry,"[65] according to Jay R. Howard. While Cornerstone offered exposure for an unestablished genre such as punk, the festival also created a home for musicians and fans who had none. The result affected how other Christian festivals operate, many now offering more cutting-edge music.

In some ways Cornerstone had to accept a certain amount of commercialism and merchandising for survival. But Howard argues that it remained an "alternative to the mainstream of CCM if not countercultural to it."[66] And for Linda LaFianza and Shari Lloyd, Cornerstone was the "bedrock of the hard music scene for Christians."[67] Thus it challenged how CCM was conceived and provided a space where evangelicals could experiment with nonmainstream musical styles.

Despite Cornerstone's cultural reach, there has of course already been a Christian presence in mainstream popular music. The list of rhythm & blues artists who count gospel music among their beloved styles is too lengthy to include. Continuing the trend of sacred-to-mainstream, the "Christian rock star" has become fairly commonplace: Bono, Barry McGuire, Bruce Cockburn, Mark Farner (Grand Funk Railroad), Kerry Livgren (Kansas), Dave Mustaine (Megadeth), Brian "Head" Welch (Korn), Alice Cooper—this merely scrapes the surface of evangelicals who occupy the hallowed halls of classic rock.

Popular rock bands are not typically known for public declarations of faith. And we may never know why these declarations remain scarce. But

THE CHRISTIAN WOODSTOCK

FIGURE 6.4 Cornerstone Festival side stage under a tent. © 2010 Cornerstone Press/Jesus People USA Evangelical Covenant Church; all rights reserved.

given the polarizing effect on a society wrought by culture wars, it is little wonder artists of faith either keep low profiles or simply nestle into the comfortable world of the CCM mainstream. Their choice of home, however, must be tethered to their choice of ideology. Politically conservative rockers such as Ted Nugent notwithstanding, overt conservatism does not bode well in the largely centrist cultural mainstream. And the right-leaning world of CCM has been thoroughly relegated to niche status, often owing to lyrics drenched with religious dogma—an approach that simply does not endear would-be pop stars to a broadcast market. The world of Cornerstone inverted ideological paradigms in such a way that CCMers who began in Nashville—the epicenter of CCM—now either live the indie rock dream or have been handed the keys to the kingdom of general market success. But another group had already established such precedent. This group went on to establish a progressively ecumenical model in their music and branding, proving inspirational for musicians disenchanted with the world of conservative, evangelical Christianity.

THE CHRISTIAN WOODSTOCK

U2's 1987 release of *The Joshua Tree* was what Andrew Beaujon refers to as "a generational touch point."[68] The band had nothing to do with CCM or its industry. But when it became a "world-beating phenomenon, Christian music's 'legalistic' tendencies—the strict adherence to what many fundamentalists consider biblical law—again emerged."[69] Christian radio stations tend to play songs by U2 only if performed by Christian bands, notes Beaujon. Despite Bono's humanitarianism, some evangelicals often bristle at the fact that he swears, drinks, and smokes, a lifestyle anathema to the American version of evangelical Christianity.

Bono did not initially find favor with conservative evangelicals, but the tide changed as more evangelical youth saw a new paradigm in U2. A world-beating phenomenon indeed. But one artist firmly ensconced within CCM proper had also planted the seeds for a wider conception of faith-based expression. Born Charles William Ashworth, author/musician/producer Charlie Peacock is one of the most noteworthy producers in the CCM universe, and he has produced groups that now enjoy significant crossover success—an accomplishment not unlikely, given his own early success with general market record labels.[70] Along with his widely acclaimed portfolio (which includes Amy Grant, Switchfoot, and The Civil Wars), Peacock has been instrumental in challenging the sacred/secular divide upon which the Gospel Music Association and the Christian music industry are built. He is among those who have encouraged Christian musicians to make art for its own sake (transformational) and opposes utilitarian views, which posit that music's sole purpose is to edify Christians, missionize non-Christians, and serve religious worship. Peacock questions this functional approach, seeking to produce artists who operate based on a holistic evangelical worldview without particularizing that worldview. Particularization tends to oversimplify Christianity with songs containing clichés and narrowly defined depictions of what he believes should be broader approaches to a biblical worldview. Thus he is the high priest of transformational CCM, representing the totality of the human experience.

Genres have been redefined, the urgency of Jesus music has been reconsidered, and business models are changing. So how will CCM fare in the future? "Young Christian baby-boomers and Gen-X once in love with the music abandoned it in adulthood and have not returned," writes Peacock.

He continues, comparing the longevity of CCM to classics in the general market:

> As a result, legacy artist catalogs (ranging from Larry Norman to Amy Grant to dcTalk and beyond) do not and will not have the staying power of their mainstream counterparts such as The Beatles, The Eagles, Elton John, Led Zeppelin, Celine Dion, James Taylor, Bob Dylan, Bruce Springsteen and U2. All these artists, and a hundred others, remain popular and economically viable today. Sadly, the pattern does not hold true for what was contemporary Christian music.[71]

Cornerstone was instrumental in Peacock's rise to fame, providing a model that released him from the constraints of CCM proper. LaFianza and Lloyd have highlighted the impetus behind Peacock's genesis. He invested "all his money into a project, packing the van with cassettes and heading east to C'stone [Cornerstone], where the reception was very warm. He went on to be a very influential producer in Nashville."[72] As a venue, the festival nurtured the latent desires of artists like Peacock, consequently creating this paradigm shift in Christian pop. As bands began to cross over into the general market, CCM's status quo was challenged. Cornerstone's progeny would go on to complicate how these "new paradigm groups" were to be categorized and marketed: Sixpence None the Richer, P.O.D., Underoath, Family Force Five, mewithoutyou, Pedro the Lion (David Bazan), Danielson Family, Eisley, Fireflight, Pillar, MxPx, and Earthsuit, a group that later became the Grammy Award–nominated group MuteMath.

Cornerstone worked toward cultural inclusion while taking care to proceed judiciously. Showcasing mainstream and indie artists, the festival pushed the envelope while simultaneously restraining itself, to appease the parent culture. Yes, festival staff proceeded with caution, aware of how heterodox expression might be perceived. Yet they still managed to make waves. While Cornerstone certainly bears little resemblance to mainstream festival counterparts such as Creation, and while the festival is relatively progressive (musically, politically, and theologically), it cannot be counted among other

Christian gatherings such as Wild Goose, an interfaith festival also inspired by Cornerstone's forbearer, Greenbelt.[73]

DIVERSITY, COMMUNITY, AND REPRESENTATION: COUNTERCULTURAL EVANGELICALISM?

Despite iconoclasm, Cornerstone maintained the appeal of being a serious Christian arts festival. Other evangelical Christian music festivals are structured based on the model of opening acts and headliners, many having charted well in the CCM industry. These events do not offer festivalgoers the freedom to build make shift stages or create serendipitous performances. Exploring how artists were represented at Cornerstone might provide insight into the JPUSA community, Christian music, and postmodern forms of evangelicalism. Did the festival mirror what is happening within some sectors of evangelical Christianity? This calls for a cultural studies approach. JPUSA and American culture are situated as "texts" within a larger story. In considering the various positions on postmodern analyses of text, Lawrence Grossberg recalls one theory—that

> any interpretation . . . is an articulation, an active insertion of a practice into a set of contextual relations that determines the identity and effects of both the text and the context. Articulation is the continuous deconstruction and reconstruction of contexts. These articulated connections are sometimes fought over, consciously or unconsciously, but in any case, an articulation is always accomplished . . . and will always have political consequences.[74]

The evolution of the JPUSA community, the Cornerstone Festival, and Christian pop music has had political consequences. Consider the lyrics previously discussed. Consider the ways in which Cornerstone as a "text" responded to cultural pluralism, then inspired Christian artists to engage postmodernity in more progressive ways. Rather than deciphering "meaning" and "representation" based on encoding (the production of meaning) and decoding (the consumption of meaning), we reserve final judgment on texts merely based on differentiating between what Grossberg refers to as "intended or preferred meanings" and "received or effective meanings," arguing that articulation of a text is an "ongoing struggle to produce the text by inserting it into a network of 'naturalized' relations. Encoding is a continuous force (e.g., producers continue to make statements), and decoding is already active in the efforts to encode. One cannot separate the materiality of a text from its appropriation, nor can one separate structures from practices."[75]

Although structures and practices cannot be separated (according to Grossberg), we all continue to interpret movements and communities through the grid of their language and how they present their messages. And so we are tempted to locate either the intended or received meanings of lyrics that have been coded as "Christian." The way concerts were produced at Cornerstone might tell us something about our particular sociopolitical contexts and ourselves.

While the process of interpreting lyrics, persons, or events may appear futile, it is possible to locate the general spirit of Cornerstone within the broader tradition of evangelical expression. Grossberg sensitizes this study to the fact that Cornerstone was already situated within a preexisting reality (one inspired by the same forces it resists) and was a product of innumerable subjectivities. Put plainly, those who have interpreted Cornerstone have done so within the grid of what is commonly understood as "Christian" music. Methods used to determine a song, a band, or the festival's intended meanings are useful only because they are measured *against* the appellation of CCM and the edicts already established by contemporary, establishment evangelicalism.

While one may remain suspicious of how fans have interpreted the festival, the crux of meaning still falls to individuals, each engaged in a social dialectic. For Grossberg, the postmodern "reduces reality and ideology to a question of affect: whether and how particular ideological elements matter is not determined by their meanings but by how they can be incorporated into particular *mattering maps* [emphasis added], particular affective structures." But then Grossberg challenges critics whose postmodernity ends in mere fragmentation and purposeless nihilism. We need sites dedicated to human struggle and discourse, even if the struggle is thought futile. In this regard, Cornerstone is "postmodern" (or post-Enlightenment) as it avoids strict musical and ideological dogma.[76]

The fans of Cornerstone categorized music groups and the festival as both "Christian" and "evangelical" by virtue of historical connections to what these terms actually mean and imply. Given this, it is possible to interpret the event based on the common elements of Christian music and evangelicalism. And we can do this by investigating a longtime affiliate of this community. Eric Pement is a former member of JPUSA, was a contributing writer for *Cornerstone* magazine, and taught at festival seminars for seventeen years. Pement notes that Cornerstone was "an artistically progressive, musically stimulating, and spiritually envigorating [*sic*] annual arts festival." He goes on to emphasize what he perceived as a distinct change in the festival's direction, one that involved "less emphasis on teaching seminars now than there was in the past, and the speakers and workshop leaders are less evangelical than they were in earlier years and more oriented toward Emergent church, contemplative spirituality, and non-evangelical forms of faith." Cornerstone's ability to provide a venue where unknown music groups could "quickly achieve prominence" was significant. But according to his personal understanding of what the original mission implied, Cornerstone's evangelical position and its challenge to CCM eventually changed. Its resistance to the Christian music industry was once about maintaining strict moral codes for bands wishing to perform.[77] Then, as the years wore on, that standard ceased to be as important, according to Pement's recollection. But this is not a change that is specific to this community or event. Pement's account is similar to other complaints about the direction of evangelical Christianity and the CCM industry.

Christian rock has always had its fair share of critics, from evangelicals to fundamentalists to secularists. And this criticism most certainly found its way to the festival. A few years before the festival's closing, a group of protestors began to appear, whose critiques concerned the gathering's "worldly" entertainment and, to the chagrin of many other conservatives, positive discussion forums about Halloween. But while many interpreted the event as either an alternative to secular culture or a haven for a subculture within the evangelical subculture, Pement and the editors for *The Phantom Tollbooth* ended up recategorizing the festival within the evangelical paradigm. But is there a different way of casting the event within the large-yet-specific Protestant subculture?

Cornerstone's status as a gathering that countered the mainstream is admissible only if the analysis presupposes a particular understanding of how structures are resisted and how evangelical Christianity ought to be defined. We can apply Grossberg's study, recognizing that this festival has been inserted into a set of "contextual relations that determines the identity and effects of both the text and the context."[78] Put simply, the festival remains *countercultural* only if CCM remains a *mainstream expression*. But Cornerstone may have, in the words of historian Jon Pahl, actually relied on the mainstream for its oppositional identity.[79] Moreover, it remained evangelical only if the center of evangelicalism shifted to become more ecumenical. And this is true for Christian music as well. As our culture shifts—as social discourse changes the ideological landscape—it is possible that groups once associated with Cornerstone either will have to reinvent themselves or will cease to be what I would like to call "new paradigm, faith-based music." In other words, the "new paradigm" will become normative.

For Cornerstone and JPUSA, the struggle to be defined against what has been perceived as a dominant parent culture (establishment evangelicalism and CCM) is significant. Mainstream and subcultural expressions often include "different cultural practices, as well as different popular sensibilities," writes Grossberg, and are "constantly opposing, undercutting, and reinflecting each other within the unstable formation of every-day life."[80] It is this sense of ongoing opposition and reflexivity that inspired the Cornerstone staff to allow and encourage more diversity than other evangelical festivals, with the hope of inculcating attendees with the ability to express deeply held doubts and fears within the context of temporary community. For John Herrin, Cornerstone was "more open to give people a little room to figure out who they are and what they are."[81] While it was still limited in its ecumenism, the festival demonstrated both ideological and artistic openness. It ruptured what other Christian festivals are unwilling to squeeze.

Festivals often celebrate events and ideas, attempting to reinvent or represent how society should or could operate. Evangelical gatherings are no different. For countercultural Christian music Cornerstone served as a counternarrative to society's official story. That is, the staff attempted to offer their own version of Christian artistic expression that countered what the Christian culture industry viewed as "official," even if it undermined what was commonly understood as "Christianly" music. CNN.com observed that "staunchly conservative critics also suggest it seems nobody is very Christian here. . . . It is often difficult to find or at least to hear any reference to God or Jesus in songs at Cornerstone. And many musicians want it that way." This was, in part, due to Cornerstone's clear attempt to free the artist. In considering the bands that performed throughout the years, Herrin notes, "I don't think they would really categorize themselves as Christian bands. They're really just bands that are made up of Christians. And . . . maybe not all the members are Christians."[82] Though JPUSA actively sought to offer a spiritual haven for bands whose members were not always Christian, the overarching goal was to create a different version of faith-based music: socially conscious, progressive, and at times metaphorical. "Let's put on a show," said Cornerstone veteran Terry Scott Taylor.[83]

Andrew Beaujon argued that Cornerstone was largely white, middle class, representing the cleanest cut kids he had ever seen at an event purported to be countercultural.[84] Despite this perception, Herrin considered Cornerstone within the context of Christian festivals: "ours is not 'cookie cutter.'" Other festivals, he says, present a sort of "church camp goes to music festival." This shopworn formula is needed for mainstream festivals, if they are to continue drawing hordes of church youth groups, many of them enjoying middle-class, disposable income. But JPUSA's desire was to offer something very different. "From the very beginning," recalls Herrin, "Cornerstone was always dedicated to trying to bring out more of what we felt were kind of really gifted people that didn't necessarily fit into the Christian music industry."[85] Other Christian festivals bear the marks of the polish now common to commercial CCM. Cornerstone, on the other hand, offered an alternative to both mainstream Christian festivals and to what is often expected of secular rock festivals. The event's 1984 genesis intrigued not only evangelicals but also the media. Don McLeese, rock critic for the *Chicago Sun-Times*, observed:

> Woodstock idealism aside, rock festivals are usually a mess. They're often marked by drug overdoses, alcohol overindulgences and the sort of open nudity and rampant sexuality that one generally doesn't experience in polite society. . . . At the Lake County Fairgrounds this weekend, there's a rock festival that is expected to be well-attended, well-behaved and full of purpose. . . . Unannounced before the festival, the "surprise" headliner of Cornerstone '84 is Kerry Livgren, formerly of Kansas, who is debuting his new A.D. band tomorrow night.[86]

To be fair, Beaujon also gives Cornerstone a resounding thumbs-up that would satisfy secular metal heads: "For anyone used to the minimum-security-prison ambiance of most rock festivals, it's a surprise to see stocked merchandise tables left unattended at night. But if you take away the safe environment, the reasonably priced food and the sober teenage virgins, Cornerstone is a lot like Ozzfest."[87]

For JPUSA and Cornerstoners, other evangelical festivals merely cater to the masses, lacking the edge of the counterculture, the spirit of the Jesus Movement, the democratizing impulse of DIY music, or the probing minds of the brooding postmodern. Thus Cornerstone was a bastion of Christian artistic eclecticism that exemplified an emerging evangelical tolerance. Many groups once showcased at the event may never enjoy mainstream radio play, satisfied with their own chosen subcultural home, content (in their youth) to live as wandering minstrels. But others still harbor dreams of general market success, without the ministerial expectations of the Gospel Music Association foisted on every lyrical utterance.

But despite their iconoclasm, JPUSA and Cornerstone ended up connecting to the cultural mainstream. The festival office paid the bills by booking mainstream acts. Concert stages made use of electricity sold by the establishment. Internet surfers were able to view concerts via webcams. A slick website was used for advertising. But the festival still insisted on maintaining a subversive appeal. Most events such as this tend to showcase about 80 percent of their music from the main stage. But to its credit, Cornerstone tried to offer a different model. Although many attended precisely for those mainstream groups, it is clear the primary focus was directed toward the side stages; each celebrated a diversity of musical styles: rock, heavy metal, punk, hard core, death metal, black metal, folk, jazz, blues, world music, Celtic, rave, industrial, hip hop, and some—well, I'm not sure what they were. This was a subculture within two subcultures: establishment evangelicalism and CCM.

As gatherings go, this bore some similarities to nineteenth-century revival meetings that functioned oppositionally. Both the Protestant Reformation and the Second Great Awakening have been compared to the Jesus Movement. Among other impulses that defined the Second Great Awakening, there was a populism that countered what was perceived as outdated expressions; there was a lack of vernacular connection to real individuals. When considering both the Second Awakening and new paradigm Christianity, Donald Miller notes how "in both instances, establishment religion is rejected."[88]

A good number of Jesus Movement veterans remain respectful (even ecumenical) when considering the church universal. But many have also been quite vocal about the failings of the traditional church. JPUSA and Christian leaders who once attended Cornerstone have identified festivals that simply mirror mainstream society, even though they often purport to *counter* mainstream society. At Cornerstone the net was cast wide as staff sought to include as many expressions as could be managed, which included serendipitous parades and makeshift generator stages. When one considers the evangelical parent culture, it becomes readily apparent that the Cornerstone phenomenon was certainly countercultural. But what was the festival actually countering? Were festivalgoers changing society or being changed? Or were they simply experiencing that which they did not and could not experience in the workaday world? Evangelical Christianity has been built on a lengthy history of experiential and experimental, culturally relevant religion. That is part of what defines it. So what did the festival actually oppose, other than crass commercialism and CCM? According to Doug

Rossinow, when accounting for the fevered dialogic we now associate with the 1960s and 1970s, "a counterculture was, by definition, both marginal and oppositional."[89] Cornerstone was both.

Since its genesis, this event attempted to offer an experience reminiscent of both Jesus-freak and countercultural sensibilities. Recalling Victor Turner's *The Ritual Process: Structure and Anti-Structure*, Stephen Marini crystallizes Turner's position by suggesting that people engaged in antistructure "experience spiritual and social realities far more fluid and flexible than the normal."[90] Those who attended this festival might have experienced what Turner refers to as a liminal moment, one in which those engaged in the process experience a sense of communitas, employing an egalitarianism otherwise not experienced in everyday life. Young evangelicals were able to stage dive, avoid showers, sport tattoos and body piercing, and even question their faith. So, if nothing else, Cornerstone offered those raised within structure to engage antistructure—to experiment (within festival guidelines) without social consequence. These moments of respite may have encouraged and challenged festivalgoers who were raised within firm belief-systems. More than this, festivalgoers were able to glimpse another world, one operating contrary to establishment evangelicalism and mainstream CCM.

CONCLUSION

Cornerstone's turn toward the "postmodern" continued JPUSA's heritage of evolution and (not surprisingly) kept the festival (until its untimely demise) on the fringes of evangelicalism. If postmodernism can be reduced to style over substance and surface over depth, then at first blush, the festival qualified—if one's analysis is merely based on how audiences receive and respond to messages. While the staff entertained postmodern critical theory, festivalgoers were far more cautious of a perceived growing liberalism. The sense of community, however, overshadowed ideological differences expressed at Cornerstone. Timothy Miller's account of the hippie experience appropriately contextualizes the spiritual impulse, connecting it to nineteenth-century evangelical emphases on embodied religion. In like manner, Cornerstone exhibited a collective religious experience where serious fans valued authenticity and sought the Spirit.

But despite attempts at pluralism, the leaders of Cornerstone held to a thoroughgoing Christian orthodoxy. And despite any potential polarization between liberal and conservative attendees, the event remained largely evangelical. But evangelicalism is not monolithic. Rather, it is a complex nexus of shifting views and competing opinions symptomatic of postmodernity or, more precisely, democracy and pluralism. While Cornerstone decidedly privileged a particular worldview, the festival was once a gathering that appeared to exemplify the evolution of American politics and religion. It was a space where social discourse was encouraged and, to a certain extent, ultimate meaning and cherished definitions remapped, as power relations were eventually revealed—Dorothy discovered the wizard's true identity. Various ideas once held as common or normative were negotiated through perennial discussions about faith and philosophy, uncomfortable and challenging as they may have been. Thus it was far deeper than the postmodern.

As noted earlier, other communal experiments throughout the 1960s and 1970s either disbanded or faded into cultural obscurity. Many expected the world to end within their lifetime. Others hoped communal experiments might result in an eventual radical shift in society. The failure of communes to deliver on their predications, however, did not bode well for communities oriented solely around apocalyptic expectancy. While other Jesus communes focused on the end, JPUSA focused on the present, seeking to preach the gospel to the disenfranchised. JPUSA's concern for on-the-ground human need has carried it successfully into the twenty-first century. Along with the mission to aid the homeless population in Uptown, the task of planning Cornerstone provided a sense of purpose for the community. But how can we appropriately locate JPUSA (as expressed at Cornerstone) within the broader world of evangelical Christianity, a movement always redefined? More to the point, how will JPUSA fare in the wake of Cornerstone's demise? And what does this death imply about other progressive forms of faith and art? Indeed, others will fill the gap. Current attempts include diehard festivalgoers who have formed "Occupy Cornerstone," a social network for fans seeking to maintain this extended "family." And then there is AudioFeed, a new festival designed by a former fan. While it is not intended to replace the festival, it hopes to fill an empty space left in the wake of Cornerstone's closing.

Neither modern nor postmodern categorizations seem to effectively capture what JPUSA and the festival represent. For Grossberg, no structure is completely stable or unstable. The complexity of history and the human equation make any final position untenable. When considering how JPUSA or Cornerstone might be classified, one must consider the fluidity of both. Each classification is dependent on a number of variables. What remained consistent, however, was JPUSA's ability to transfer its Jesus Movement ethos to Cornerstone. The emphasis on community, iconoclasm, and the spirit and populism divorced from the corporate establishment (evidenced by generator stages) all demonstrate that JPUSA offered something very different from the establishment. Even when attempts were made to recode establishment forms of music and ethos to fit the cultural mainstream, efforts were blunted by side-stage presentations, each carrying the aura of an authenticity that questioned the corporate sensibilities of the main stage.

JPUSA's conspicuous presence at the festival—its ubiquity—allowed festivalgoers to glimpse *individual* representatives of a countercultural ethos. The festival had a history of attracting seekers, occasioning within each an awareness of their own liminality. And this created a sort of revolving-door scenario for the JPUSA community. Some sought healing, purpose, and a different way of experiencing "church." The fact that young seekers are often attracted to the romance of JPUSA might account for its longevity and success, even if seekers remain for only a brief period of time. Through Cornerstone, JPUSA engaged culture, unlike other communal experiments. Given the festival's structure and ethos, JPUSA was able to offer what it considers to be truly countercultural, challenging the saliency of the CCM industry and establishment evangelicalism. The vision resulted in an annual gathering that provided a venue for free artistic expression, regardless of style or lyrical content. Festival seminars served to help festivalgoers develop new understandings of what "sacred" music might be while also challenging political and theological paradigms. Cornerstone's history complicates definitions commonly attributed to Christian music. The result has been a burgeoning subculture of musicians under the *influence* of evangelical faith who rise to the challenge of performing in venues largely disassociated from what is often expected of those who claim evangelical distinction. And through their music, these pioneers championed the ideals associated with the Left, emphasizing social justice over and above simple expository preaching and missionizing often connected to evangelical Christianity. Whether by accident or by design, Cornerstone questioned the category of (or the need for) the "Christian band."

Clearly JPUSA's social activism reinforced a commitment to a way of living and a brand of Christianity quite alien to establishment evangelicalism. This has provided communards a reason for being, inspiring them to engage enterprise (through their businesses) while agreeing to a life of simplicity and voluntary poverty. Cornerstone once kept the community connected to the larger culture and, unlike other Jesus communes, offered an ongoing context whereby their connection to the larger culture maintained sociocultural relevance. But two factors might threaten JPUSA's continuance. Since Cornerstone has folded, JPUSA might lose a larger sociocultural frame of reference. This has the potential to affect the community negatively, creating the possibility of insularity. Second, many of JPUSA's second-generation communards are leaving the community. And those who remain will determine the direction of the community. The next chapter considers the testimonies offered by current and former second-generation communards and explores the community's parallels to American evangelicalism and pop culture.

7
THE FUTURE: EX-MEMBERS, SECOND GENERATION, AND SOCIAL DYNAMICS

✷ ✷ ✷

To a certain extent, exploring the potential future of JPUSA helps shed light on the future of any religious organization attempting to navigate a delicate (even elegant) balance among orthodoxy, democracy, and pluralism. So far JPUSA'S longevity can be connected to a commitment to aiding Uptown's homeless population, a steady influx of new members, mission businesses, and a sustained affiliation with the parent denomination. Its businesses provide the capital needed to sustain the group, freeing members to operate missions such as Cornerstone Community Outreach. This shelter represents a perennial need, ensuring a collective commitment from the faithful. The Evangelical Covenant Church keeps the commune from becoming isolationist. And until its untimely demise, the Cornerstone Festival attracted new members who contributed to labor, if only briefly. Perhaps the legacy of the festival will continue to attract fans to JPUSA halls in the foreseeable future. But the community's future will likely be determined by its rising generations. After all, given the leadership council's aversion to the democratic process, one wonders how future leaders will be decided. And considering the rapid exodus of second-generation members, it is no stretch to wonder who will prove seasoned enough to lead the community.

Given the fluidity of American society, accommodation to the surrounding culture is equally necessary for JPUSA to remain successful. The way it manages communal structure and sociocultural change determines how its noncommunal constituency, second-generation communards, and former members perceive it. If JPUSA resists change, it is possible that some second-generation communards will leave to seek a life experience that (for them) accurately represents the real world. But if the community continues to accommodate sociocultural shifts (reinventing its ethos), there is an equal risk that first-generation members will still leave the community. And this has already happened.

While cultural evolution has, for the most part, sustained the commune in terms of cultural relevance, an über-differentiation may only serve to deteriorate membership. Thus change is needed, but only incrementally. The first signs of what could be considered a tension between tradition and progress can be seen in JPUSA's second generation. Throughout this process I have relied on the testimonies of individuals. While the comments of founding members are informative when considering JPUSA's history, structure, and longevity, the stories of second-generation communards offer the perspective of those who did not choose this sort of life. And this provides greater insight into what the future might hold for JPUSA. Historian James D. Chancellor agrees that individual testimonies are important for documenting historical accounts: "If we are to find the soul of faith, to discover the power of religious ideas, the depth and intensity of religious moods and motivations, and the complexities of the religiously centered life, then we must abandon an intellectual imperialism that denies faith adherents the right to interpret their own experiences."[1] In no small way, getting a handle on how this community has navigated pluralism sheds light on the complexities of American culture.

THE SECOND GENERATION: GROWING UP IN COMMUNITY

As with other countercultural experiments JPUSA experienced its "long sixties." And this period would have (perhaps) lasted longer, had the group taken a cue from Catholic missionaries. Put simply, these young Jesus freaks were attempting to swim upstream, so to speak. Life on the road; voluntary poverty; a decision to settle in the inner city of a major metropolis; outreach to the homeless and all manner of social outcasts. The trek was the stuff of radical missions. And then they had children.

Whether JPUSA founders should have married and had children is quite beyond the scope of this book. But one thing is clear: raising children within this environment must have been challenging. Still, to a certain extent, the commune needs someone to pick up the torch. While communal sustainability is indelibly linked to commitment mechanisms, the dedication of second-generation communards will ultimately determine JPUSA's fate, or at least its cultural relevance. Founding members commit to core principles, with the exception of those who choose to leave. Leaders must consider how mantles of leadership are to be handed down, how the next generation will be trained, and at what age. For the JPUSA council, there is no immediate need to determine what the emerging leadership will look like. According to John Herrin, the founders are in the prime of their lives. And for many in leadership, God remains firmly in control. So if we are to interpret JPUSA's future based on how committed second-generation members are to the cause, it is important to understand how they perceive their own lives within the community.

At very early ages some noticed theirs was a different sort of life. Between eight and nine Scarlett Shelby (daughter of John and Tina Herrin) knew her life differed from those of other children—others did not live in houses shared by teachers and pastors. Now twenty-two and a mother, Shelby sees communal life as offering safety, despite the inner-city location. Comparisons to the "outside world" extend well beyond what is perceived as shared or breached space. Recollections of how children perceive communal living are often situated within dichotomies established by how "normalcy" is constructed and remembered, at least by adult communards looking back on childhood with either fondness or distaste. Recalling an early awareness of differentiation, Nathan Cameron remembers visiting his grandparents during family gatherings:

> I was about six or seven. I remember the moment very distinctly. . . . My grandparents lived in Wisconsin . . . every once in a while we would go

up and visit them. My idea of life up to that point was living this communal life. We all lived in one big building, and all my friends were just a door away down the hall, and we all just kind of lived together and played together and did everything together. And I would go up to my grandma's house, and everybody had their own house, and everybody had their own car, and everything was separate. And so I kind of thought . . . it was like vacation. Everybody got out of the city to go to Grandma's house, to kind of get away from it all, and then they would go home.[2]

Nathan's moment of differentiation came when he realized that his family and friends were different. At the end of visits to family and friends, he would return to the commune while others were able to remain within their own private escapes.

So there were several kids who lived next door to my grandmother . . . we would all play . . . but I thought that was vacation. I thought all these kids, when I left, they left too and went back to their communities. I remember [when] I was about six or seven . . . I said, "Oh, so what community do you live in? . . . Where do you go when you're done hanging out here?" All of a sudden I was just like, "Wait a minute. You mean you don't have to go back to that? This is where you get to stay all the time?" . . . It was kind of a traumatic moment for me. . . . I had to go back into the city and poverty . . . a place where I didn't have my own space, a place where I lived in a room with five other kids. We had to share everything. . . . I remember having a very hard time wanting to go home and it being a very difficult thing for me. . . . I felt . . . like I was trapped . . . and I wanted out but I couldn't get out because I wasn't an adult. . . . I didn't choose this life.[3]

Although Nathan's childhood was a difficult one, as an adult he continues to value communal living. His father, Tom Cameron, earned his law degree while living in the commune. (JPUSA felt he should gain practical experience working with a law firm, thus preparing him to serve as in-house council). While employed, Cameron and his family attended company parties held at homes owned by successful lawyers. After he saw how financially secure families lived, the disparity between the upper and lower classes became even more pronounced. And the chasm between the wealthy and those living in Uptown served as new inspiration.

It's not surprising that many second-generation communards differ from founding members. Veteran communards often come from broken backgrounds, and they developed a particular expression of communal living within the broader context of the Jesus Movement.[4] Second-generation JPUSA communards do not have this framework. For founders, the goal was a familial context, a family-like structure that offered support for new Christians who had previously struggled with drug abuse and a general lack of direction. But for the kids, this was simply not the case. They are the demographic within JPUSA whose world was not ordered around the need for an extended family and spiritual accountability. Thus the constant need for close proximity (members are encouraged to remain close to one other person)[5] is, to some extent, lost on the second generation. Daughter of founding members Glenn and Wendi Kaiser, Ami Moss (twenty-eight and married) struggled with her lack of privacy. She grew up sharing a room with her siblings and other children. For Ami, matters of privacy and family often blur when considering school and home. Teachers for JPUSA's school live in the same building, are part of the same "family," and are connected to their students in ways unlike children raised in noncommunal situations.

For many not born in the community, adjusting amounted to a trial by fire. Children born in JPUSA are often quite close, creating a challenge for newcomers seeking acceptance. The son of mother Carol Trott and stepfather Jon Trott, Christopher Wiitala joined between 1986 and 1987, along with his brother and mother. For Wiitala the process of adjusting to communal life was dependent on his ability to make friends with those who had been born and raised in a very tight-knit group. Unlike others, he has been able to tour with his music group (promoted by JPUSA's record label Grrr), periodically escaping the confines of Uptown Chicago. His perception of life in the community differs from that of others of his generation. For example, touring with his band has offered an ongoing measure of comparison to the "outside world." But upon returning he is confronted with members who assume there has been an unbroken connection. That is, communards assume they are connected to one another by virtue of their shared experience. Everyone is "family" simply by virtue of living in the same bounded community, all experiencing the "joy of the Lord."[6] And this level of intergroup connection signals how common living spaces are often perceived, and even taken for granted.

Shared space and the lack of privacy notwithstanding, life in JPUSA promises a level of familial connections that, many argue, benefit the children. As with any large family, these kids are raised by a number of individuals and families. For them, it takes a village—and this is a positive thing. Scarlett Shelby is grateful for growing up in a community where her children remain under the watchful eye of like-minded members of the same extended family. But some second-generation members feel this can be taken too far. Wiitala recalls his frustration with how some parents make a grand assumption—that others will automatically watch (or discipline) children who are not their own. (The assumption is they are all "family.") Boundaries are breached when this taken-for-grantedness causes communards to cross lines of privacy (clothes are borrowed) or assumptions are made pertaining to childcare (children are watched by "the community," not unlike daycare).[7] To be blunt, Wiitala considers some members of JPUSA presumptuous regarding the level and depth of interpersonal connections, or even the trustworthiness of those designated as part of "the family" when providing care for JPUSA children. Still, others say families in the commune provide greater levels of childcare than Wiitala has suggested.

Rising generations hold quite particular perceptions of life in JPUSA that influence their own self-identity. Each memory they share offers a glimpse into communal life through the eyes of childhood, squaring notions of the social norm with the reality of life in Uptown. What remains a pressing matter (one that may very well decide their fate) is the developing ideological chasm between founders and many second-generation communards, differences now materializing in the glaring light of pluralism. And it is this same sort of ideological tension that polarizes baby boomers and "millennials" in American society. When considering communal identity, millennials have, according to the Pew Research Center, "begun to forge theirs: confident, self-expressive, liberal, upbeat and receptive to new ideas and ways of living."[8]

FOUNDING MEMBERS AND SECOND GENERATION: THE DIFFERENCES

Cultural accommodation is often necessary for a group such as this to survive, particularly if they are urban-based. But in classically generation-gap form, values held by the younger members often create a measure of tension, resulting in either communal change or fragmentation. Are these the future leaders? It goes without saying that many of them hold values similar to those of the founders, though often reflective of their own generation's ability to filter ideas with nuance. But in many cases, differentiation often forecasts what amounts to dissatisfaction, as the up-and-coming generation compares their personal worlds to that of the founders and their communal world to the outside. This creates a struggle, since this is part of a relationship that must always reinvent itself, "subject to continual revision," says Kanter, as the external environment remains in a constant state of cultural flux.[9]

The result of this continual *differentiation* has warranted dialogue among all members of the community. For example, many leaders differ on what can be considered minor issues (denominational particulars, eschatology, and political theory) but still agree on historic Christian orthodoxy. On the other hand, second-generation perspectives on social issues are of evidentiary value when considering how this generation has been affected by exposure to the outside world and, more specifically, pluralism. For example, many of them are quite flexible on topics such as abortion and homosexuality. And in pragmatic fashion that is fundamentally "progressive," they are quick to note that problems associated with war and poverty far outweigh the more pedestrian "pet sins" held by baby boomers. Tamzen Trott argues that while JPUSA holds to the core ethos of following Jesus, difference and flexibility contribute to both positive and negative aspects of community

THE FUTURE

structure and life. The reason for JPUSA's longevity, she says, is its ability to assimilate cultural moments deemed important by the wider youth subculture. On the other hand, younger members (and this also includes Tamzen) still insist that the council's "acceptance" of theological and cultural difference is not as fluid as one might think. More to the point, while some feel they are free to question beliefs, others feel relatively silenced.

Any so-called newfound freedoms are created to help JPUSA negotiate between structures established by their shared values and what has shifted in the broader culture. Flexibility retains members, but it has also caused second-generation members to consider what is available to them outside of communal life. Thus cultural assimilation and accommodation simultaneously appeases younger members while also highlighting differences between communal and noncommunal life. And while the commune has been able to change with the culture over the years, those changes might not have come early enough. Musing over the various restrictions placed on JPUSA youth in earlier years, Shelby recalled a time when each floor of Friendly Towers had one community television, used only for viewing old movies or fantasy epochs such as the *Dark Crystal* and *Harry Potter*. (This strikes her as ironic, considering that many conservative evangelicals often consider the magical world of Harry Potter antithetical to Christian teaching. But JPUSA, she points out, finds value in fantasy, given its interest in the works of medievalist tale spinners such as C. S. Lewis and J. R. R. Tolkien.) Indeed, the leaders once considered network sitcoms (enjoyed by many evangelicals who demonize the *Harry Potter* series) more dangerous than media that utilize fantasy and magic to convey "larger truths." But over the years the community has lifted these restrictions, going on to allow televisions in individual apartments without strict guidelines pertaining to content.

Both Shelby and Tamzen say others within their peer group share their perspective on social issues. While many of them agree on matters of civil and ecclesiastical polity, over half hold different cultural values. For example, Tamzen and others her age support gay marriage. Even more surprising, they believe the Bible should not be taken literally. Still, some hold fast to a more conservative approach. Nathan does not favor gay marriage but remains conflicted, given his friendship with some who are in same-sex relationships. Despite his attempt at tolerance, he firmly believes that homosexuality is a sin. Nevertheless, he recognizes the complexity of the issue, recalling gay friends who have better relationships than many married heterosexual couples.

Although the council maintains their conservative position on same-sex relations, those who disagree on "secondary issues" are not asked to leave, unless these differences lead to conflict. Despite this rather shopworn position on marriage, the difference between JPUSA and other conservative evangelicals is that JPUSA seeks to avoid intolerant rhetoric, welcoming open, civil dialogue regarding what it agrees to be a matter a bit more complex than evangelicals often admit. For the group, homosexuality may be a sin, but no more than overeating. This explains Jon Trott's recalcitrant reaction to homophobes, to the extent that he considers them inimical to the cause of Christianity and the teachings of Jesus. While founders agree that Christian conviction and sexual orientation are not mutually exclusive, they maintain that Christians should seek healing and "deliverance."[10] But Tamzen and some of her peers remain insistent: one can be gay, be Christian, and remain close to God, without the need for repentance, deliverance, or behavioral modification.

Contrary to many evangelicals, Jon Trott considers the church's "battle" over gay marriage to lack a certain moral clarity, arguing the church's position should remain separate and distinct from what is largely a civil matter. Uncomfortable with foisting his views of marriage on others, he says that if the love of Jesus is to be observed, choices must be respected. While his views on homosexuality are more tolerant of complexities often attached to debates concerning sexual preference, conservative evangelicals maintain that unchecked tolerance often leads to a slippery slope. Trott notes that this is a typical retort from the Religious Right. He recalls how some will question his position of tolerance, suggesting that tolerance becomes a slippery slope that leads to "child sex or murder." His response hints at frustration with what he views as flawed questions to what is self-evident. He writes: "We all know what we're talkin' about here . . . two consenting adults" who want to be "recognized by the state as a couple." Having a "high view of scripture" (despite his recognition of the failings of language), he leaves it at that. Trott accepts civil unions and believes the church should maintain a different definition of marriage but welcomes open dialogue from both the gay and "ex-gay" communities.[11]

Along with social issues, many second-generation communards even diverge on matters of religious belief. Reinforced by the forces of pluralism, ideological change has continued with rising generations. Skeptical about categories, Tamzen does not consider herself a Christian. But despite her skepticism, she still believes in a God with whom she has a relationship. Yes, her position might be viewed as more radical than those of many of her peers. But then there are others (former members) who have become atheists. Their extreme position is a reaction to the rigidities associated with religious *certainty* and expectations of holiness. Ironically, these rigidities have not dulled the activist impulse in Tamzen. Noting an interest in pursuing a degree in social work, she hopes to continue working with the homeless, independent of any particular religious orientation. Her "call" is quite personal; from an early age children raised in JPUSA are made aware of poverty and violence.

While many raised in JPUSA feel they have been nurtured in a hermitage of sorts, in many ways Nathan Cameron's story shows us that these kids are not protected from the "real world" but are often exposed to more reality than are suburbanites. Along with social ills associated with inner-city life, young members of JPUSA inherit a paradigm of living established by elders influenced by patterns of personal crisis and redemption. A historical nod to the existential crisis that defined much of the counterculture, many founders were raised in broken homes, developed broken lives, and joined the commune after struggling with some form of addiction. In short, they needed answers and structure. Hoping to create this semi-utopia, leaders penned rules to govern activities that, for them, represented dysfunction. For example, Nathan notes that while contextually necessary (given the alcoholism among some of the homeless seeking housing with JPUSA), extremism prevailed as JPUSA leaders universally demonized alcohol. But, as with sexuality, alcohol became negotiable, at least for the second generation. Nathan's generation is not a product of abuse or disaffectedness. Raised in a stable, loving home, Nathan and many of his peers do not consider alcohol sinful, nor is it connected to a life of dissidence or abuse. In fact, in recent years some community leaders have softened their position on the matter after having attended denominational events where alcohol was served. Still (and understandably), JPUSA maintains a policy of teetotalism within the walls of the community, given its outreach to those who struggle with many forms of addiction. These rules, according to Christopher Wiitala, were set in place "for the weakest person."[12]

Although many second-generation members differ from the founders on social and cultural values, some maintain similar versions while exhibiting a more tolerant version of the same ethic. And while the majority differs from founders on these issues, most tend to agree on the basic tenets of historic (albeit more tolerant) evangelical Christianity. To put this into perspective, commitment to the same "larger cause," so it seems, has not been enough to retain a significant presence among second-generation members. Indeed, many feel called to serve humanity, but this "calling" has not sufficiently translated into commitment to JPUSA.

HOW COMMITTED ARE THEY?

Only 15 percent of those raised in JPUSA have actually remained.[13] Still, the constant exposure to Uptown's poverty and perceptions of an ill-equipped church culture (unmotivated to follow Jesus in service to the poor) create what historian James Chancellor refers to as a "continual crisis environment."[14] This crisis environment (while chiding the church by illuminating its inadequacy) serves to keep founders engaged in their mission and mobilizes travelers and seekers to embrace JPUSA's higher calling. Committed to fully identifying with the poor, founders and travelers dedicate themselves to Jesus by serving the homeless. However, those in the second generation do not always share a sense of divine mandate felt by founders and travelers. Though dedicated to her neighbors and friends within the commune, Scarlett Shelby hopes to chart a different sort of humanitarianism. A pre-med student with hopes of becoming a physician, she plans to leave the community; as is the case with many of her peers, she does not feel called to a life of service defined by communal living.

Although the notion of divine calling is significant when attempting to locate the intentions of this generation, in the end a recurring sentiment concerning the lack of freedom highlights second-generation perceptions of communalism as an organizing premise. In fact, most second-generation members feel constricted by communal rules, and they hope to find their own identity outside of communal life. A seasoned first-generation communard, Susan (her real name has been withheld), notes that it was common for second-generation members to desire more freedom after high school:

> I think it's because they're so close here. They see the same people from the time they start school until they graduate—it's the same people in their class. We're just now allowing them to have a little bit more freedom to move about in the city. Normally, it's a pretty tight supervision that they're given, so they always want to see what is out there. When they graduate they want to try something new. They want to watch every movie that we didn't let them see. They just want more freedom. And so, they're trying to experience everything that there is.[15]

Indeed, on reaching adulthood many raised within these walls decide to leave. But so do those who have chosen to join as adults. Of all adult members, 23 percent have left the community in recent years, many of whom simply felt a divine unction to move on. Others simply sought more freedom, more money, or more voice in how they spent what little money was allotted. In the end, younger members tend to articulate the same sentiment—the desire for a different manner of living. The difference between communal and noncommunal adolescent rites of independence is that those raised within noncommunal environments can measure their bounded existence (family life) against scenarios not defined by a daily bounded experience. That is, for noncommunal youth (with the possible exception of small, noncommunitarian rural scenarios), the lines between home, school, church, and other activities are often quite distinct. But for youth raised in communes such as JPUSA, all elements of weekly life are collapsed into one holistic mass; lines are blurred, reaffirming that all areas of life are part of one collective experience. This sort of deindividuation is necessary for successful communal longevity, says Kanter. Considering the most successful nineteenth-century communes, she notes that the "most enduring communes [are] also the most centralized and the most tightly controlled."[16]

Highly centralized communes that have used authoritarian control, regardless of their reason, have indeed been more successful than other groups where organizational structure was, at best, ephemeral. But with respect to multigenerational contexts, the effectiveness of highly centralized authority-structures may prove indeterminate. While control mechanisms have served to buttress JPUSA since 1972, concentrated power (the council) and boundaries intended to maintain commitment now repel rising generations. Some second-generation communards leave the community after graduating from high school, only to return for a brief stay. At age fifteen (in 2010), Tamzen realized that she did not choose communal life. After completing high school she left to experience life on her own. Tamzen notes that over 50 percent of her peers share her desire to leave the community. Although brief periods of experiencing noncommunal life often result in the decision to leave JPUSA, children of the founders are encouraged to experience life outside the community to gain both perspective and experience; those who return do so based on their own choosing.

Many have left, but others have embraced the life in hopes of maintaining organic (familial) connections lost in a postindustrial world. Like many of her peers Tiana Coleman was able to compare her life to that of noncommunal children at an early age while still enjoying the close proximity of lifelong friends in JPUSA. And like Coleman, Joel Williams has fond memories, comparing communal life to that in a small town—in the middle of a big city. For Williams and others, there is one constant that attracts and repels—the "blessing and curse of living so close together," working toward the common goal of providing for the poor, a task in which they take pride despite the lack of anonymity.[17]

THE FUTURE

In his critique of the community, sociologist Ronald Enroth argued that members of JPUSA who prepare to leave are often viewed with disdain, labeled apostate, or spiritually remanded.[18] But Susan holds no ill will toward her children who have left, recognizing that Christian faith extends beyond the community. Of course she speaks as a mother. But others recall members who have moved on, and in most cases the parting of ways was amicable. Although some former members had negative experiences when leaving, others were wished well. This is not to dismiss other accounts, but these accounts are often rife with emotion. Communal life is much like marriage, warranting such commitment that when breached, the result is the feeling of loss compared to divorce.

Recognizing the mass exodus of second-generation members, Susan has wondered how the group might retain younger members. How can they keep the attraction? If leaders had created a structure of gradual change (allowing youth certain freedoms and luxuries incrementally), Susan muses, teenagers might not have felt the need to "gorge" themselves with things previously denied, resulting in dissatisfaction with life in JPUSA. Thus authoritarian structure (often needed in social contexts defined by missions to the dysfunctional) results in a sort of encapsulated chamber. If this "pressure valve" (tightly bounded rules) is opened slowly, says Susan, youth may experience gradual depressurization.[19] This incremental allowance of freedom and access to previously banned parts of culture amounts to what Kanter refers to as "controlled acculturation."[20]

Regardless of the methods behind the original authoritarian structure, the *reason* was primarily to guard JPUSA youth from "worldly" temptations.[21] This sentiment of protection is common for both youth and adults living in communal scenarios. According to Kanter, "outside society, a changing, turbulent, seductive place, poses a particular threat to the existence of utopian communities, so that most successful communities of the past have developed sets of insulating boundaries—rules and structural arrangements that minimized contact with the outside."[22] Of course, this in no way implies that the group has evolved into some sort of compound. Its members are not shielded from the outside world in the literal sense.

Confronted daily by inner-city life, these urban activists are able to return home to process images and experiences with the help of emotional mediation, via the support of a community defined by a collective experience. A sound practice for any group hoping to shore up long-term membership, this communal "tether" helps the faithful interpret society through JPUSA's quite particular paradigmatic grid. Ironically, these paradigms have retained founding members but also contribute to a curious exodus among rising generations. Thus controlled acculturation provides everyone with a new means, nurturing dedication to the community while acquiescing to the dominant culture. But this might still prove problematic.

When considering peer commitments Scarlett Shelby makes a distinction between the *generation* and the actual year a person is born, noting that many born during the late 1970s and early 1980s tend to remain while those born during the late 1980s and early 1990s tend to leave, having had more experiences outside of JPUSA. Owing to lifted restrictions on television and music and the rise of the Internet, JPUSA youth were increasingly exposed to what they were missing. And so the perspectives of the second generation are mixed, varied perspectives often developing based on when the individuals were born and when they came of age living "in community."[23]

FORMER MEMBERS: STRUCTURE, AUTHORITY, AND ALLEGATIONS OF ABUSE

Over half choose to leave JPUSA. And many who remain still appear open to the possibility of another sort of life. Despite disagreements on social or theological matters, many have considered their alternatives, always examining the difficulties of communal life. But what of those who have left JPUSA? Perceptions of former communards add unique perspectives, when considering the community's history and general potential, even if the catalysts for departure often shape those perceptions. JPUSA instituted these affirmative boundaries, but distinctions between the commune and the outside world often create cognitive dissonance for many who still live within the safe walls of Friendly Towers.

THE FUTURE

Communards join willingly, often only to find communal life to be incompatible with their own sense of individualism. And while many former members are from the second generation, there are also those who joined as adults. After spending a significant amount of time in JPUSA, these were able to measure communal life against their previously established understandings of community and structure. Now fifty-two, Scott (his real name has been withheld) lives in a rural area. In 1982 he had a desire to change the world. Having been raised a Mennonite, it is perhaps not a stretch to consider that he had implanted within him the seeds for social justice, though his parents were "very anxious" about his decision to join JPUSA. Scott does not pretend that communal life was easy.

As they considered what is "normative" to American individualism (not to mention avarice), some who left the commune did so in response to their own struggle with what is fundamental to communal life. Like other members, for Scott the difficulties (while partly ideological) amounted to the need for privacy. "The worst part about LIVING in community," writes Scott, "was possibly the lack of privacy. You were always 'on.' You ate breakfast with the same people, you worked with them, you worshiped with them, shared a crowded dorm-room, and went on vacation with them."[24]

Many were attracted to JPUSA in hopes of fulfilling a desire to serve God in a life wholly counter to American society. But then the individualism endemic to American culture often challenges the utopian vision. Scott's account of life in JPUSA reveals a disconnect between the communitarian dream and the American premium placed on the independent, autonomous self:

> During my tenure there was a strict "buddy" rule, so you were never, ever alone. Even in the bathroom, there would be a line outside waiting to get in. Plus, as you can imagine, sharing everything could be very inconvenient. As someone once said (a Soviet communist, I think): "That which belongs to everyone, belongs to no-one." So everything was dirty, broken, noisy, overcrowded, and behind schedule. Imagine sharing a car with 500 other people. It could be vexing, to say the least. So not only were you always "on" you were always "on" in the midst of some major or minor inconvenience.

THE FUTURE

A great opportunity to die to oneself and become more like Christ, for certain, but no picnic.

As with any organization, those who have moved on hold varied perceptions unique to their own experiences. Burnout and frustrations over JPUSA's lack of democracy resulted in Scott's decision to leave in 1998. He does remain in contact with his JPUSA friends, and he considers the most memorable part of that life to be "intense feeling of camaraderie," recalling life in JPUSA as a "foretaste of heaven." He continues:

> A group of believers united in spirit, sharing everything and working towards common goals. Absolutely some of the best times of my life were there, and shared with a score of friends. I never laughed so much in my entire life. I don't even know what to compare it too, but similar to a college residence building, except intergenerational with kids riding bikes up and down the halls.

It appears, however, that this foretaste of Heaven has often been overshadowed by eroded personal boundaries. After having a child, Elaine grew ever aware that privacy was something of a luxury. But overall her experiences (including the choice to leave) were positive. Still, these recollections are more complex, especially when looking to lifelong members whose core identities developed with JPUSA. Eric Pement joined in 1976 at the age of twenty-one. During his time in the community, he was a contributing writer and editor for *Cornerstone* magazine. At the time, life in the community provided "a crucible for growth, it offered the time needed for Bible study, prayer, and fulltime evangelism without having to work a secular job." As with other former members, the lack of privacy, mobility, and the erasure of personal boundaries became too much to handle.

> No one owned their personal car, and vehicles were corporately shared but poorly maintained. We had no money to take public transportation as we wanted, and many things I would have wanted to do (in ministry or out-

reach) were hampered by not being able to travel as freely as I would have done living independently.[25]

Many view this lack of privacy as a necessary inconvenience. As for the power of the council, this was simply a different way to govern. Still, others note that JPUSA leaders have overstepped their bounds. These former communards nurse deep-seated frustrations concerning a lack of voice afforded rank-and-file members. And for them, insult to injury included dogmatic policies, disciplinary action (if those polices were not followed), and an environment that prioritized the collective over and above one's need to explore individual identity. In fact, this tension between the public and private extended to entire families whose storied lives continue to unfold in the shadow of JPUSA's memory. In the 1970s Barbara Pement was a journalist hired by an affiliate of ABC in Battle Creek, Michigan. After visiting Chicago and meeting JPUSA missionaries on the street, Pement (already a Christian) considered leaving her position as continuity director at ABC. She joined JPUSA in 1977 at the age of twenty-four. In the beginning, legalistic rules, she recalled fondly, "kept us on the straight and narrow" to such an extent that that she and others obeyed because they "loved Jesus so much and wanted to please Him." Many were "out of control" in their lives before joining. And they "welcomed the reigning in." JPUSA was once a very different community, one that focused more on evangelism:

> In the early years serving Jesus was all about changing lives, seeing your faith become alive and vibrant. Personal daily Bible reading increased intimacy with Christ. . . . Resurrection Band and Cornerstone Newspaper/Magazine, our musical and literary voice[s] were on the front lines of effective evangelism and encouragement to believers around the world. Bible study discussions, singing songs about God's love, telling others about Jesus characterized the reality of our fervor.[26]

Pement says that over time "a subtle shift took place." As time wore on, life "in Jesus People became less about Jesus and more about . . . I don't know . . . something else." She considers one possibility: this shift occurred after young members had children and then, questioning the status quo, reconsidered how JPUSA's children were allowed to mature. "We wanted our children to love Jesus too and that wasn't going to happen just because we had surrounded our closed society with ultra strict rules. Rules without relationship breeds rebellion."

JPUSA children did not experience the same intense relationship with Jesus as did the founders. For both young and old, communal law trumped personal growth during the early years. "In the young days of Jesus People," writes Barbara Pement, "a person who bucked the rules or had another opinion was seen as unfit for the purposes of remaining in Jesus People. 'Submit or split' we used to say, meaning 'just do as you're told or leave.' Back then we had no patience for people who were not serious about obedience to God."[27] This way of managing communards was intended to stifle resistance. After all, many of them bucked authority in their pre-Christian lives. So, submit or split. "The rule was a good idea at the time," she recalls, "because it weeded out those who were not serious about their commitment."[28] This method of management was intended to discourage laziness and provide an incentive to work. Indeed, some wanted to question the structure. But "there could be no honesty in raising serious discussion about certain long-held practices," says Pement. The leaders were immovable on communal policy: "Provoking challenges were viewed as mutiny or 'causing dissention' [sic]. Maintaining the structure of the commune took precedence over the architecture of our lives. The Foundation that had begun firmly, had changed. Was the commitment to Jesus? Or to Jesus People USA? What's the difference?"

Clearly this method of governance elicited mixed feelings and produced mixed results. Still, Barbara Pement maintains that strict guidelines were needed to maintain holiness and commitment to the original cause. But for her, this setup strengthened the *commune*, not the *individual*, which complicates their attempts at balancing the collective and the person. Pement's children did not grow spiritually in JPUSA. In fact, after leaving JPUSA, her children changed. "The difference upon exiting is as night and day. Relatives noticed it right away, and even friends who had never lived or visited Jesus People," writes Pement. "My children blossomed becoming more outgoing."[29] Though strict boundaries served to incentivize communal commitment in the earlier years, they worked in reverse as time wore on. Thus if individuals are disincentivized because of overly rigid boundaries, then planned mechanisms no longer serve their purpose of solidifying communal dedication.

While some recall a relatively positive experience (often punctuated by periods of ill-conceived leadership or theologically colored missteps), others carry negative memories, which are quite profound. According to other former members, strict guidelines intended to safeguard members from worldly temptation created the opposite effect, resulting in dysfunction. But to what extent? Remember, JPUSA is a product of the Jesus Movement and, to some extent, most of the cultural conservatism commonly associated with baby boom evangelicals. Given this love affair with the inimitable written Word (the literalism associated with neo-evangelicalism), JPUSA's council has historically operated based on certain "implied" expectations of behavior and doctrine. As a result, some former members have expressed frustration over how the community perceived and defined them (as individuals), to the extent that certain levels of dogmatism stunted individual growth. Following the lead of his parents, Jaime Prater chose to leave the community. His documentary *No Place to Call Home* explores some of the stories told by various persons raised in JPUSA. Life in JPUSA was "the most amazing, wonderful, awful, fantastic, horrible, brilliant experience of my life," says Prater.[30] The film explores the pain felt by some former members. Now adults, these members recall a childhood that was both interesting and tumultuous. While they certainly recall the bond felt within the community, it is clear they are haunted with painful memories that fall short of being fully resolved. As children and teenagers, freedom was far from reach. They always played within the walls of JPUSA. And if they went anywhere, it was in a group accompanied by an adult. Rules were made for the weakest people, recalls Lizzy Jones (Prater), even though the truly "weakest members," to them, were fresh from the street, bedraggled, hungover, addicted. But this lack of freedom, she says, extended even to the life of the mind.

Lizzy started to find contradictions in the Bible. And she asked questions. Avoiding her investigation, leaders "shut her down." She would think, "Why aren't you answering my questions?"[31] For Allyson Jackson, growing up in JPUSA was akin to a fascist police state, for each person feared being sent away to live on the Farm—if suspected of questioning JPUSA's structure or, more seriously, the Bible. "I was not allowed to question anything pertaining to the Bible and Christianity," says Prater. Others maintain that no one could challenge the leaders. If they said you were lying, the matter was closed. No appeal.

Most of us nurse painful memories of our youth. And the threat of being "shipped off" appears to be a fairly common threat for wayward children. Still, these former members recall with measures of emotional pain how spankings were commonplace. They would, says Angel Harold, get "the rod" if questions were missed in school or they did not eat or drink what they were given. "When kids were disciplined or spanked with the rod," say Sheila and Dennis Braggs, "you had no idea of what was going on, who was spanking the kid, what they got spanked for . . . looking back, we were naïve about the people that we were trusting." But this is little different from the expectations meted out by the overseers of a Catholic monastery or the discipline employed by nuns seeking to mold children into the likeness of Christ. It is true that we tend to recall our childhoods with both fondness and disdain, and we also heap disdain (or at least how we perceive the misdeeds afforded us) on our parents. But for these former communards, the complaint seems to go beyond mere adolescent angst or the need for personal space or freedom. It also extends to parenting techniques. Dennis and Sheila Bragg vividly recall the helpless feeling they had as parents. "We entrusted our lives to someone who we respected as an authority," they say. All parental decisions were surrendered to those in authority. Now looking back, the Braggs are astounded. "What in the world were we doing as parents? Why did we allow this to happen?" Parents were not given the tools on how to be better parents, says Dennis, and you didn't have the authority to be the parent you wanted to be. The role of parent was simply taken away. The whole group functioned as the parent, says Sheila. Parents were not allowed to raise their children how they saw fit, according to Lottie Jones.

She was afraid. If she did not abide by JPUSA rules of child rearing, she recalls, her family would be kicked out on the street, without a place to go.

Those who once held leadership positions over the children also appear to lament the overly rigid structure. Barbara Pement has certainly outlined the ways in which JPUSA children were not afforded the proper course of maturation. But others (such as a JPUSA teacher) appear to be troubled by the level of underdevelopment now apparent in second-generation members who have come of age. First, kids did not know about sex until the age of sixteen. Second, in Prater's estimation, parents wanted to shield their kids from bad experiences often connected to their storied pasts, then reacted with force to kids who asked ticklish questions about sexuality or, more seriously, entertained their own sexual identity. In fact, says one, it was a sin for girls to like boys at the tender age of fourteen. This seems rather tame, or even commonplace, when stacked against the sexually repressed 1950s American culture. In short, this is nothing especially new or surprising. But according to Emma Snyder, a former JPUSA teacher, this pattern extended well beyond merely sheltering little ones from a would-be hostile world, to the point that young people were often underprepared for life outside the commune. According to her, teens were never adequately prepared for college, nor were they trained in the proper way to compose resumes and secure employment. This is not surprising since all members were assured work within the community. They were, in her estimation, discouraged from leaving JPUSA and attending college.

The lack of training is a common thread. Some testimonies emphasize how this style of governance squelched any possibility for personal maturation, to the extent of dysfunction. Unable to locate any personal identity, former communard Maurica Bytnar hates herself. "I don't know who I am, because I was never allowed to figure out who I am." But more to the point of human development, there lives a pesky topic with which many Christians (historically) have scarcely dealt. Sexuality and sexual identity is often a reoccurring theme in tightly bounded communities. And to a certain extent these topics are deeply rooted in how human sexuality is often understood or interpreted within a biblical context. For example, although they embrace LGBT individuals (loving them as Jesus would), they remain firmly opposed to the "lifestyles." This is not surprising, considering JPUSA's theological position, not to mention the imperative for collective agreement. But again, this is not uncommon. Conservative Catholics and Protestants frown on homosexuality and any deviation from what is considered to be "biblical" examples of family and sexuality. Furthermore, various Pentecostal Christians often consider deviation from "normative" Christian behavior to be demonic. But for Jaime Prater the matter went beyond a theological position.

Raised in JPUSA, Prater recalls the turmoil involved in making his sexual orientation public. After he expressed his feelings at a young age, the community, he says, all but abandoned him. But there is more to the story. Prater recalls being sexually abused. And the staff never handled the matter because they never believed it, he argues. Prater is under no illusion that stories can be contested or that families will react to what they feel is inappropriate behavior. And given his interest in men at a young age, he understands why parents in the community were wary. More to the point, he understands why JPUSA leadership and families felt the need to require supervision of his playtime, particularly if spent around other children. Still, Prater laments the way he was treated. When he was between the ages of twelve and fifteen, his mother was told to keep him in a sort of isolation. Life was structured around his room and his mother's constant presence and supervision, and the community's apparent shunning did little service for his emotional well-being. Their approach to the matter, says Prater, amounted to separation. "Let's take him out of society make him feel like he is . . . unfit, make him feel like he is different, he is unlovable, that he is unworthy, that he's not normal. And that's what they did, which affects me to this day, to this moment." Prater holds no ill will but believes the leaders were simply afraid and did not know what to do.

Perhaps the most disturbing testimony can be found in Prater's interview with former member Justin Denton. Denton is among a number of former members who maintain they were sexually abused as children. His testimony amounts to a recollection of three men who forced Denton to perform oral sex on them. The following is an excerpt from Prater's documentary.

THE FUTURE

DENTON: I had to be like nine or ten, . . . or eleven maybe . . . still foggy but, that was like the worst, as far as like being molested as a kid. Seriously fucked my head up.

PRATER: Was it an adult?

DENTON: Yeah, it was an adult . . . it was quite a few . . . the Chelsea building is a tower of hell to me, because of what happened to me there . . . there was two or three of them.

PRATER: Were they all men?

DENTON: Yeah . . . he asked me to come in there, and he had his friend in there. It happened more than once. They made me give them oral sex . . . that'll fuck your brain up real bad.

PRATER: Did you tell anybody?

DENTON: No . . . all three of em made me do that . . . they called me their girlfriend, that they made me their girlfriend. They said if I said anything to anybody . . . one of them asked the other one to tell em what they do to kids that tell about that kind of thing.

PRATER: How long did it go on for?

DENTON: I don't really know the period of time. . . . I know it happened and it wasn't brief . . . it's still pretty foggy . . . there is a shadow that lives in the heart of that place.

Others have come forward with vivid memories about sexual abuse, claiming that fringe members were primarily the guilty parties. But as with Prater, the burden of proof was on the victim, resulting in what these former members estimate was a sort of shunning from both peers and adults. Along with Prater, some of those interviewed recall sexual and psychological abuse that, they say, often went untreated and unresolved. The fault of the community, say ex-members, amounts to an ill-conceived way of handling misdeeds. Put simply, these former members feel that abuse was covered up (or victims were not believed), thus highlighting a disturbing possibility: the ministry was more important than the members. But many have come forward. Heather Kool (Mount) was sexually assaulted by a member but says a leader has since apologized, stating they should have believed her and offered counseling, without isolating her. Now living in Georgia, Kool "filed . . . civil suit against JPUSA and the ECC," writes Timothy C. Morgan, "seeking $100,000 in damages. Other survivors may sign on to the litigation. In total, Prater has accounts of abuse from 73 individuals and has hosted a private area on Facebook, where survivors share their stories."[32]

Contemporary media brings with it swift results. "Two lawsuits have been filed against Jesus People in Cook County Circuit Court," writes Judith Valente. "The suits also name the Evangelical Covenant Church, headquartered outside of Chicago. Jesus People has been a member congregation of that church since 1989. In one of the suits, Heather Kool . . . alleges she was repeatedly sexually abused as a child by a resident of the community while living there with her mother."[33]

Along with terrible memories of abuse, these members remain haunted, noting how a sense of loneliness (the feeling that they were not heard) extended to the way disabilities were handled. Jared Harmon recalls that "life was good, but then I got diagnosed with ADD and ADHD at the age of four." Harmon did not feel liked. "I didn't get invited to a lot of birthday parties, 'cause I was ADD or 'cause I was hyper, and I acted out, ya know? A lot of parents kind of shunned me away, didn't let me play with their kids or anything." Wondering what he did wrong, he thought, "If that's what they think I am, I might as well just play the part."[34] For others, isolation also extended to a sort of class-based circle of acceptance. Jaime Prater's mother, Mary Prater, reasons that JPUSA operated based on in-groups and out-groups. "You didn't have any friends of the pastor's kids." Her kids were "on the outs." Dealing with her son Jaime's isolation, she was at her wit's end. "It became like this nightmare. I decided, I'm not doing this any more . . . there was no real basis for it. . . . Jamie's never done anything. . . . He's been impulsive. He's said things. But he's not done anything. . . . there are kids in this community that have done terrible things, they're not in isolation. . . . It was just a nightmare."[35]

It is certainly common for any tight-knit community to create a framework whereby all members are measured. And for those in leadership, the flock's spiritual maturation (to some extent) is in their hands.[36] And as might be expected, some have reacted in extreme measure. Jennifer Cadieux hated life in JPUSA. After pretending to go for a jog, she fled in 1981, only to discover that she hated life outside almost as much.[37] But as with any secular or religious organization, order is expected. While rigid ideological boundaries often define communal structures, some argue that when a member attempts to probe beyond established norms, he or she is met with tension from leadership. Allyson Jackson maintains that questioning the norm was simply off limits.[38] And as we have seen, some former communards say that leaders have often viewed nonconformity as spiritual dissent.[39] A tacit gag order, according to some, quashes attempts at iconoclasm, if ideological boundaries are carried to their conclusion.

Despite dogmatic peculiarities, these structures have served to reinforce a community susceptible to disintegration. Historian Malcolm Magee notes that communes (or churches) in locations such as this must, in the interest of survival, operate as a fortress. While JPUSA continues to engage culture, it must simultaneously guard against what it considers threatening to weaker members. Thus while JPUSA policies and beliefs might be viewed as anathema to the mainstream (though they have liberalized over the years), a history of failed communal experiments reinforces the belief that rigid structures are still needed. According to Kanter, "the function of strong norms, highly developed programs for behavior, elaborate ideologies, and centralized authority is not only to promote total commitment but also to provide certainty, clarity, and security for members of groups that have rejected the established order."[40]

I am not arguing for or against JPUSA's particular structural mechanisms. Rather, I argue that these mechanisms have been necessary to maintain communal cohesiveness to date. This is needed for collectives defined against "established" models of community. But as we have seen, these mechanisms may have contributed to individual dissent. Despite the testimony of Barbara Pement, controlled acculturation appears to be an acceptable balance, one that maintains a communally bounded existence while also valuing the growth of individual communards (a balance between Gemeinschaft and Gesellschaft). But the voices of dissent represent only one side of the story.

While some former members argue that JPUSA's structure stunts personal growth, robbing individuals of identity and proper maturation, others maintain that the community freely explores ideas, and they are open to thoughts expressed by the rank-and-file. Chitu Okoli considers his decision to join at the age of twenty-one to be a significant life-choice. He sought "to live simply in order to live a life as simple disciples [*sic*] of Christ." Unlike other former members who have expressed discontent with JPUSA's leaders, Okoli's perception is quite different. For him, communards "were not afraid to express their opinions to the leaders. There was never a sense of intimidation or of some topics being taboo." However, some discontented members did engage in critical meetings with leadership. The result was that the discontented were asked to move on since "it was obvious that they were unhappy with the way things were, and after unfruitful discussions, it seemed best to the leaders for them to peacefully move on rather than building up pent-up resentments." Okoli continues, recalling a specific situation where the reasons for conflict were openly disclosed:

> I learnt about a couple of these situations involving people who were close to me, I directly approached pastors to ask about them, and they were very open in explaining the situation to me from their point of view; there was nothing taboo about my asking about these sensitive situations, even though they did not directly involve me. Misunderstandings happen, and that, unfortunately is part of our unperfected life as Christians. However, I personally never felt in any way intimidated by the leaders at JPUSA.[41]

But while Okoli insists that questions and opinions offered by the rank-and-file were valued, Barbara Pement maintains they were not, arguing that mistakes made by communards only exacerbated the matter. Writes Pement: "Unfortunately, a person can be labeled for life there. It is kind of like the 'unforgiving spouse' who remembers the one bad thing you did and brings it up on a regular basis on numerous occasions whether the current issue at hand warrants it or not."[42] Although both Pement and Okoli have different accounts of structure and authority (one positive and one negative), it is clear that a rigid structure once existed—and still does, to some extent. And although Okoli decided to leave, his assessment of the community allows further extrapolation regarding perceptions of council authority and community sustainability.

History demonstrates that excessive control may contribute to a commune's demise. But Okoli's argument for JPUSA's sustainability is based on his understanding of divine guidance and how he differentiates their organizational structure (such as the avoidance of a single-leader model) from other communal experiments. For him, "the practice of consensus brings in one accord, which is a master key to the blessings in God's New Testament economy. . . . JPUSA struck gold on this point." He goes on to note the importance of "commitment to practice oneness with the rest of the Body of Christ" and observes how ecumenism has sustained JPUSA:

> Other than the spiritual blessing, seeking oneness with other believers, especially those who are different from us in practice and specific beliefs, saves us from overstressing things that really are not that important. It is altogether too easy for an intention[al] community to think that is the "proper" Christian way to live, and to thus recluse themselves from those outside of them. However, by actively seeking fellowship with other believers, JPUSA has been protected from the frog-in-the-well syndrome, from seeing only their own virtues and not those of others.[43]

Okoli reasons that JPUSA's decision to seek fellowship with other Christian communities saved it from dissolution. However, JPUSA's self-conscious identification as a commune, or "intentional community,"[44] overshadowed its original signifier as merely a group of inner-city missionaries. Overall the variety of perspectives held by former members is symptomatic of an organic, changing community. Their testimonies suggest that everyone experienced very different lives from one another while in JPUSA, each perceiving the commune quite subjectively. For Scott, JPUSA was a "foretaste of heaven." For Barbara Pement, JPUSA became a "spiritually dark place." Okoli "appreciate[s] their sincerity." For Jaime Prater, life in JPUSA was "amazing, wonderful, awful, fantastic, horrible, [and] brilliant." And for Mary Prater, it was a nightmare. But ultimately the sentiment that has inspired ex-members to form negative opinions about JPUSA's "experiment" is rooted in the rather varied interpretations of freedom and democracy, and these interpretations also affect how well other American communities thrive in the shadow of pluralism.

Sociologist Anson Shupe notes that the premise on which communal societies are built are often either misunderstood by disgruntled communards and the outside world or are dismissed when the communal premise conflicts with personal ideas about freedom, and the boundaries that distinguish public property from private property. Shupe reasons that one must keep in mind that communitarian lifestyles are often "interpreted by persons familiar only with a predominantly contractual culture." Thus "testimonies of angry, disillusioned ex-members of intense covenantal groups always have to be taken with a grain of salt." Second, "covenantal communities," writes Shupe, "are predicated on different premises and assumptions than are contractual communities." Consequently, "actions that are part of the discipline and sharing of resources in a covenantal community like JPUSA can be made to sound abusive under the glaring light of contractual logic. Contractuals can make covenantals seem odd, deviant, even dangerous because the natures of their social organizations are very different."[45]

Still, allegations of abuse may not go away anytime soon. And a great many former members (who were raised in JPUSA) have clearly been traumatized. But strong opinions about JPUSA are by no means confined to ex-members, second-generation communards hoping to leave, or journalistic exposés. Some residents of Uptown have also made virulent remarks about the commune's tactics. According to some reports, JPUSA's tactics (its fight on behalf of Uptown's impoverished families) are often perceived as arrogant, even confrontational. Along with neighborhood dissent concerning JPUSA's methods of aiding low-income families, some residents simply dislike the commune because of its affiliation with a former SDSer and Black Panther, Alderwoman Helen Shiller. How JPUSA is perceived, then, is a matter of both personal perspective and neighborhood agenda.

Clearly JPUSA's structure of authority has received significant attention over the years as former communards have spoken out about personal experiences with the commune. And while views about personal boundaries and council authority depend on each individual circumstance, there remains a consistent thread of agreement: supporters and opponents all seem to suggest that the authority held by the council was in some way or another rather extensive. Moreover, both sides maintain that personal boundaries such as privacy, space, and a sense of individuality were somehow breached. These testimonies tell us something: as with any organization, some members will gain satisfaction, some will recall fond memories, some will become disgruntled, and others (the wounded ones) will lose themselves.

WHAT ABOUT THE FUTURE?

Given the tattered relationship American culture has had with radical social experiments, a burning question remains: can JPUSA sustain this? To some extent our immediate impulse is to consider how this specific group will weather our ever-changing cultural landscape. On the other hand, it may prove useful to consider how their social philosophy might benefit other communities who seek new approaches to social problems largely unrealized or undiscovered by politicians and pundits. And perhaps this begins with transferring the radical social ethos to the safe enclaves of the silent majority: suburbia. A local church in a suburb of Chicago now employs the sixty-something Rez Band guitarist Stu Heiss. He joined JPUSA in 1974 at the age of twenty-five seeking to be "discipled"[46] by fellow-believers, with high hopes of realizing a more authentic experience with God. JPUSA offered this. Heiss attended a Rez Band show before joining the community, later becoming the group's lead guitarist. After years of serving Rez and JPUSA, Heiss came to value the role of the local church, observing that local, suburban expressions of Christianity should be more involved in outreach programs similar to JPUSA's. And to a certain extent, this is the point of the book. As we shall see, American evangelicals are beginning to grow weary of serving the Republican Party. More to the point, they are seeking a more practical form of Christianity that is at once orthodox and politically progressive.

Communities like JPUSA, according to Heiss, often rise to meet challenges left unmet by the local church. This is precisely where JPUSA and the Evangelical Left arguably differ from evangelical conservatism, a force that absolutely insists on emphasizing the power of individual salvation to meet human need. Like JPUSA's matriarch Dawn (Herrin) Mortimer, Stu

THE FUTURE

Heiss believes the evangelical church has misunderstood the totality of the Christian mission, one that includes social justice in service to the poor. Feeling a burden to help the local church engage social justice as a holistic understanding of the Gospel, Heiss left JPUSA in 2002 and currently holds a staff position with the Christian and Missionary Alliance–affiliated Lombard Bible Church. Although his family has had to adjust to suburban living (a radical shift from life in an inner-city commune), this seminary-trained, suburban pastor values his new context, remains in contact with the community, and at times performs reunion shows with Rez Band.

There are varying degrees of opinion when considering how former communards perceive JPUSA's ongoing mission. Some argue that JPUSA has drifted from its original calling. But Okoli and Scott both insist that the overall thrust remains consistent. Heiss continues to value JPUSA's ministry, reasoning that the mission-mindedness of the community must continue to be transplanted into the local church. For him, JPUSA's uniquely radical approach to humanitarianism is often absent in local, suburban expressions of the church. And although the future of the commune is enslaved to the stridence of youthful indecision (exemplified in travelers and rising generations), JPUSA's collective resolve is unabated, for it represents a level of charity significant to those who seek cogent models of social activism.

Given the rapid exodus of the second generation, JPUSA must strategize about how it is to carry out its mission in Uptown. Perhaps more important, it will likely have to exercise demons of the past and offer apologies to former members, whose painful memories now seem to define their lives. Then, after the dust settles, it must begin to consider who will occupy those cherished positions on the leadership council. This creates the possibility for a new communal structure, one inspired by drifters who join the community in search of a meaningful life, some hoping to locate the Mecca, the epicenter of what I am calling "new paradigm faith-music." Also referred to as "crusties" and "festival freeloaders,"[47] these seekers bring new blood into the community, and a new labor force. But do they offer any sense of continuity in the face of second-generation exodus? Do they provide stability? And are they safe?

Drifters often remain for no more than a few months, or at the most a year. As with early JPUSA, every generation has young people who are

THE FUTURE

disenchanted with the church, dropouts and antiestablishment seekers. For Curtis Mortimer, JPUSA offers an experience where there are adults who understand and accept youth where they are. For many of these "dropouts," JPUSA is a rest stop where they can find healing. But to what end? And at what cost? While some have found healing and a home, others (particularly some who were born and raised in JPUSA) feel their own self-exploration was severely hampered, as was the case with Maurica Byntar, a former communard unable to locate her own identity.

It is no wonder emotions are high and identities have been undermined. After all, seekers who join the community are often damaged, in need of serious emotional and psychological healing. But as a number of ex-members have stated, the process of accepting new members into the fold involves little more than paying lip service to the rules of the community. Certainly nothing like a background check! And this, they rightly argue, creates an environment where children are exposed to potential threats.

Indeed, dysfunction can occur in any social context, and Byntar's case is by no means inconsequential when attempting to ascertain flawed mechanisms that may contribute to organizational demise. However, new JPUSA efforts such as Project 12 may prove effective in curtailing problems associated with identity-formation. A training program designed for both members and nonmembers seeking internship opportunities, Project 12 exemplifies how the commune now offers scenarios for youth to gain biblical training and practical application. Young students embrace JPUSA's ethos of offering assistance to families in Uptown who struggle with poverty. Project 12's core principle is the biblical verse Matthew 25:40: "The King will reply, 'I tell you the truth, whatever you did for one of the least of these brothers of mine, you did for me.'"[48] As a result, programs such as this might contribute to bolstering the identities of those raised in the commune and serve as a commitment mechanism for drifters, inspiring them to remain in JPUSA. This may go a long way in solving the identity problem. But JPUSA may also have to create new mechanisms to curtail any potential influx of drifters whose mental and emotional damage may place youth (children) in harm's way.

As a rule, social experiments often attract seekers in search of purpose, identity, and a sense of belonging. Every year JPUSA welcomes newcomers

THE FUTURE

in search of a number of scenarios: a community based on the New Testament model; alternative ways of experiencing church; an outlet to serve the homeless; a place of personal healing. Whatever the case, aspects of this lifestyle that once attracted new communards now often repel those who find communal rules beyond expectation. In the end, JPUSA's future is indelibly linked to how they choose to handle newcomers as the second generation leaves. More than this, it is how they will mediate the psychosocial problems smuggled in by drifters. And given allegations from wounded ex-members, JPUSA will have to reconsider its outreach to these drifters as long as there are children living in the community.

Since the second-generation members of *any* community cannot be counted on to continue what founding members established, there must be an emphasis placed on recruitment. This is self-evident. And it certainly goes without saying that postmodern Christianity has evolved independent of any particular group or movement. But postmodern *evangelicalism* has been given a cultural boost through movements like emergent Christianity, a "conversation" popularized by youth who found their ideological footing at events such as the Cornerstone Festival. Young "postmoderns" appear to be in JPUSA's future, as well as the future of other expressions of progressive Christianity. But will this endear these new spiritual trailblazers to establishment evangelicalism?

That JPUSA has changed since 1972 accounts for why it has remained culturally relevant—and why some veteran members have chosen to leave. The community has evolved politically and theologically, demonstrating how diversity of opinion within the commune has strengthened their resolve. But these differences (particularly when measured against the evangelical subculture) may prove problematic as JPUSA continues to garner support from the parent culture, in hopes of avoiding insularity. Some evangelicals (particularly those in the countercult community) believe JPUSA has drifted in its core beliefs. More specifically, according to ex-member Eric Pement, ideological change (which may have kept JPUSA culturally relevant) could actually have contributed to decline in membership. "Over time the community's complexion, goals, and orientation started to change," says Pement, "and things which were minor or nonexistent in early years became increasingly troublesome as the years progressed." The possible catalyst for JPUSA's differentiation from conservative evangelicalism may be related to its decision to drop a core belief from its public statement of faith. Between 1978 and 2003, article 1 of JPUSA's statement of faith, writes Pement, "included belief in the inerrancy of Scripture, and an affirmation of the Chicago Statement on Biblical Inerrancy."[49] But the article was removed around 2003. It now reads: "*We believe* that the Bible is the uniquely inspired, authoritative Word of God and is the only perfect rule for faith, doctrine, and conduct." For the more conservative evangelical, the omission of the word "inerrancy" is tantamount to theological liberalism.[50]

Pement views theological change in JPUSA as significant in terms of its identity. "The JPUSA community in its earlier years," he writes, was "dedicated as an evangelistic missionary organization, working as a Christian community." The commune expected that missionaries "would believe in the Bible and have a high view of Scripture, and when one no longer shared those convictions, they should probably find a different calling or occupation." Communards who diverged on these matters were expected to move out. Pement goes on, suggesting that JPUSA's shift in identity and purpose are connected to changes in theology. He writes:

> As the community shifted from being a missionary training center and evangelistic outreach, and developed a self-identity as an intentional community, the emphasis on evangelism, Biblical study, mission work, and support for church planting diminished, permitting a greater latitude in one's views of Scripture.[51]

According to Pement, in its infancy JPUSA was strictly a missionary group. But the increased focus on a communal orientation, he argues, created a scenario for a different view of scripture, as well as an emerging ecumenism. Put another way, Pement's statement suggests that JPUSA's decision to remove what is fundamental to some forms of evangelicalism (what historian David Bebbington refers to as biblicism)[52] is rooted in the community's history of engaging cultural pluralism. But his reason for leaving was unrelated to these changes: "My wife had been unhappy with living at JPUSA and we wanted better opportunities for our children. I also felt that I had been unproductive for several years and had 'plateaued' in my outreach and I thought I could serve the Lord more effectively in another capacity."[53]

In the end, Pement's observation as a former member provides a unique context. As one who joined during the 1970s, he has weathered the various critiques that have beset the commune. As one who has raised children in both communal and noncommunal contexts, he offers insight into how youth are affected by authority in different contexts. And as one who was a contributing writer for *Cornerstone*, he offers a nuanced perspective on the current life of the community and its potential future.

Pement believes that, to some extent, JPUSA's philosophical changes negatively affected attendance at the Cornerstone Festival. According to his estimation, between 1995 and 2012 attendance dropped from its high of twenty-four thousand. But JPUSA pastor Neil Taylor maintains that Cornerstone actually enjoyed larger numbers throughout the late 1990s until 2001. Moreover, festival director John Herrin estimates that the festival never reached over nineteen thousand (despite what many claim), noting that the higher numbers were always "a bit hyped."[54] Regardless, from 2001 until Cornerstone closed its doors in 2012, numbers dropped to half of what they once were, a decline attributed to post-9/11 fear of travel and large gatherings, not to mention an increase in gas prices.

Pement insists that like JPUSA, the Cornerstone Festival eventually drifted from its evangelical distinction. Indeed, throughout the 1990s the festival did appear more "evangelical," depending on how the term is defined, of course. So Pement's attempt to connect the decline in festival attendance to ideological change is not without merit. Herrin agrees that the festival's shift might account for low attendance in the final years. But any significant change in attendance, he reasons, should be attributed to festivalgoers and not to Cornerstone. "Hippies are getting older and some more conservative," says Herrin. "Cornerstone has never marched to the beat of mainstream evangelicalism nor conservative politics. I am sure that has alienated some folks over the years as we have drifted apart."[55] This bifurcation cannot be underestimated. But while baby boom Jesus freaks appear to be becoming more conservative, arguably they have always *been* conservative, now merely more attuned to theological differences when compared to the ahistorical persuasions of the 1970s Jesus freak. Although JPUSA and its Jesus-freak cohorts are growing apart ideologically, others (whether baby boom or Generation X) collapse the difference with the increasing influence of emergent and progressive Christianity, albeit incrementally.

Despite his assessment of JPUSA's change, Pement remains sympathetic toward the commune. Attempting to connect the group's divergence from the original mission, he notes what he perceives as a decline in communal membership. According to him, membership dropped from over 500 to somewhere between 350 and 400 since his departure in July 2000. He makes no explicit connection between this decline and ideological shifts but argues that to suggest JPUSA is *thriving* is "too strong a term." Rather, "the community is still active, still engaged, still functioning and offering a supportive communal context for its members."[56] But leaders offer a different account. Recalling a history of steady growth, JPUSA pastor Neil Taylor holds that the numbers are simply not this drastic. From 1972 the small community of 30 grew to 200 by the end of the 1970s. By the 1980s membership remained around 400, peaking at 425 during the 1990s. And despite the demise of the Cornerstone Festival, JPUSA membership still averages 400, intermittently dropping to 375, much like a local church, according to Taylor and Herrin. While Pement appears to at least imply some connection between JPUSA's change in mission and decline in membership, others hold that JPUSA's ability to adapt actually contributed to longevity. Its members are able to nurture long-standing convictions (e.g., Christian orthodoxy) while also holding them under the microscope of public opinion, always reexamining their own assumptions, unlike other Jesus Movement communal experiments.

There is no doubt the community has survived critiques from former members and others living in Uptown. While it has been praised and condemned, JPUSA has (to this point) outlived other groups that also developed under the auspices of the Book of Acts. Thus JPUSA's future is dependent on a number of variables, much like the American evangelical church and Christian pop media. Despite varied perceptions held by former members, the commune's success may simply be a result of their attempt to find a balance between the particulars of American individualism and the collectivism called for in the Book of Acts. In a 1976 issue of *Cornerstone* magazine, JPUSA publicly voiced its attempt at balancing individualism and collectivism, quoting Dietrich Bonhoeffer's *The Cost of Discipleship*: "the disciples of Jesus must not fondly imagine that they can simply run away from the world and huddle together in a little band."[57] Hoping to realize Bonhoeffer's vision, JPUSA sought balance as it avoided becoming a "sheltered cloister" or an advocate of a purely "social gospel.[58]

Remaining connected to the culture has certainly sustained the group since 1972. But is it enough? Is there a limit to any attempt at a New Testament semi-utopia? Kanter has argued that a communal enclave of "warm, close, supportive relationships—does not always occur according to scenario. Reality modifies the dream."[59] In other words, although JPUSA beliefs occasion an ongoing negotiation with the parent culture—allowing periodic reinvention to remain relevant and sustainable—its choice of lifestyle conflicts with what is expected by the establishment. American culture and communal perceptions change in unexpected ways, necessitating JPUSA to reinvent the community in hopes of effectively keeping pace with any "reality" that might "modify the dream." Kanter observes that "the assumptions they [the commune] make about what is possible and desirable in social life challenge the assumptions made by other sectors of American society."[60] Therefore it is prudent for JPUSA (or any group) to recognize how it is perceived by the dominant culture and how its challenge might threaten the established order. In so doing, it remains abreast of scenarios that could spell organizational demise.

CONCLUSION

Documentaries about religious radicalism continue to titillate. We are, after all, consumers of the fantastic, particularly as it feeds our curiosities about how others attempt to find a suitable balance between orthodox belief and pluralism. And it is also important to monitor communities of faith, bearing in mind that success and failure nip at the heels of any human endeavor, particularly when that endeavor involves tortured souls. But why does it matter? Because the future of this community (how they navigate cultural change) tells us something about how religious commitment within any group will fare in the future, as the United States becomes increasingly multicultural. And so a thing that bolsters a group or chips away at its foundation reveals something about our own nature. We know that second-generation communards are leaving JPUSA, and it retains an estimated 15 percent of the second generation. If any viable future is to be realized, the council will have to identify new leaders and a core rank-and-file, many of whom tend to be itinerant. Still, though they bring fresh energy and perspective, drifters do not remain long enough to warrant receiving any mantle of leadership. Besides, if the testimonies offered by ex-members are any indication, some drifters may prove to be dangerous. So who will assume the mantle of leadership? Second-generation communards can rarely be counted on to continue the life of any community. It appears that leadership must focus efforts on recruitment and find a way to retain new members.

While JPUSA leaders have demonstrated an ability to change communal ethos (in keeping with their desire to remain relevant), public perception may create difficulties for them to maintain a positive (or more specifically orthodox) image with evangelical constituency. Negative press brought by former members, journalists, and Ronald Enroth oddly served to rally evangelical support for JPUSA.[61] But then, many who can be counted as JPUSA's "public" once attended the Cornerstone Festival. And they may very well rescue the community from their own past.

The commitment of second-generation communards and negative representations advanced by former members may have an impact on JPUSA's future, but this is not binding. What is most pivotal, if Kanter's assertions are correct, concerns the role played by JPUSA's "fringe members," how the council decides to appropriately monitor their activities, and how they intend to protect the children. Comprehensive studies on communes, instantiated by scholars such as Rosabeth Moss Kanter and Timothy Miller, reveal the instability of groups whose structural mechanisms increase the likelihood of in-grown membership and insularity. Put another way, fresh blood is needed. Since second-generation members do not choose communal life, and since they were not "converted to believe in the community's ideals after weighing the alternatives," they are "not necessarily the most reliable source of committed adults to perpetuate the community," according to Kanter. Thus recruitment of new (mentally stable) members remains the more viable option for continuance, though this approach is also problematic. New members can become disillusioned, resulting in the introduction of "discordant element[s] into the community." And this has most certainly happened.[62]

Studies on communes have demonstrated the inevitability of societal pressure, competing forces with which communal enclaves must contend. JPUSA now practices controlled acculturation, allowing youth to gradually evolve with society, and to form individual identities while maintaining basic tenets that define the community. The longevity of any close-knit group is often determined by an ability to approximate what is at stake, accommodate the surroundings, and absorb particular, carefully chosen elements into the collective. However, it is equally important for communes to understand the value of allowing individual members the freedom to mature (independent of how the surrounding culture is perceived) while still maintaining a boundary, albeit negotiable and porous. Furthermore, communities like JPUSA must also maintain amicable relations with former members for whom life has been altered by mechanisms originally intended to discourage dissent and departure, and whose lives have been damaged by mismanagement of dangerous individuals and situations. Finally, political and theological difference must be mediated, allowing members to voice their differences and their concerns without fear of retribution. In so doing, discordant opinions fade into the gray of ecumenism, a cordiality once practiced at Cornerstone and now (because of Cornerstone) found in the CCM industry.

These approaches to both circumstances and environment are, I contend, admissible evidence that accounts for JPUSA's self-conception and potential for continued longevity. But more than this, the accounts offered by second-generation and ex-communards validate my own suspicions. Despite its methods, JPUSA's journey leftward problematizes how evangelicalism is often conceived and challenges how faith-based music is commonly

THE FUTURE

understood. Its success will largely be determined by how other evangelicals perceive it. And *this* is dependent on what evangelical Christianity will look like in the coming years. In many ways, JPUSA's successes, failures, and cultural influence parallel changes now occurring within the vast subculture of American evangelicalism. Our journey into the world of JPUSA offers insight into the differences between conservatism and liberalism and highlights distinct differences between these rather tired classifications and the so-called Evangelical Left.

8

CONCLUSION

✶ ✶ ✶

That JPUSA has continued well beyond its 1972 genesis is reminiscent of other religious groups who, despite travail, managed to survive. But how? And why does it even matter? First, as interest in the Jesus Movement waned, JPUSA's urban location allowed the community to attract youth who still held countercultural values, many seeking a lifestyle wholly at odds with mainstream American culture. Second, it is clear that a communal way of living is sustainable, if variables such as generational differences are considered. Third, it is possible for intentional communities to survive longer than once expected. Fourth, even communities dedicated to an unwavering principle can respond to and evolve with American culture, given the complexities associated with pluralism.

In the beginning JPUSA was thoroughly evangelical, aesthetically countercultural, and politically ambiguous—with the exception of its left-leaning models of social activism. Indeed, coreligionists also considered JPUSA evangelical. Yet as the 1980s came to a close, its ability to deemphasize the importance of theological positions (such as the Rapture) created a significant difference between its community and other Jesus freaks. Moreover, JPUSA's communal ethic and leftism placed it outside the parameters putative to establishment evangelicalism. While the choice to live out of a common purse was in keeping with what was established by the New

CONCLUSION

Testament, JPUSA's form of socialism was not in keeping with the established order or with a largely right-leaning evangelicalism. Rather than engage in what theorists such as Werner Sombart and Max Weber refer to as a "profit-based" economy, the commune embraced a subsistence economy. And their soul-winning efforts became part of a larger, holistic understanding of the Christian gospel, as the emerging leadership sought to meet the practical needs of Chicago's homeless. Thus the purpose of "business" has not been profit seeking for its own sake, nor work for its own sake (in the Weberian sense). Rather, JPUSA engages enterprise to sustain the commune and to fund efforts to offer aid to Uptown's low-income population. Consequently the burgeoning commune diverged from their Jesus Movement progenitors' belief in the Rapture, a position that placed tremendous emphasis on the second coming of Christ, to the exclusion of social justice. Contrary to this upward gaze, Uptown became JPUSA's mission field, one that established a perennial context for communards to realize a concrete sense of purpose, transcending ephemeral ideology. In keeping with the edicts of both the counterculture and (to a certain extent) a conflation of holiness doctrine and Catholic social teachings, JPUSA's austere commitment mechanisms (maintained by affirmative boundary distinctions) have served to keep members mobilized in service to the homeless in Chicago's 46th Ward. The shelter program creates a symbiotic relationship between communards and commune, reinforcing commitment to a larger cause. Faithful members believe their responsibilities are connected to the whole; when one fails a task, they fail their "family" and, more specifically, a divinely inspired dedication to serve the less fortunate. Stated simply, everyone is acutely aware that their contributions to the overall mission cannot be underestimated.[1]

The fact that JPUSA is interstitial—that it remains culturally relevant while cloistered—is important when considering how communal life (or local communities, for that matter) can be understood. More specifically, that JPUSA is service-based rather than retreat-based confirms Kanter's thesis: successful communes must avoid insularity while simultaneously affirming negotiable boundaries, a sentiment that can easily be applied to an evangelical subculture now treading the tumultuous waters of pluralism. Emergent

CONCLUSION

Christians (as one example) maintain certain ideological boundaries, but they are porous, often negotiated based on sociocultural contexts.

While boundaries have sustained JPUSA since 1972, the negotiability of these boundaries has also contributed to an ever-eroding commitment among younger members. And to some extent, that this bounded (guarded) community chose to minister to drifters served it well, as it created a revolving door of members, but it has come with a price. As we have seen, allegations of sexual abuse of minors are certainly enough to cause one to question an environment that places children in proximity to new members, whose backgrounds are often tattered and broken. The result has been a recent outpouring from former members, most of them still recovering from what they insist was a childhood that no one should endure. But what of those who still call JPUSA home? Will the youth pick up the torch? As my previous work indicates,[2] the second generation plays an immediate and paramount role in the commune's future, and JPUSA must also consider how communards are to interact with the wider culture (how the commune influences and is influenced), particularly given their contingencies: retention of members; future relations with evangelicals subjected to postmodern Christianity; an embattled CCM industry. Put simply, social movement organizations (SMOs) "not only mediate the effects of the environment but are partially determined by the environment," writes sociologist David F. Gordon.[3]

Although JPUSA has weathered criticism and a growing tide of potential litigation, its core purpose and mission to serve the neighborhood of Uptown may very well stave off disillusionment within the commune, or at least keep newcomers actively engaged. Along with maintaining commitment mechanisms and an organizational model of "multiple eldership," JPUSA's ability to appropriately evolve with the dominant culture will keep it culturally relevant and, perhaps, socially active. Evidence of this can certainly be found in its music. But it also appears in the newly emerging leadership structure.

We have seen JPUSA develop over the years, beginning with one charismatic leader, later to embrace the plurality of leadership as seen in the council. But given the premium placed on balancing the public and the private,

CONCLUSION

the community and the individual, it comes as no shock that this or any group would find their way to a political middle ground—the gray space between black and white. In recent years the leadership has chosen to decentralize authority, creating a number of committees intended to provide oversight for JPUSA's various businesses, ministries, and duties associated with daily life in the community. But remember, if they evolve too quickly (allowing too many freedoms for those raised in the commune), new generations may seek another way of life when they reach adulthood.

A bounded community, JPUSA has instituted and nurtured belief systems designed to stave off temptation. But those mechanisms (whether intentional or incidental) designed to contribute to communal longevity appear to be having the opposite effect as members continue to leave. Thus if the council places more value on the architecture of the commune than on the formation of the individual, JPUSA may run the risk of alienating future leaders of the community. More to the point, if the testimonies offered by those who have come forward with allegations are true—if the leaders have a history of protecting the ministry and hiding the problems—what sort of new dynamic will emerge between the Evangelical Covenant Church and its noteworthy satellite community called JPUSA?

Kanter's theory of sustainability is applicable to JPUSA's survival *since* 1972. As a service commune, JPUSA's boundaries and activism have provided its members with a grand cause that outweighs propensities to elevate individual leaders. Not surprising, these believers must contend with a rapidly shifting culture while remaining true to their ethos, particularly when the problem of sustainability remains ever-present. After all, they will only remain an active, culturally-engaged commune if they retain viable members able to work in JPUSA businesses, assuming those businesses and ministries continue to garner support from constituents, evangelical or otherwise. Kanter correctly argues that for communes to remain healthy in the face of environmental change, they must "deal with changes in the external society, from choosing to ignore them to incorporating them."[4] If JPUSA remained cloistered (rural or urban), it would have likely folded long ago.

For this group, interaction with a pluralistic world may serve to strengthen and weaken collective commitment. But will mechanisms that allowed JPUSA to survive contribute to its demise as rising generations refuse to acquiesce? Since second-generation members of a commune do not choose communal life, they are an unreliable source to perpetuate a community, says Kanter. And as we have seen, some former members measured life in the commune against what was perceived as effective structures or belief-systems, communal or otherwise.[5]

Ultimately, courting new members and maintaining a consistent ethic of acculturation account not only for communal survival but also for the longevity of any organization or movement. Noting the cultural impact of the Jesus Movement, historian Larry Eskridge underscores the reciprocal element (religion influencing culture and vice versa) that was common to early Jesus freaks, many of whom made use of and benefited from American popular culture: "Indeed, the Jesus Person 'style' continued to prosper as a distinct evangelical youth culture with concerts, coffeehouses, newspapers, bumper stickers, crosses, and Bible studies."[6] In like manner, JPUSA remarkably demonstrates how cultural connections can have an impact on and change both a particular group and larger movements, such as American evangelicalism and evangelically based popular music. But the long-term effect remains to be seen. What is clear, however, is that this community must navigate a precarious sociocultural position. And in like manner, evangelical Christianity must constantly negotiate with the larger culture (reinventing itself) while simultaneously affirming its distinctives.[7]

JPUSA and the Cornerstone Festival have both occupied a different ideological space, one that does not conform solely to conservative establishment evangelicalism, Jesus-freak millenarianism, or theologically liberal Christianity. The tired Right-Left binary offers us very little when attempting to ultimately locate JPUSA within the broad swath of U.S. religious history. Moreover, despite its somewhat interstitial enclave of resistance, JPUSA's goal (as it pertains to culture and ideas) has been to use *Cornerstone* magazine (before it went out of publication) and the festival (before it folded) as mechanisms to challenge long-held paradigms. In *Rapture Ready*, journalist Daniel Radosh comes to this conclusion about Cornerstone: "The open-minded, intellectually adventurous spirit of Cornerstone may still be a

CONCLUSION

small force in evangelical culture, but it seems poised to become influential beyond its size. The younger demographic that's drawn here will soon grow into positions of leadership in the church and society."[8]

Indeed, many within the younger demographic already occupy positions of leadership. After all, Cornerstone was voicing an "open-minded, intellectually adventurous spirit" since its genesis. But while the 1980s and 1990s represented a time when the event was unapologetically evangelical and theologically conservative, the close of the century solidified Cornerstone's ability to engage in a different manner of inquiry, one subject to the searing eyes of literary criticism. Radosh's observation may be a bit late, but his sentiment rings true: although conservative evangelicalism maintains a cultural foothold, many fans of Cornerstone (though by no means all) began to view rightist forms of Christianity as dubious, controlled by politically driven demagogues.

Evangelical Christian culture and belief have evolved as a result of a number of dialectical processes, as well as the power of material culture. As products of this culture, JPUSA and Cornerstone set into motion a process that inspired new musical forms (particularly of the indie brand) largely divorced from industry gatekeepers. In so doing, they challenged the "Christ Against Culture" approach to social engagement. Historian Mark Allan Powell has accurately commented on evangelicalism's propensity to adopt this model of cultural interaction: "I have found one of the Achilles' heels of American evangelicalism to be its adoption of the 'Christ Against Culture' model, which Niebuhr effectively critiques. But it is an unnecessary weakness, born of a defensive posture that evangelicalism should be able to transcend." Powell goes on to explain a rather curious point: evangelicals appear to enjoy significant social power while simultaneously complaining "about how marginalized they are within modern society." And this is quite evident in CCM. He concludes by addressing JPUSA's role in this drama:

> My point is, evangelicals perpetuate the "Christ Against Culture" model insofar as it helps them advance their agenda—but ultimately it is very limiting, and a number of evangelicals are beginning to realize this. JPUSA

appears to have been born as a Christ Against Culture movement—but through Cornerstone they evolved toward adoption of a more dialogical vision. This could be the future of evangelicalism in America.[9]

JPUSA and Cornerstone provide evidence that new forms of evangelical belief and expression have been emerging. And this social impact continues to extend to evangelical popular music. As a result, two forms of evangelically inspired music have emerged: a form of CCM disconnected from the CCM signifier yet still connected to conservative, establishment evangelicalism, and a form rendered unrecognizable owing to the forces of pluralism. The latter form can be traced to subcultural music groups once showcased at the Cornerstone Festival, many of which teetered between a robust commitment to Christian social justice, on the one hand, and roundly evangelical theological affinities, on the other. And so JPUSA's progeny extends well beyond Chicago's 46th Ward, expressing the ethos of the commune and the festival through music groups now marketed to the general public.[10]

A thoroughgoing left-wing humanitarianism was always evident at Cornerstone. The event served to maintain a spirit arguably extinguished in the wake of post–Jesus Movement circumstances: the rapid growth of individualism, the compressing of evangelicalism and nationalism into an identifiable whole, and the commercialization of popular evangelical music. In the wake of this, Cornerstone provided an alternative to mainstream evangelical festivals, created an outlet for independent musicians, and proffered one possible way to redefine what it means to categorize music as either evangelical or Christian.

The music industry is now filled with artists whose beginnings can be traced to the evangelical subculture, and it is conceivable that Cornerstone contributed to a remapping of how evangelical music is represented; the festival indeed challenged boundaries established by the gatekeepers of gospel music and theologies cherished by traditionalists. The inimitability of Rez Band, The 77s, Charlie Peacock, Sixpence None the Richer, and P.O.D. only served to inspire younger artists to try harder, to attempt mimicry as they breach long-standing barriers, and as they rupture the binaries of sa-

CONCLUSION

cred and secular. And this was certainly made possible by JPUSA's unique approach to political and religious belief.

As the commune's theology continues to mirror a postmodern ethos, one wonders how JPUSA will fare in the future. While I argue that its ability to engage social justice and evolve has kept it alive and relevant, its success largely depends on what the world will look like—what evangelicalism will look like. As the 1990s came to a close, Cornerstone seminars entertained postmodern critical theory and establishment paradigms were questioned. For a growing numbers of JPUSA members and festivalgoers, the dialectical approach to knowledge led not to certainty but to more questions. JPUSA and members of the Evangelical Left began to avoid the cognitive, Enlightenment-inspired religion of fundamentalism (read conservative evangelicalism), favoring the contemplative spirit of a postmodern Christianity that (as result of the theoretical) embraced ambiguity while remaining faithful to a modified form of evangelical Christianity. Ironically, Jesus freaks throughout the late 1960s and 1970s also challenged establishment paradigms. Like post-1990s JPUSA, early converts also avoided Enlightenment-inspired epistemologies—but their challenge was to the religion of mainline liberals, favoring the experientialism of pentecostals. Similar in many ways, each expression can be considered different based on what was being *countered*. Early Jesus freaks questioned the liberal mainline; JPUSA questions establishment evangelicalism.

As with Jesus freaks of the 1960s and 1970s, the Evangelical Left and emergent Christianity emphasize faith over certitude, creating an ironic impulse that historian Donald Miller refers to as "postmodern primitivism."[11] This is not to suggest, however, that JPUSA and others on the left have entered with fundamentalists into what Miller considers a "precritical worldview." Rather, it is "to disavow the hegemony of the socially constructed 'rational' mind."[12] It is within this space that faith and hope live. After all, the crisis of representation also affects the scientific method. Empirical, measurable evidence also falls prey to the ravages of time and text. Thus in the absence of certainty (in anything), faith is the only option—at least for the postmodern Christian. And, ironically, many of these seekers (especially

CONCLUSION

millennials) are returning to High Church models of faith. Having been marketed to throughout their lives, the evangelical tendency toward the cultural vernacular now falls on deaf ears. They are "not easily impressed with consumerism or performances," says blogger Rachel Held Evans. She writes:

> Time and again, the assumption among Christian leaders, and evangelical leaders in particular, is that the key to drawing twenty-somethings back to church is simply to make a few style updates—edgier music, more casual services, a coffee shop in the fellowship hall, a pastor who wears skinny jeans, an updated Web site that includes online giving.[13]

Ironically, for the postmodern, millennial generation (and for many in Generation X), the critique sounds strikingly similar to what conservatives once said—that true holiness has somehow eluded today's faithful. Evans continues:

> We want an end to the culture wars. We want a truce between science and faith. We want to be known for what we stand for, not what we are against. We want to ask questions that don't have predetermined answers. We want churches that emphasize an allegiance to the kingdom of God over an allegiance to a single political party or a single nation. We want our LGBT friends to feel truly welcome in our faith communities. We want to be challenged to live lives of holiness, not only when it comes to sex, but also when it comes to living simply, caring for the poor and oppressed, pursuing reconciliation, engaging in creation care and becoming peacemakers. You can't hand us a latte and then go about business as usual and expect us to stick around. We're not leaving the church because we don't find the cool factor there; we're leaving the church because we don't find Jesus there.

Indeed, this sentiment has been echoed in a number of circles that are part of the polysemous Evangelical Left. These new attempts to wrest orthodoxy from the hands of the Religious Right has become apparent in the emergent church, the emerging church, liberal evangelicalism, New Monasticism, and the so-called Slow Church Movement. Each is symptomatic of a larger crisis among evangelicals (and other persons of faith) who continue to balance their belief systems with a robust acceptance of all things modern and postmodern.

Clearly JPUSA is among those who have tried to locate a middle ground (a gray area) between the mainstream and the fringe while retaining particular fundamentals that situate them within the evangelical paradigm. In like manner, the Evangelical Left now negotiates a position that is not fully liberal, conservative, or evangelical. Cultural theorist Lawrence Grossberg attempts to explain how belief is mediated in the midst of postmodernity:

> It is only if we begin to recognize the complex relations between affect and ideology that we can make sense of people's emotional life, their desiring life, and their struggles to find the energy to survive, let alone struggle. It is only in the terms of these relations that we can understand people's need and ability to maintain a "faith" in something beyond their immediate existence. Such faith, which is at least part of what is involved in political struggle, depends upon affective investments that are articulated into but not constituted by structures of meaning."[14]

JPUSA's postmodernism (controlled as it might be) amounts to an acceptance of the culture as it is. Group members no longer base Christian belief on evidentiary polemics but embrace the mystery. This long-suffering community embraces pluralism while continuing to believe that ultimate meaning undergirds their purpose in life. For Grossberg, the balance between the postmodern crisis and a meaningful life is in locating *purpose* in the midst of the crisis. "It is not that nothing matters," writes Grossberg, "but that it does not matter what does, as long as something does."[15] Put another way, *what* matters is not the point, so long as we find *something* that matters. For JPUSA, this "something" remains a dedication to the communal life in service to the less fortunate.

As we have seen, the JPUSA community occupies a rather nebulous space, which is symptomatic of something that is uniquely American. They have entered that uncomfortable area between the binaries of white and black. But the gray of uncertainty allows a certain wiggle room, providing a sliver of an opening where different forms of social activism can flourish, and where new expressions of faith-based music can emerge. JPUSA is then best located in a space that combines the culture-engaging impulse of post–Jesus Movement, establishment evangelicalism, and the fringe expressions of isolationist, Jesus-freak communitarianism. Despite this liminality, JPUSA has been able to retain the spirit of the Jesus Movement. In the end, this creates new questions: (1) What is the future of evangelical popular music, given the forces of pluralism? Despite the growth of emergent Christianity and the Evangelical Left, conservative forms of belief and popular expression remain quite successful. Although conservative forms of evangelical pop culture remain strong, music groups spawned by Cornerstone now serve as counterweights for evangelical fans, offering them alternatives to long-held paradigms. That Cornerstone in many ways contributed to the remapping of CCM is evident. Various music groups now successful in the general market developed an initial fan base at the festival. And given the success of these "secular" faith-based bands, will CCM groups finally be absorbed into the secular mainstream? It is difficult to determine any lasting effect of Cornerstone's influence. However, that evangelical Christianity and evangelical popular culture are changing in response to pluralism is clear. (2) Is it accurate to suggest that through Cornerstone, JPUSA contributed to an upsurge in the Evangelical Left, or at least more interest in emergent Christianity? Many who attended the festival were *traditional* evangelicals. But when postmodern theory was openly discussed (within a social space defined by commonly held belief-systems), the festival would later influence festivalgoers and musicians in ways unlike other evangelical events. Furthermore, JPUSA and Cornerstone have both proven to be inconvenient for establishment evangelicals. In short, JPUSA's philosophy nuances the categories of "CCM" and "evangelical."

Despite decline in festival attendance, in its remaining years Cornerstone attracted an increasing number of left-leaning, emergent Christians. And though it was once celebrated as a bastion of subcultural theological conservatism, the Evangelical Left gained a foothold. But in the wake of untimely demise (and in the shadow of a largely conservative Christian music industry), the Left may have to rely on start-ups like the Wildgoose Festival or the PAPA Festival, if progressive forms of Christianity (and its popular music) are to advance in any significant way. Unlike Cornerstone, both of these embrace the LGBT community. But like Cornerstone and JPUSA, they embrace a near-anarcho-socialist position. The PAPA Festival holds to an ideal that is in defiance of the current world economic system, says *Washington Post* journalist Julia Duin, "which organizers think benefits the rich. Thus, PAPA has set up a 'bartering tent,' where people can bring things they've made to trade, avoiding money." Recalling her days in the Jesus Movement, Duin understands: "No one understood why we wanted to live in households and share our salaries. While the emphasis seems to have shifted—back then, the main concern was to get folks filled with the Holy Spirit; here it's peace and justice—the sentiment is familiar."[16]

As for subcultural evangelicals who lament the demise of a venue that celebrated independent music, it is likely that niche will be filled again—someone will certainly pick up the torch. One such attempt is AudioFeed, a new endeavor in Champaign-Urbana, Illinois, founded by a former "Cornerstoner." It is, according to its Facebook page, "a music festival built by some people who loved Cornerstone and wanted to see all their friends and favorite bands in one place again."[17] And it is tempting to consider how JPUSA will interact with the new festival. Could it become yet another recruiting ground? Perhaps. Still, JPUSA must continue to romance a new generation by developing scenarios that attract those whose ultimate calling is connected to social justice. And as long as it has children living in its community, JPUSA may have to reconsider how it ministers to the homeless, drifters, seekers, and the like.

That the evangelical subculture has become culturally pliable is not surprising. Philip Goff and Alan Heimert maintain that as historians reengage assumptions about the past, the ground shifts as the discipline of religious history continues to "shape and to be shaped by larger social and cultural forces." They go on to state that further study "uncovers today's strange bedfellows, evangelicals and postmodernists, who together have launched a forceful objection to long-standing historical assumptions and paradigms."[18] Within this new historical context, categories and movements are in some ways compressed into manageable signifiers. In other ways, they are broadened to include as many other categories as possible (to satisfy pluralism), thus losing any cohesive distinctiveness. The evolution of JPUSA underscores how cultural evolution may affect the evangelical parent culture. The Religious Right (and associated cultural products) remains influential in the United States. But a new generation has chosen to part ways, choosing to ally with emergent and progressive forms of religious faith. In so doing, they signal the coming of new definitions, new delineations, new boundaries, new allegiances, new reformations, and new forms of popular culture. The idea that pluralism has influenced evangelical Christianity may be overplayed, but the sentiment remains strong.

NOTES

✱ ✱ ✱

1. INTRODUCTION

1. Colleen McDannell, *Material Christianity: Religion and Popular Culture in America* (New Haven: Yale University Press, 1995), 222–23.
2. Noreen Cornfield, "The Success of Urban Communes," *Journal of Marriage and Family* 45, no. 1 (February 1983): 115–26.
3. In *Witnessing Suburbia: Conservative and Christian Youth Culture* (Berkeley: University of California Press, 2009), Eileen Luhr has noted how some initially dismissed the Jesus Movement as a youth phenomenon destined to dissolve. She concludes that the movement ultimately created a new form of evangelical popular culture that would fuel the rise of a new suburban conservative youth culture, portending the empowerment of the new Religious Right.
4. Ibid., 162.
5. Melani McAlister, "What Is Your Heart For? Affect and Internationalism in the Evangelical Public Sphere," *American Literary History* 20, no. 4 (Winter 2008): 870–95.
6. Jason Bivens, *Religion of Fear: The Politics of Horror in Conservative Evangelicalism* (New York: Oxford University Press, 2008).
7. Marcia Pally, "The New Evangelicals," *New York Times*, December 9, 2011. http://campaignstops.blogs.nytimes.com/2011/12/09/the-new-evangelicals/.

2. THE LARGEST AMERICAN COMMUNE

1. Donald E. Miller, *Reinventing American Protestantism: Christianity in the New Millennium* (Berkeley: University of California Press, 1999), 11–12.

2. THE LARGEST AMERICAN COMMUNE

2. This chapter is a slightly revised version of my article of the same title in *VOLUME! The French Journal of Popular Music Studies* 9, no. 2 (2012). It was also published in Sheila Whiteley and Jedediah Sklower, eds., *Countercultures and Popular Music* (Farnham, UK: Ashgate, 2014), 109–22.
3. See Shawn Young, "Into the Grey: The Left, Progressivism, and Christian Rock in Uptown Chicago," *Religions* 3, no. 2 (2012): 498–522.
4. Timothy Miller, *The 60s Communes: Hippies and Beyond* (Syracuse: Syracuse University Press, 1999), 99.
5. Young, "Into the Grey."
6. Rosabeth Moss Kanter, *Commitment and Community: Communes and Utopias in Sociological Perspective* (Cambridge: Harvard University Press, 1972), 75. Emphasis added.
7. Doug Rossinow, *The Politics of Authenticity: Liberalism, Christianity and the New Left in America* (New York: Columbia University Press, 1998), 53, 82, 150, 151.
8. Barry Shenker, *Intentional Communities: Ideology and Alienation in Communal Societies* (Boston: Routledge & Kegan Paul, 1986), 10.
9. Anson Shupe, "Jesus People USA," in *Sects, Cults, and Spiritual Communities: A Sociological Analysis*, ed. William W. Zellner and Marc Petrowsky (Westport, Conn: Praeger, 1998), 27.
10. Miller, *60s Communes*, xiii.
11. Ibid., xxiv.
12. Ibid., 148.
13. Larry Eskridge, "God's Forever Family: The Jesus People Movement in America 1966–1977" (Ph.D. diss., University of Stirling, 2005), 304–5.
14. Jedidiah Abdul Muhib Palosaari, "Notes," October 15, 1973. http://ml-in.facebook.com/notes.php?id=513198705&start=480&hash=6224177f16565d53de95d0d2a43d331b.
15. Mark Allan Powell, *The Encyclopedia of Contemporary Christian Music* (Peabody, Mass.: Hendrickson, 2002), 753.
16. Jon Trott, "Part 1(a): Birth and Rebirth," *A History of Jesus People USA*. http://www.jpusa.org/lessons1a.html. Originally printed in "Jesus People Here for Public Rallies," from a Houghton-Hancock, Michigan, area newspaper (name and date unknown).
17. Tom Cameron, interview by author, digital recording, Chicago, March 21, 2010.
18. John Herrin, interview by author, digital recording, Chicago, March 10, 2009.
19. Trott, "Part 1(a): Birth and Rebirth."
20. Ibid.
21. Ibid.
22. Herrin, interview, March 10, 2009.
23. Ibid.

2. THE LARGEST AMERICAN COMMUNE

24. Powell, *Encyclopedia*, 752–54.
25. Herrin, interview, March 10, 2009.
26. Jon Trott, "Part 2: House and Home," *A History of Jesus People USA.* http://www.jpusa.org/lessons2.html.
27. Herrin, interview, March 10, 2009.
28. Trott, "Part 1(a): Birth and Rebirth."
29. Ibid.
30. Jon Trott, "Part 1(b): Quest for Balance," *A History of Jesus People USA.* http://www.jpusa.org/lessons1b.html.
31. Jon Trott, interview by author, digital recording. Chicago, March 11, 2009.
32. David Gordon, "A Comparison of the Effects of Urban and Suburban Location on Structure and Identity in Two Jesus People Groups" (Ph.D. diss., University of Chicago, 1978), 40–41.
33. Cameron, interview, March 21, 2010.
34. Gordon, "Comparison."
35. Jon Trott, "Part 4: Authority, Freedom and Uptown," *A History of Jesus People USA.* http://www.jpusa.org/lessons4.html. Originally printed in Lesley Sussman, "Jesus Group Buys Hotel, Vows Rehab," *Uptown News*, April 17, 1979, 1.
36. David K. Fremon, *Chicago Politics Ward by Ward* (Bloomington: Indiana University Press, 1988), 124.
37. Ibid., 303–7.
38. Trott, "Part 4: Authority, Freedom and Uptown," 1.
39. Jon Trott, "Part 5: Who Is My Neighbor?" *A History of Jesus People USA.* http://www.jpusa.org/lessons5.html.
40. Trott, interview, March 11, 2009.
41. Ben Joravsky, "Upscaling Uptown: Can Developers of Subsidized Housing Escape HUD Rules by Prepaying Their Mortgages?" *Chicago Reader*, March 24, 1988. http://www.chicagoreader.com/chicago/upscaling-uptown-can-developers-of-subsidized-housing-escape-hud-rules-by-prepaying-their-mortgages/Content?oid=871958.
42. Trott, "Part 5: Who Is My Neighbor?"
43. Jon Trott, "Part 7: Action—Social and Political, I," *A History of Jesus People USA.* http://www.jpusa.org/lessons7.html. Originally printed in Newsletter, "Note from Chicago," 1984, Jesus People USA, Chicago. Trott also cites Todd Gitlin and Nanci Hollander, *Uptown: Poor Whites in Chicago* (New York: Harper & Row, 1970). Trott states that Gitlin worked in Uptown between 1965 and 1970, creating "an indictment against Chicago's destructive housing policy." This is included in the notes section to "Part 7."
44. Trott, "Part 7: Action—Social and Political, I.
45. Trott, "Part 7: Action—Social and Political, I." Originally printed in *Rev Rag*, October 4, 1987; November 8, 1987.
46. Ibid.

47. Laurie Abraham, "Refugee Families Face Eviction by Rehabber," *Chicago Sun-Times*, August 1986.
48. Michael Loftin, "Coalition Formed to Fight Displacement," *The Voice Speaks: The Newsletter of Voice of the People in Uptown* (Spring 1987): 1. Voice of the People is a low-income housing developer.
49. Fremon, *Chicago Politics*, 309.
50. Ibid., 303–7.
51. Jon Trott. "Part 8: Action—Social and Political, II," *A History of Jesus People USA*. http://www.jpusa.org/lessons8.html.
52. Ibid.
53. Ibid.
54. Herrin, interview, March 10, 2009.
55. John Herrin, email, June 6, 2013.
56. Glenn Kaiser, interview by author, digital recording, Chicago, March 11, 2009.
57. Howard Zinn, "Marxism and the New Left," in *Dissent: Explorations in the History of Radicalism*, ed. Alfred L. Young (DeKalb: Northern Illinois Press, 1968), 371.
58. This is a statement taken from the Bible in the book of Matthew 25:40 (New International Version): "The King will reply, 'I tell you the truth, whatever you did for one of the least of these brothers of mine, you did for me.'" The phrase "least of these" is one that inspires leaders of JPUSA to engage in social justice.

3. THE BLESSING AND CURSE OF COMMUNITY

1. Fremon, *Chicago Politics*, 303–7.
2. Steven M. Tipton, *Getting Saved from the Sixties: The Transformation of Moral Meaning in American Culture* (Berkeley: University of California Press, 1982).
3. This was a millenarian group oriented around Tony and Susan Alamo. In some cases, Jewish messianic converts embraced a staunch Christian fundamentalism. Tony Alamo (formerly Bernie Lazar Hoffman) and his wife Susan were two of the more radical converts during the Jesus Movement. They were exclusivist preachers claiming that hippie evangelism began with *them* in 1965, and that they were the "true" catalysts of the movement. The Alamo Christian Foundation in California earned the title "exclusivist" by working to distance itself from other Jesus Movement camps, adopting a hardline position while denouncing other evangelical groups.
4. Young, "Into the Grey." Also see Timothy Miller, "A Communitarian Conundrum: Why a World That Wants and Needs Community Doesn't Get It," paper presented at the Thirty-Seventh Annual Conference of the Communal Studies Association, New Harmony, Ind., September 30–October 2, 2010.
5. Kanter, *Commitment and Community*, 174.
6. Jean Vanier, http://larcheusa.org/who-we-are.html.

3. THE BLESSING AND CURSE OF COMMUNITY

7. Ibid.
8. http://www.rebaplacefellowship.org/Who_We_Are.
9. Kanter, *Commitment and Community*, 191, 195, 200.
10. Nathan Cameron, interview by author, digital recording, Chicago, March 20, 2010.
11. Curtis Mortimer, interview by author, digital recording, Chicago, March 21, 2010.
12. Dorena Sadeghi, interview by author, digital recording, Chicago, March 6, 2010.
13. Raye Clemente, interview by author, digital recording, Chicago, March 5, 2010.
14. Neil Taylor, interview by author, digital recording, Chicago, March 7, 2010.
15. Tom Cameron, interview by author, digital recording, Chicago, March 21, 2010.
16. Lyda Jackson, interview by author, digital recording, Chicago, March 7, 2010.
17. Joshua Davenport, interview by author, digital recording, Chicago, March 6, 2010.
18. "Susan" [pseud.], interview by author, digital recording, Chicago, March 21, 2010.
19. Colleen Davick, interview by author, digital recording, Chicago, March 10, 2009.
20. Aaron Tharp, interview by author, digital recording, Chicago, March 5, 2010.
21. http://weknowthegoodguys.com/We_Know_the_Good_Guys_FAQ.php.
22. Ibid.
23. Rosabeth Moss Kanter, "Supercorp: Book Review and Author Interview," *News Center*, November 3, 2009, interview, Sean Silverthorne, http://www.moneycontrol.com/news/book-review/supercorp-book-reviewauthor-interview_422139-1.html.
24. Tim Bock, *Unless the Lord Build the House: The Story of Jesus People USA's Mission-Business, and How I Was Part of It*, 2nd ed. (Chicago: Jesus People USA Full Gospel Ministries, 2009), 92–93.
25. Cornerstone Community Outreach, *Mission Statement.* http://www.ccolife.org/blog/cco.
26. Kirsten Scharnberg, "Commune's Iron Grip Tests Faith of Converts," *Chicago Tribune*, April 1, 2001. http://articles.chicagotribune.com/2001–04–01/news/0104010382_1_needy-youth-commune-spiritualism.
27. Jimmy Carter, "Mental Health Systems Act Remarks on Signing S. 1177 into Law," October 7, 1980. http://www.presidency.ucsb.edu/ws/index.php?pid=45228.
28. Alexandar R. Thomas, "Ronald Reagan and the Commitment of the Mentally Ill: Capital, Interest Groups, and the Eclipse of Social Policy," *Electronic Journal of Sociology* 3 (1998). http://www.sociology.org/content/vol003.004/thomas.html.

3. THE BLESSING AND CURSE OF COMMUNITY

29. Ibid.
30. Sandy Ramsey, interview by author, digital recording, Chicago, March 7, 2010.
31. David Baumgartner, email, March 29, 2010.
32. First published in *Cornerstone* 22, no. 102/103 (1994): 19–21, except for the signature portions after the last paragraph of text. Cornerstone Communications, http://www.cornerstonemag.com/features/iss103/covenant.htm.
33. Dawn Mortimer, interview with author, Chicago, March 21, 2010.
34. Ibid.
35. Ibid.
36. Ibid.
37. Project 12 (P-12) is a training program designed for both members and nonmembers seeking internships opportunities.
38. Neil Taylor, email, April 7, 2010.
39. Scott [pseud.], email, March 13, 2010.
40. "Stephen" [pseud.], email, April 16, 2010.
41. Miller, *60s Communes*, 167.
42. Hugh Gardner, *The Children of Prosperity: Thirteen Modern American Communes* (New York: St. Martin's Press, 1978).
43. Scharnberg, "Commune's Iron Grip."
44. Anson Shupe, William A. Stacey, and Susan E. Darnel, eds., *Bad Pastors: Clergy Misconduct in Modern America* (New York: New York University Press, 2000), 163.
45. Timothy Miller, *Response from Timothy Miller, Professor of Religious Studies, University of Kansas*. JPUSA archived letters provided by communard Lyda Jackson, September 2010.
46. *Response for Scholars at the Communal Studies Association*. JPUSA archived letters provided by communard Lyda Jackson, September 2010.
47. Jon Trott, "Is Abuse About Truth or Story: Or Both? One Intentional Community's Painful Experiences with False Accusations," in Shupe, Stacey, and Darnell, *Bad Pastors*, 173. http://muse.jhu.edu/books/9780814786697.
48. Ibid., 174.
49. Jon Trott has argued that many of these allegations are weak owing to Enroth's inability or unwillingness to specify the nature of abuse. Furthermore, Trott and Shupe have argued that Enroth's method is unsound because he identified only with the "victims" and created "narrative accounts" as "literal history." Trott points out that Enroth admitted to combining stories to "make a more compelling narrative," thus calling into question the validity of individual charges. See ibid., 170.
50. http://www.angelfire.com/zine/jpusainfo/constitution_intro.html.
51. Jon Trott, email, April 11, 2010.
52. "Work and Taxes." http://www.jpusa.org/covenant.html.
53. Trott, email, April 11, 2010.

54. Eric Pement, email, June 15, 2010.
55. Barbara Pement, email, June 29, 2010.
56. Taylor, interview, March 7, 2010.
57. Trott, email, April 11, 2010.
58. Jean Vanier, *Community and Growth*, rev. ed. (New York: Paulist Press, 1996), 222.
59. John Herrin, email, June 6, 2013.
60. Ibid.
61. Dawn and Curtis Mortimer, interview by author, digital recording, Chicago, March 21, 2010.
62. Trott, "Part1(b): Quest for Balance."
63. Kanter, *Commitment and Community*, 201.
64. Ibid., 64–66.
65. "Susan" [pseud.], interview, March 21, 2010.
66. Lyda Jackson, interview, March 7, 2010.
67. Clemente, interview, March 5, 2010.
68. Nathan Cameron, interview, March 20, 2010.
69. Taylor, interview, March 7, 2010.
70. Tom Cameron, interview, March 21, 2010.
71. Dawn and Curtis Mortimer, interview, March 21, 2010.
72. Glen van Alkemade, interview by author, digital recording, Chicago, March 21, 2010.
73. Ibid.
74. Miller, *60s Communes*.
75. Chris Spicer, interview by author, digital recording, Chicago, March 7, 2010.
76. Stu Heiss, interview by author, digital recording, Chicago, March 20, 2010.
77. Ibid.
78. Wendi Kaiser, interview by author, digital recording, Chicago, March 7, 2010.
79. Scott [pseud.], email, March 13, 2010.
80. Ibid.
81. Kanter, *Commitment and Community*, 188.

4. BIG SHOULDERS, BIG COMMUNITY

1. James Davidson Hunter, *Evangelicalism: The Coming Generation* (Chicago: University of Chicago Press, 1993).
2. Certainly Revivalism was initially associated with the Burned Over District. However, I am distinguishing the Midwest for its own history of religious and political populism.
3. George M. Marsden, *Religion and American Culture* (Belmont, Calif.: Wadsworth/Thomson Learning, 2001), 116.

4. BIG SHOULDERS, BIG COMMUNITY

4. According to this position, history is divided into various dispensations; thus one is able to determine an approximate time for the End of Days. Moody assisted in the founding of Bible institutes that trained young ministers in this doctrine, bolstering young evangelists to weather the storm of modernity's critique of biblical literalism. The Moody Bible Institute in Chicago is one of the more notable examples. These were training grounds for ministry of the *soul*. While social activism was valued, programs to provide aid for the poor were viewed as secondary to salvation of the human soul.
5. Jay Grimstead, "How the International Council on Biblical Inerrancy Began." http://65.175.91.69/Reformation_net/Pages/ICBI_Background.htm. Grimstead was a personal friend of and colaborer with the late apologist Francis Schaeffer. Papers from Summit II were published in Earl D. Radmacher and Robert D. Preus, eds., *Hermeneutics, Inerrancy, and the Bible* (Grand Rapids: Zondervan, 1984). Papers from Summit III were published in Kenneth S. Kantzer, ed., *Applying the Scriptures* (Grand Rapids: Zondervan, 1987).
6. "Records of the International Council on Biblical Inerrancy." http://library.dts.edu/Pages/TL/Special/ICBI.shtml.
7. Biles, Roger, *Richard J. Daley: Politics, Race, and Governing Chicago* (DeKalb: Northern Illinois University Press, 1995), 7.
8. David W. Stowe and Malcolm Magee, "David W. Stowe: A Conversation About the Jesus Movement with Malcolm Magee," April 17, 2013. http://uncpressblog.com/2013/04/17/david-w-stowe-a-conversation-about-the-jesus-movement-with-malcolm-magee/.
9. Todd Gitlin, *The Sixties: Years of Hope, Days of Rage* (New York: Bantam Books, 1993), 436, 437.
10. Evidence of this can be found in Randall Balmer, *Thy Kingdom Come: An Evangelical's Lament: How the Religious Right Distorts the Faith and Threatens America*. (New York: Basic Books, 2006); Eskridge, "God's Forever Family"; and David W. Stowe, *No Sympathy for the Devil: Christian Pop Music and the Transformation of American Evangelicalism* (Chapel Hill: University of North Carolina Press, 2011).
11. Stowe and Magee, "Conversation."
12. Ibid. Emphasis added.
13. Balmer, *Thy Kingdom Come*, 147.
14. Gitlin, *The Sixties*, 84.
15. James J. Farrell, *The Spirit of the Sixties: The Making of Postwar Radicalism* (New York: Routledge, 1997), 28.
16. See Todd Gitlin and Nanci Hollander, *Uptown: Poor Whites in Chicago* (New York: Harper & Row, 1970).
17. Rossinow, *Politics of Authenticity*, 302.
18. See Gitlin and Hollander, *Uptown*.
19. Cornfield, "Urban Communes," 115–26.

20. Jon Trott, "Life's Lessons: A History of Jesus People USA: Part Five: Who Is My Neighbor?" *Cornerstone* 24, no. 107: 45.
21. Thomas, "Ronald Reagan."
22. Ibid.
23. Trott, "Part 7: Action—Social and Political, I."
24. Thomas, "Ronald Reagan."
25. Trott, "Part 7: Action—Social and Political, I."
26. Ibid.
27. Ibid.
28. Herrin, interview, March 10, 2009.
29. Ibid.
30. Gitlin, *The Sixties*, 326.
31. Jim Wallis, *God's Politics: Why the Right Gets It Wrong and the Left Doesn't Get It* (New York: HarperCollins, 2005), 34.
32. Ibid., 3.
33. Ibid., 5.
34. Ibid., xxiii.
35. Jon Trott, email, January 15, 2010.
36. Ibid.
37. Marsden, *Religion*, 248–49. Emphasis added.
38. Balmer, *Thy Kingdom Come*, 105. I thank the journal *Religions* for giving me permission to reprint part of this section from Young, "Into the Grey," 498–522.
39. Students for a Democratic Society, *Port Huron Statement*, June 15, 1962. http://history.hanover.edu/courses/excerpts/111hur.html.
40. "Uptown," *Cornerstone* 6, no. 40:4.
41. Kanter, *Commitment and Community*, 191.
42. Jon Trott, "Part 2: House and Home." *A History of Jesus People USA.* http://www.jpusa.org/lessons2.html. Emphasis added.
43. Sanctified protestation known as "flirty fishing," plural marriage known "sharing," and allegations of pedophilia.
44. See James D. Chancellor, *Life in the Family: An Oral History of the Children of God* (Syracuse: Syracuse University Press, 2000).
45. Raye Clemente, interview by author, digital recording, Chicago, March 5, 2010.
46. Joshua Davenport, interview by author, digital recording, Chicago, March 6, 2010.
47. Otto Jensen, interview by author, digital recording, Chicago, March 10, 2009.
48. Dietrich Bonhoeffer, *The Cost of Discipleship* (New York: Simon & Schuster, 1959), 191.
49. Jon Trott quotes Bonhoeffer in "House and Home." The quote can also be found in "Citizens of Two Worlds," *Cornerstone* 5, no. 30: 4–5.
50. Kantner, *Commitment and Community*, 213.
51. Jon Trott, email, June 21, 2010.

4. BIG SHOULDERS, BIG COMMUNITY

52. "In the End . . . Man Created Chicago," *Cornerstone* no. 22: 8.
53. Over the years, many articles in *Cornerstone* dealt with unresolved poverty. See Mike Hertenstein and Chris Ramsey, "Want in the Land of Plenty," *Cornerstone* 12, no. 69: 6–9; "That American Way," *Cornerstone* 6, no. 41: 15; "Behind the Velvet Curtain-Suburbia," *Cornerstone* 7, no. 42: 15; Larry Bishop, "The American Myth," *Cornerstone* 9, no. 53: 16–18; Larry Bishop, "The Delusion of Desire," *Cornerstone* 10, no. 58: 30–32; Jon Trott, "Progress & Poverty," *Cornerstone* no. 59: 58–60.
54. "Uptown," 4.
55. See the sections on businesses and structure in chapter 3. I thank my wife, Martha Young, who helped me flesh out this idea.
56. Zinn, "Marxism," 371.

5. THEOLOGY, POLITICS, AND CULTURE

1. Gordon, "Comparison."
2. I use this term in an attempt to explain how JPUSA balances social outreach to the poor with an equal appreciation for spiritual mindedness.
3. Gordon, "Comparison."
4. Alex R. Schaefer, "Evangelicalism, Social Reform and the US Welfare State, 1970–1996," in *Religious and Secular Reform in America: Ideas, Beliefs and Social Change*, ed. David K. Adams and Cornelis A. Van Minnen (New York: New York University Press, 1999), 254.
5. Stowe and Magee, "Conversation."
6. D. G. Hart, *Deconstructing Evangelicalism: Conservative Protestantism in the Age of Billy Graham* (Grand Rapids: Baker Books, 2005).
7. Nathan O. Hatch, *The Democratization of American Christianity* (New Haven: Yale University Press, 1989).
8. Emergent Christianity represents a "conversation" among evangelicals who are disenchanted with traditional, conservative evangelicalism and the Religious Right. More significantly, emergent represents an attempt by evangelicals to engage postmodernity, cultural pluralism, and literary deconstruction while retaining Christian belief—even orthodoxy—albeit defined differently. Some describe themselves as "postevangelical." See works by Brian McLaren, Tony Jones, Phyllis Tickle, Marcus Borg, Mark Driscoll, Robert Webber, and Jenell Williams Paris.
9. David W. Bebbington, *The Dominance of Evangelicalism: The Age of Spurgeon and Moody* (Downers Grove, Ill.: InterVarsity Press, 2005).
10. Jon Trott began to distance himself from evangelicalism after George W. Bush came into office.
11. Preston Shires, *Hippies of the Religious Right* (Waco: Baylor University Press, 2007).

5. THEOLOGY, POLITICS, AND CULTURE

12. Marsden, *Religion*.
13. Shires, *Hippies*, 113.
14. A parallel universe also formed among Christians in the New Left as members of the YMCA at the University of Texas at Austin read the works of Albert Camus, Paul Tillich, and Martin Luther King, Jr. See Rossinow, *Politics of Authenticity*.
15. Shires, *Hippies*, 51.
16. Miller, *American Protestantism*, 22.
17. Ibid., 22–23.
18. Ronald M. Enroth, *The Jesus People: Old-Time Religion in the Age of* Aquarius (Grand Rapids: Eerdmans, 1972), 168. H. Richard Niebuhr originally used the term in *Christ and Culture* (New York: Harper & Row, 1951.
19. Grant Wacker, "The Functions of Faith in Primitive Pentecostalism." *Harvard Theological Review* 77, no. 3/4 (July–October 1984): 368.
20. Ibid., 369.
21. Shires, *Hippies*, 153–55, 108. Emphasis added.
22. Stowe, *No Sympathy*, 70–74.
23. Ibid., 70–71.
24. Ibid., 70–74.
25. Glenn Kaiser, email, February 22, 2010.
26. Gordon, "Comparison," 85.
27. It is believed that the tribulation will be a time of great suffering caused by the anti-Christ. Some believe Christians will be raptured before while others believe they will be raptured after.
28. Kaiser, email, February 22, 2010.
29. Otto Jensen, interview by author, digital recording, Chicago, March 10, 2009. George Marsden classifies this "kingdom now" thinking as a liberal position in *Reforming Fundamentalism: Fuller Seminary and the New Evangelicalism* (Grand Rapids: Eerdmans, 1987), 81.
30. Jon Trott, bluechristian.blogspot.com, January 14, 2008.
31. Emergent theology is best understood as an evangelical attempt to retain elements of orthodox Christianity while also accepting postmodern critical theory and cultural pluralism. For more on this, see Brian McLaren, *A Generous Orthodoxy* (Grand Rapids: Zondervan, 2006), or John R. Franke, *Manifold Witness: The Plurality of Truth* (Nashville: Abingdon Press, 2009).
32. Jon Trott, interview by author, digital recording, Chicago, March 11, 2009.
33. Ibid.
34. Shari Lloyd and Linda LaFianza, email, February 18, 2010.
35. See Young, "Into the Grey," 498–522. Also Jon Trott, email, January 15, 2010.
36. See Stowe, *No Sympathy*; Shires, *Hippies*; Balmer, *Thy Kingdom Come*; and Duane Murray Oldfield, *The Right and the Righteous: The Christian Right Confronts the Republican Party* (Lanham, Md.: Rowman & Littlefield, 1996).

5. THEOLOGY, POLITICS, AND CULTURE

37. See Balmer, *Thy Kingdom Come*. This work demonstrates that the Right has essentially co-opted evangelicalism, creating a caricature of the evangelical Christian. This distortion causes nonevangelicals to associate evangelicalism with political coalitions rather than historically defined evangelical Christianity, which has been more concerned with individual conversion rather than nationalistic power structures seeking to create a mythic "Christian nation."
38. For example, some JPUSA communards argue that abortion can be resolved by adopting a leftist orientation. Jon Trott encapsulates what many in JPUSA believe regarding this issue in a blog titled "President Obama, Health Care, Abortion, and the Right's Credibility Gap," *Blue Christian on a Red Background*, September 10, 2009. http://bluechristian.blogspot.com. Trott has also explained this position in an email correspondence with me on May 16, 2010. This combination of leftist politics and an antiabortion position is not unprecedented. The Farm, headed by countercultural icon Stephen Gaskin, is a commune near Summertown, Tennessee, and was antiabortion, offering a home for single, pregnant mothers in an attempt to offer assistance. See Miller, *60s Communes*, 120.
39. Trott, interview, March 11, 2009. The quotes immediately below are all from this interview.
40. Perkins is also the president of the John M. Perkins Foundation for Reconciliation and Development. He began his relationship with JPUSA when the Rez Band was on the road and then, though aged, continued to lecture at the festival.
41. Trott, interview, March 11, 2009.
42. Colleen Davick, interview by author, digital recording, Chicago, March 10, 2009.
43. Like other conservative evangelical Christians, many early Jesus freaks (though not all) believed that the United States was intended to be a Christian nation, one that needed to return to God. Many converts became part of baby boomer evangelical Christianity, much of which believed the nation had become highjacked by secular humanism. Ironically, those on the left, such as Jim Wallis, Anthony Campolo, and Randall Balmer, believe the Religious Right highjacked Christianity.
44. For an understanding of the relationship between Christian eschatology in American society and social reform, see David S. Katz and Richard H. Popkin, *Messianic Revolution: Radical Religious Politics to the End of the Second Millennium* (New York: Hill & Wang, 1999); Shires, *Hippies*; Balmer, *Thy Kingdom Come*; and Oldfield, *Right and the Righteous*.
45. Kaiser, email, February 22, 2010.
46. Trott, interview, March 11, 2009. Quotes immediately below are all from this interview.
47. Ibid.
48. John Herrin, interview by author, digital recording, Chicago, March 10, 2009.

5. THEOLOGY, POLITICS, AND CULTURE

49. Pauline Lipman, *The New Political Economy: Neoliberalism, Race, and the Right to City* (New York: Routledge, 2011), 7.
50. Ibid., 9.
51. Ibid., 19.
52. Ibid., 23.
53. Ibid., 25.
54. Ibid.
55. Ibid., 66–67.
56. Chancellor, *Life in the Family*, 11, 17, 101–3, 106–7, 140–42, 150, 282.
57. Members of the Children of God (mostly women, though not only) were encouraged to engage in prostitution for the purpose of missionizing. The practice, referencing the biblical call to becoming "fishers of men," attracted new members. While many in COG still view the doctrine as sound, the practice is no longer used. See ibid., 9–11, 16–17, 22–23, 116, 119–27, 128–30.
58. See ibid.; and John W. Drakeford, *Children of Doom: A Sobering Look at the Commune Movement* (Nashville: Broadman Press, 1972).
59. Before the Religious Right came to power, notable conservative ministers (particularly Southern Baptists) were actually prochoice, owing to their acceptance of the separation of church and state. Historian Randall Balmer has demonstrated that social issues such as abortion were popularized merely to mobilize conservative voters in service to the culture war. Contrary to other histories pertaining to the Religious Right, the movement formed in response to Bob Jones University's policies, which amounted to de facto racial segregation. *Roe v. Wade* merely served as a convenient (and less controversial) issue around which to rally conservatives. See Balmer, *Thy Kingdom Come*.
60. Gordon, "Comparison," 51–52.
61. John Herrin, email, November 15, 2010.
62. Glen van Alkemade, interview by author, digital recording, Chicago, March 21, 2010.
63. Marsden, *Religion*, 276.
64. Ibid. Marsden also deals with the matter of evangelical and fundamentalist Christianity's relationship to culture and society in *Fundamentalism and American Culture: The Shaping of Twentieth-Century Evangelicalism, 1870–1925*, 2nd ed. (Oxford: Oxford University Press, 2006), and *Reforming Fundamentalism*.
65. Frank Schaeffer, "The Only Thing Evangelicals Will Never Forgive Is Not Hating the 'Other,'" *Religion Dispatches* (2009). http://www.religiondispatches.org/archive/rdbook/2097/the_only_thing_evangelicals_will_never_forgive_is_not_hating_the_%E2%80%-9Cother%E2%80%9D/?page=2.
66. These two paragraphs are from Young, "Apocalyptic Music," 51–67.
67. The work of Timothy Miller and Barry Shenker explores the communal impulse to create the model society, with the hope that the larger culture will follow.

5. THEOLOGY, POLITICS, AND CULTURE

68. Jon Pahl, *Empire of Sacrifice: The Religious Origins of American Violence* (New York: New York University Press, 2010).
69. Brian McLaren, "Why I'm Voting for Barack Obama . . . and I Hope You Will too: Reason 4: The Environment." http://www.brianmclaren.net/archives/ blog/why-im-voting-for-barack-obama-a-2.html. See also Brian McLaren, *A Generous Orthodoxy* (Grand Rapids: Zondervan, 2004).
70. Many leaders of the Evangelical Left, such as Randall Balmer, Jim Wallis, Tony Jones, and, to lesser degrees, Anthony Campolo, and Brian McLaren, have gone further in their acceptance of situations where abortion might be the only alternative (with varying degrees, as does JPUSA). What is more distinct is the difference in opinion over gay marriage and how homosexuality is generally considered. Although some leaders and many second-generation members of JPUSA have more tolerant views on same-sex unions (when compared with the views of conservative evangelicals), the Evangelical Left often extends tolerance to the acceptance of gay marriage and discounts the oft-held belief that homosexuality represents a "struggle" or "sin."
71. By this I intend to suggest that some evangelicals during the Jesus Movement (particularly those during the rise of the Religious Right) engaged social issues with an agenda that was largely Restorationist. While many remained premillennialists, they also attempted to engineer the kingdom of God by building coalitions meant to create legislation that would satisfy special interest groups on the Right. The goal was to restore the nation to its mythical roots of a Christian nation, reengage social activism, albeit a different kind (when compared with nineteenth-century progressives), while also affirming millenarianism.
72. For detailed examples of Christian isolationists, see Chancellor, *Life in the Family*, and Drakeford, *Children of Doom*. Donald E. Miller notes the differences between "new paradigm" and megachurch rightists and the social liberalism of the mainline in *American Protestantism*. A good source for understanding the rapid rise to power within the ranks of evangelicalism is Michael D. Lindsay's *Faith in the Halls of Power: How Evangelicals Joined the American Elite* (New York: Oxford University Press, 2007).
73. Kaiser, email, February 22, 2010.
74. James Davidson Hunter, *Evangelicalism: The Coming Generation* (Chicago: University of Chicago Press, 1993), 41.
75. Miller, *American Protestantism*, 109.
76. For more on this, see Balmer, *Thy Kingdom Come*, 195. See also Lindsay, *Faith*; and Luhr, *Witnessing Suburbia*.
77. Stowe, *No Sympathy*, 77.
78. Jim Wallis, "The Global Church and America's War," September 13, 2001. http:// www.huffingtonpost.com/jim-wallis/the-global-church-and-ame_b_64326 .html.

79. Brian McLaren, "Needed: Christians Thinking Differently About the Future," June 3, 2010. http://www.huffingtonpost.com/brian-d-mclaren/christian-eschatology_b_598868.html.
80. Ibid.
81. There is a history of apathy toward social justice, as well as a suspicion of those who preach doctrines of social reform rather than individual reform. This, of course, predates Jesus freaks. Some of the most immediate predecessors are Moody, Darby, Spurgeon, and the Puritans. Those who have often been skeptical of global efforts toward peace and justice have cited 1 Thessalonians 5:3: "While people are saying, 'Peace and safety,' destruction will come on them suddenly, as labor pains on a pregnant woman, and they will not escape" (NIV).
82. Herrin, interview, March 10, 2009.
83. Joshua Davenport, interview by author, digital recording. Chicago, March 6, 2010.
84. Communards such as Raye Clemente and Tamzen Trott have expressed a desire to help the homeless. The desire to serve is independent of any religious belief or impulse.
85. Christian Smith, *American Evangelicalism Embattled and Thriving* (Chicago: University of Chicago Press, 1998), 106, 107. Smith alters Peter Berger's concept of plausibility structures of religious belief as related to "sacred canopie" (see *The Sacred Canopy* [New York: Anchor, 1967]) to argue that the metaphor of a "sacred umbrella" is more useful in describing religious belief within the context of modernity. Smith argues that belief is sustainable and manageable by evaluating practices and worldviews not in relation to "everyone conceivable" but merely to "members of their own reference group. Although JPUSA engages the "real world," its "sacred umbrellas" provide a mobile mechanism that reminds its members of their community of support, which validates religious belief, unlike other persons of faith who must negotiate modernity without an ever-present ideological anchor—one that governs one's entire existence. That is, communal living provides ongoing reinforcement of belief.
86. Preston Shires and Ronald Enroth provide evidence that suggests that early Jesus Movement converts engaged society for the purpose of securing converts before the rapture. JPUSA, on the other hand, engages society with the hope of bettering society.

6. THE CHRISTIAN WOODSTOCK

1. Luhr, *Witnessing Suburbia*, 71.
2. Marsden, *Religion*, 68.
3. Ibid., 189.
4. Oldfield, *Right and the Righteous*, 49–50.

6. THE CHRISTIAN WOODSTOCK

5. Luhr, *Witnessing Suburbia*, 33.
6. Ibid., 101.
7. Ibid., 136.
8. Young, "Apocalyptic Music, 51–67.
9. Andrew Beaujon, *Body Piercing Saved My Life: Inside the Phenomenon of Christian Rock* (Cambridge, Mass.: Da Capo Press, 2006), 179–81.
10. Eskridge, "God's Forever Family," 20.
11. Beaujon, *Body Piercing*, 34.
12. http://www.amygrant.com/music.
13. Beaujon, *Body Piercing*, 31.
14. Ibid., 32.
15. Jay R. Howard, and John M. Streck, *Apostles of Rock: The Splintered World of Contemporary Christian Music* (Lexington: University Press of Kentucky, 1999), 49.
16. Bill Mankin. "Peace, Love and . . . We Can All Join In: How Rock Festivals Helped Change America," *Like the Dew: A Journal of Southern Culture and Politics*, March 4, 2012. http://likethedew.com/2012/03/04/we-can-all-join-in-how-rock-festivals-helped-change-america/.
17. John G. Turner. "The Christian Woodstock," *Wall Street Journal*, January 18, 2008.
18. Ibid.
19. Shires, *Hippies*, 121.
20. Ichthus, "The Ichthus Music Festival Is Back! Creation Festivals Helps Keep the Ichthus Festival Legacy Alive!" http://ichthus.org/.
21. Javier Espinoza, "The Beat Goes On," *Wall Street Journal*, July 5, 2013. http://online.wsj.com/article/SB10001424127887324436104578579112994316642.html?KEYWORDS=rock+festivals.
22. Ibid.
23. "'Family Guy' and Terror; Stars and Addiction; 'Holy Hollywood'; Interview with Actor Stephen Baldwin." *Showbiz Tonight*. Transcripts. Show aired October 2, 2006. http://transcripts.cnn.com/TRANSCRIPTS/0610/02/sbt.01.html.
24. During the 1970s and 1980s, the contemporary Christian music industry and the Gospel Music Association produced music that put forth an obvious Christian message, mentioning the word "Jesus" as often as possible. Musicians who sought to compose songs using metaphor and ambiguity were typically not labeled "Christian" when considering categories and marketing. During the 1990s more Christian musicians felt freer to compose songs that dealt with a number of topics. Cornerstone antedates this.
25. Jon Trott, "Part 6: Cornerstone Festival," *A History of Jesus People USA*. http://www.jpusa.org/lessons6.html.
26. "'Family Guy' and Terror."
27. Van Alkemade, interview, March 21, 2010.

28. Dick Hebdige, *Subculture: The Meaning of Style* (New York: Routledge, 2002), 102.
29. Hard-core music groups rupture the performer-fan relationship by inviting fans on stage. Hard-core concerts involve a stage filled with fans who share the same spotlight, implying there is no distinction between the band and the fan. In like manner, punk bands during the 1970s often spat at the audience, thus erasing lines of distinction.
30. Lawrence Grossberg, "The Affective Sensibility of Fandom," in *The Adoring Audience: Fan Culture and Popular Media*, ed. Lisa Lewis (New York: Routledge, 1992), 308.
31. Victor Turner, *The Ritual Process: Structure and Anti-Structure* (Chicago: Aldine De Gruyter, 1995), 25.
32. Simon Frith, "Towards an Aesthetic of Popular Music," in *Music and Society: The Politics of Composition, Performance, and Reception*, ed. Richard Leppert and Susan McClary (New York: Cambridge University Press, 1989), 140.
33. Ibid., 144.
34. Sarah Thornton, *Club Cultures: Music, Media and Subcultural Capital* (Middletown, Conn.: Wesleyan University Press, 1996), 18.
35. Grossberg, "Affective Sensibility," 308.
36. McAlister, "What Is Your Heart For?," 883.
37. Ibid., 883–84.
38. Lawrence Grossberg, "Putting the Pop Back into Postmodernism." *Social Text* 21 (1989): 169.
39. Alan P. Merriam, *The Anthropology of Music* (Evanston: Northwestern University Press, 1964), 213.
40. See Christopher Small, *Musicking: The Meanings of Performing and Listening* (Middletown, Conn.: Wesleyan University Press, 1998).
41. One musical example is Pedro the Lion, known for heterodoxy, leftist politics, and language often deemed unacceptable within the context of teenagers. Conservative festivalgoers have stated that they were amazed that the group was allowed to perform on the main stage, a venue often peopled by church youth groups. The more visible examples apply to the seminars. A number of theological, philosophical, and political opinions were represented at seminars. While some who attended were challenged in their own paradigms, others often engaged in robust debates.
42. Grossberg, "Putting the Pop Back into Postmodernism," 169.
43. Doug Van Pelt, email, May 30, 2010.
44. Tooth & Nail records formed as a result of Cornerstone and paved the way for a new generation of evangelical rock musicians seeking to break out of the previously cast CCM mold. See *Cornerstone Festival: Twenty Years and Counting*, prod. and dir. John J. Thompson (Nashville: Floodgate Records, 2002), DVD.
45. Mark Allan Powell, email, June 1, 2010.
46. Doug Van Pelt, email, May 29, 2010.

6. THE CHRISTIAN WOODSTOCK

47. Linda LaFianza and Shari Lloyd, email, June 4, 2010.
48. Barry Alfonso, *The Billboard Guide to Contemporary Christian Music* (New York: Billboard Books, 2002), 30.
49. "Award Eligibility: C." *GMA Dove Awards 2009–2010 Policy & Procedures Manual for GMA Professional, Associate, and Student Members.* http://www.doveawardsvoting.com/2009_Policy_Procedures_Manual.pdf.
50. Christian music producer and author Charlie Peacock has discussed the state of the Christian music industry and the debates over what qualifies as "Christian" music in *At The Crossroads: Inside the Past, Present, and Future of Contemporary Christian Music*, rev. ed. (Colorado Springs: Shaw/Waterbrook Press/Random House, 2004).
51. Mark Allan Powell, email, October 24, 2006.
52. Powell, *Encyclopedia*, 13.
53. The 77s, "Woody," Brainstorm Artists, Intl., 1992.
54. The 77s, "The Lust, the Flesh, the Eyes & the Pride of Life," Exit/Island Records, 1987.
55. Doug Van Pelt, email, June 3, 2010.
56. Van Alkemade, interview, March 21, 2010.
57. Beaujon, *Body Piercing*, 3.
58. Van Pelt, email, May 30, 2010.
59. Herrin, interview, March 10, 2009.
60. Van Pelt, email, May 30, 2010.
61. Henri Lefebvre, *The Production of Space* (Oxford: Blackwell, 1991), 59.
62. *Bleed into One*, prod. and dir. Steve Taylor, Imperial Pictures, forthcoming, documentary.
63. Van Pelt, email, May 30, 2010.
64. *Cornerstone Festival*.
65. Jay R. Howard, email, June 4, 2010.
66. Ibid.
67. LaFianza and Lloyd, email, June 4, 2010.
68. Beaujon, *Body Piercing*, 35.
69. Ibid., 36.
70. Charlie Peacock is a Grammy award–winning, multiformat songwriter and record producer. Production and songwriting credits include Switchfoot, Karl Denson's Tiny Universe, Ladysmith Black Mambazo, Béla Fleck, Leigh Nash, Al Green, Tommy and the Whale, Warren Barfield, Maeve, Sam & Ruby, Savannah, Amy Grant, Sixpence None The Richer, Sara Groves, Nikki Williams, Anna Owens, Audio Adrenaline, Sarah Masen, David Crowder Band, Avalon, Philip Bailey, dcTalk, Margaret Becker, Out of the Grey, Twila Paris, and CeCe Winans.
71. Charlie Peacock, "The Future of Christian Music: Peacock's Prognostication." *CCMmagazine.com*. http://www.ccmmagazine.com/news/stories/11571162/.

7. THE FUTURE

72. LaFianza and Lloyd, email, June 4, 2010.
73. According to this festival's website, the name "Wild Goose" can be attributed to the festival staff members' understanding of Celtic Christianity: "In the spirit of vibrant, category-defying Celtic Christianity, we saw our desire embodied in the Celtic Church's way of speaking about the enigmatic Holy Spirit: The Wild Goose, who wanders where she will. Who can tame her? No one. Far better it is to embark on a Wild Goose Chase, and see the terrain of our faith be transformed." Wild Goose Festival. http://www.wildgoosefestival.org/about-2/getting-in-touch/.
74. Grossberg, "Putting the Pop Back into Postmodernism," 168–69.
75. Ibid., 169.
76. Ibid., 181.
77. Eric Pement, email, June 15, 2010.
78. Grossberg, "Putting the Pop Back into Postmodernism," 168.
79. Jon Pahl was the respondent to my presentation on JPUSA and Cornerstone at the American Historical Association. His response was titled "Alternatives to What? New Religions and Intentional Communities in Recent American History," paper presented at the Annual Conference of the American Historical Association, Boston, January 6, 2011.
80. Grossberg, "Putting the Pop Back into Postmodernism," 179.
81. Herrin, interview, March 10, 2009.
82. "'Family Guy' and Terror."
83. Terry Scott Taylor states this in the DVD about Cornerstone when recalling how his band, Daniel Amos, would often prepare for the festival. See *Cornerstone Festival*
84. Beaujon, *Body Piercing*, 12.
85. Herrin, interview, March 10, 2009.
86. Trott, "Part 6: Cornerstone Festival." Originally printed by Don McLeese in "Praising Jesus with Heavy-Metal Beat," *Chicago Sun-Times*, June 29, 1984.
87. Andrew Beaujon. "Hallelujah Palooza Faith and Rock Mosh Together at Christian Music Festival," *Washington Post*, July 7, 2004. http://www.washingtonpost.com/wp-dyn/articles/A32667-2004Jul6.html.
88. Miller, *American Protestantism*, 11–13, 67, 180–85.
89. Rossinow, *Politics of Authenticity*, 251.
90. Stephen A. Marini, *Sacred Song in America: Religion, Music, and Public Culture* (Champaign: University of Illinois Press, 2003), 30.

7. THE FUTURE

1. Chancellor, *Life in the Family*, xxi.
2. Nathan Cameron, interview, March 20, 2010.
3. Ibid.

7. THE FUTURE

4. The Jesus Movement spawned a number of controversial groups, such as The Children of God, The Way International, the Tony and Susan Alamo Christian Foundation, and Jim Jones's Peoples Temple. These created media hype and kept evangelicals engaged in cult awareness. JPUSA has to define itself against these groups to gain favor with establishment evangelicalism.
5. In earlier years, all JPUSA communards were assigned a "buddy." Everyone has to have a buddy with them at all times.
6. Christopher Wiitala, interview by author, digital recording, Chicago, March 6, 2010.
7. While he recognizes that part of communal life includes shared property, Christopher Wiitala expressed frustration with how often privacy is breached and how it is merely assumed that a child is being watched, or that anyone asked will agree to babysit. Ibid.
8. "Millennials: A Portrait of Generation Next." February 24, 2010. http://www.pewresearch.org/millennials/.
9. Kanter, *Commitment and Community*, 144.
10. Tamzen Trott, interview by author, digital recording, Chicago, March 21, 2010; Scarlett Shelby, interview by author, digital recording, Chicago, March 7, 2010. This has also been expressed in the trailer of a forthcoming documentary about kids who have been born and raised in JPUSA: *Born: Growing Up in a Religious Commune*, trailer, prod. and dir. Jaime Prater. http://www.bornthefilm.com.
11. Jon Trott, interview by author, digital recording, Chicago, March 11, 2010.
12. Wiitala, interview, March 6, 2010. Other rules included a ban on various forms of secular music. The ban was later lifted.
13. Amy Moss, interview by author, digital recording, Chicago, March 7, 2010.
14. Chancellor, *Life in the Family*, 90.
15. "Susan" [pseud.], interview, March 21, 2010.
16. Kanter, *Commitment and Community*, 129.
17. Joel Williams, interview by author, digital recording, Chicago, March 21, 2010.
18. Ronald M. Enroth, *Recovering from Churches That Abuse* (Grand Rapids: Zondervan, 1994), 125–28.
19. "Susan" [pseud.], interview, March 31, 2010.
20. Kanter, *Commitment and Community*, 143.
21. Wiitala, interview, March 6, 2010.
22. Kanter, *Commitment and Community*, 83.
23. Shelby, interview, March 7, 2010.
24. Scott, interview.
25. Eric Pement, email, June 15, 2010.
26. Barbara Pement, email, June 28, 2010.
27. Ibid.
28. Barbara Pement, email, June 29, 2010.

7. THE FUTURE

29. Ibid.
30. *No Place to Call Home*, prod. and dir. Jaime Prater, http://www.kickstarter.com/projects/1722853758/no-place-to-call-home-growing-up-in-a-religious-co.; and *Born*.
31. *No Place to Call Home*. Quotes in subsequent paragraphs are all from this film unless otherwise noted.
32. Timothy C. Morgan. "Dozens of Children Abused at Evangelical Commune, Adult Survivors Allege," *Christianity Today*, February 28, 2014. http://www.christianitytoday.com/gleanings/2014/february/dozens-of-children-abused-at-evangelical-jpusa-jesus-people.html.
33. Judith Valente. "Jesus People Documentary Sheds Light on Religious Community's Darker Stories." *USA Today*, April 7, 2014. http://www.usatoday.com/story/news/nation/2014/04/07/jesus-people-community-documentary/7444017/.
34. *No Place to Call Home*
35. Ibid.
36. Leaders would also affirm that spiritual maturation is also the result of the Holy Spirit.
37. Kirsten Scharnberg, "Exodus from Commune Ignites Battle for Souls: Second of Two Parts," *Chicago Tribune*, April 2, 2001.
38. *Born*.
39. See ibid. and Enroth, *Recovering from Churches That Abuse*.
40. Kanter, *Commitment and Community*, 130.
41. Chitu Okoli, email, March 9, 2010.
42. Pement, email, June 28, 2010.
43. Okoli, email, March 9, 2010.
44. A minor distinction that emphasizes the choice to join or to leave. This also is a term used to disarm negative views associated with the word "commune."
45. Shupe, "Jesus People USA," 37.
46. Instructed in the ways of Christianity and held accountable during the process of training.
47. These terms have been used to describe persons who join the community a few weeks before the Cornerstone Festival for the purpose of gaining free admission to the event. Some choose to remain in the community while others leave.
48. Matthew 25:40.
49. Eric Pement, email, June 15, 2010.
50. "Jesus People USA Evangelical Covenant Church," *Our Statement of Faith*. http://www.jpusa.org/faith.html.
51. Pement, email, June 15, 2010.
52. Bebbington, *Dominance*.
53. Pement, email, June 15, 2010.
54. John Herrin, email, December 2, 2010.
55. Ibid.

7. THE FUTURE

56. Ibid.
57. Bonhoeffer, *Cost of Discipleship*, 191.
58. Jon Trott quotes this in "House and Home," *A History of Jesus People USA*. http://www.jpusa.org/lessons1b.html.
59. Kanter, *Commitment and Community*, 213.
60. Ibid.
61. Ruth Tucker, "JPUSA Is Family: Observations by Ruth Tucker," *Cornerstone* 22, no. 102/103 (1994): 41; William Backus, "Who's Abusing Who? A Letter to JPUSA from Psychologist and Author William Backus on Dr. Ronald Enroth's Methodology," *Cornerstone* 22, no. 102/103 (1994): 35–36; Jon Trott, "Is Abuse About Truth or Story: Or Both? One Intentional Community's Painful Experience with False Accusations," *Cornerstone* online. http://www.cornerstonemag.com/features/web01/truthorstory01.html.
62. Kanter, *Commitment and Community*, 146.

8. CONCLUSION

1. Young, "Into the Grey," 498–522.
2. Ibid.
3. David F. Gordon, "The Role of the Local Social Context in Social Movement Accommodation: A Case Study of Two Jesus People Groups," *Journal for the Scientific Study of Religion* 23, no. 4 (December 1984): 394.
4. Kanter, *Commitment and Community*, 142.
5. Ibid., 146.
6. Larry Eskridge, "'One Way': Billy Graham, the Jesus Generation, and the Idea of an Evangelical Youth Culture," *Church History* 67, no. 1 (March 1998): 104.
7. Part of this paragraph is from Young, "Apocalyptic Music," 109–22.
8. Daniel Radosh, *Rapture Ready: Adventures in the Parallel Universe of Christian Pop Culture* (New York: Scribner, 2008), 188.
9. Mark Allan Powell, email, January 2, 2011.
10. Music groups such as Pedro the Lion represent a nebulous form of evangelical Christianity that both affirms a certain exclusivity about Jesus while also remaining skeptical about evangelical expressions that too quickly judge the validity of other truth-claims. Thus groups like this (and others at Cornerstone) typify a gentler form of evangelical Christianity.
11. Miller, *American Protestantism*, 87.
12. Ibid., 122.
13. Rachel Held Evans. "Why Millennials Are Leaving the Church," *CNN*, July 27, 2013. http://religion.blogs.cnn.com/2013/07/27/why-millennials-are-leaving-the-church/.
14. Grossberg, "Putting the Pop Back into Postmodernism," 179.
15. Ibid., 180.

8. CONCLUSION

16. Julia Duin, "PAPA Festival Highlights Christianity, Anarchism and Community Spirit," *Washington Post*, September 1, 2011. http://articles.washingtonpost.com/2011-09-01/lifestyle/35275137_1_community-kitchen-brethren-church-christian3.
17. AudioFeed.https://www.facebook.com/Audiofeedfestival/info.
18. Philip Goff and Alan Heimert, "Revivals and Revolution: Historiographic Turns Since Alan Heimert's 'Religion and the American Mind,'" *Church History* 67, no. 4 (December 1998): 695–96.

BIBLIOGRAPHY

✴ ✴ ✴

Abraham, Laurie. "Refugee Families Face Eviction by Rehabber." *Chicago Sun-Times*, August 1986.

Adorno, Theodor W., and Max Horkheimer. "The Culture Industry: Enlightenment as Mass Deception." In *Dialectic of Enlightenment*. New York: Continuum, 1993. First published as *Dialektik der Aufklarung*, 1944.

———. *Essays on Music*. Berkeley: University of California Press, 2002.

Alfonso, Barry. *The Billboard Guide to Contemporary Christian* Music. New York: Billboard Books, 2002.

Attali, Jacques. *Noise: The Political Economy of Music*. Minneapolis: University of Minnesota Press, 1985.

"Award Eligibility: C." *GMA Dove Awards 2009–2010 Policy & Procedures Manual for GMA Professional, Associate, and Student Members*. http://www.gospelmusic.org/dovevoting//2009_Policy_Procedures_Manual.pdf.

Backus, William. "Who's Abusing Who? A Letter to JPUSA from Psychologist and Author William Backus on Dr. Ronald Enroth's Methodology." *Cornerstone* 22, no. 102/103 (1994): 35–36.

Balmer, Randall. *Thy Kingdom Come: An Evangelical's Lament: How the Religious Right Distorts the Faith and Threatens America*. New York: Basic Books, 2006.

Beaujon, Andrew. *Body Piercing Saved My Life: Inside the Phenomenon of Christian Rock*. Cambridge, Mass.: Da Capo Press, 2006.

———. "Hallelujah Palooza Faith and Rock Mosh Together at Christian Music Festival." *Washington Post*, July 7, 2004. http://www.washingtonpost.com/wp-dyn/articles/A32667-2004Jul6.html.

Bebbington, David W. *The Dominance of Evangelicalism: The Age of Spurgeon and Moody*. Downers Grove, Ill.: InterVarsity Press, 2005.

BIBLIOGRAPHY

"Behind the Velvet Curtain-Suburbia." *Cornerstone* 7, no. 42: 15.

Biles, Roger. *Richard J. Daley: Politics, Race, and Governing Chicago*. DeKalb: Northern Illinois University Press, 1995.

Bishop, Larry. "The American Myth." *Cornerstone* 9, no. 53: 16–18.

———. "The Delusion of Desire." *Cornerstone* 10, no. 58: 30–32.

Bivens, Jason. *Religion of Fear: The Politics of Horror in Conservative Evangelicalism*. New York: Oxford University Press, 2008.

Bock, Tim. *Unless the Lord Build the House: The Story of Jesus People USA's Mission-Business, and How I Was Part of It*. 2nd ed. Chicago: Jesus People USA Full Gospel Ministries, 2009.

Bonhoeffer, Dietrich. *The Cost of Discipleship*. New York: Simon & Schuster, 1959.

Carter, Jimmy. "Mental Health Systems Act Remarks on Signing S. 1177 into Law." October 7, 1980. http://www.presidency.ucsb.edu/ws/index.php?pid=45228.

Chancellor, James D. *Life in the Family: An Oral History of the Children of God*. Syracuse: Syracuse University Press, 2000.

Clifford, James. *The Predicament of Culture: Twentieth-Century Ethnography, Literature, and Art*. Cambridge: Harvard University Press, 1988.

Conover, Patrick W. "An Analysis of Communes and Intentional Communities with Particular Attention to Sexual and Genderal Relations." *Family Coordinator* 24 (October 1975): 454.

Cornfield, Noreen. "The Success of Urban Communes." *Journal of Marriage and Family* 45, no. 1 (February 1983): 115–26.

DeRogatis, Amy. "Born Again Is a Sexual Term: Demons, STDs, and God's Healing Sperm." *Journal of the American Academy of Religion* 77, no. 2 (June 2009): 275–302.

Di Sabatino, David. *The Jesus People Movement: An Annotated Bibliography and General Resource*. 2nd ed. Jester Media, 2003.

"Documenting Sources from the World Wide Web." *History of the Jesus Movement*, November 1997. http://one-way.org/jesusmovement/index.html (2004).

Drakeford, John W. *Children of Doom: A Sobering Look at the Commune Movement*. Nashville: Broadman Press, 1972.

Duin, Julia. "PAPA Festival Highlights Christianity, Anarchism and Community Spirit." *Washington Post*. September 1, 2011. http://articles.washingtonpost.com/2011-09-01/lifestyle/35275137_1_community-kitchen-brethren-church-christian.

Dyer, Richard. *Only Entertainment*. New York: Routledge, 1992.

Enroth, Ronald M. *The Jesus People: Old-Time Religion in the Age of Aquarius*. Grand Rapids: Eerdmans, 1972.

———. *Recovering from Churches That Abuse*. Grand Rapids: Zondervan, 1994.

Eskridge, Larry. "God's Forever Family: The Jesus People Movement in America 1966–1977." Ph.D. diss., University of Stirling, 2005.

———. *God's Forever Family: The Jesus People Movement in America*. Oxford: Oxford University Press, 2013.

BIBLIOGRAPHY

———. "'One Way': Billy Graham, the Jesus Generation, and the Idea of an Evangelical Youth Culture." *Church History* 67, no. 1 (March 1998): 83–106.
Espinoza, Javier. "The Beat Goes On." *Wall Street Journal*, July 5, 2013. http://online.wsj.com/article/SB10001424127887324436104578579112994316642.html
Farrell, James J. *The Spirit of the Sixties: The Making of Postwar Radicalism.* New York: Routledge, 1997.
Flake, Kathleen. *The Politics of American Religious Identity: The Seating of Senator Reed Smoot, Mormon Apostle.* Chapel Hill: University of North Carolina Press, 2004.
Former JPUSA Member. *An Open Letter to: Herbert M. Freedholm, Superintendent, Central Conference Evangelical Covenant Church.* http://www/angelfire.com/zine/jpusainfo/fletter.html. Frank, Thomas. *What's the Matter with Kansas: How Conservatives Won the Heart of America.* New York: Metropolitan Books, 2004.
Franke, John R. *Manifold Witness: The Plurality of Truth.* Nashville: Abingdon Press, 2009.
Fremon, David K. *Chicago Politics Ward by Ward.* Bloomington: Indiana University Press, 1988.
Frith, Simon. *Sound Effects: Youth, Leisure, and the Politics of Rock 'n' Roll.* New York: Pantheon Books, 1981.
———. "Towards an Aesthetic of Popular Music." In *Music and Society: The Politics of Composition, Performance, and Reception*, edited by Richard Leppert and Susan McClary, 140–44. New York: Cambridge University Press, 1989.
Gardner, Hugh. *The Children of Prosperity: Thirteen Modern American Communes.* New York: St. Martin's Press, 1978.
———. "Dropping into Utopia." *Human Behavior* 7 (March 1978): 43.
Geisler, Norman L. *Biblical Inerrancy: An Analysis of its Philosophical Roots.* Grand Rapids: Zondervan, 1981.
———. "Theological Method and Inerrancy: A Reply to Professor Holmes." *Bulletin of the Evangelical Theological Society* 11, no. 3 (Summer 1968): 139–46.
Gitlin, Todd. *The Sixties: Years of Hope, Days of Rage.* New York: Bantam Books, 1993.
Gitline, Todd, and Nanci Hollander. *Uptown: Poor Whites in Chicago.* New York: Harper & Row, 1970.
Glanzer, Perry L. "Christ and the Heavy Metal Subculture: Applying Qualitative Analysis to the Contemporary Debate about H. Richard Niebuhr's *Christ and Culture*." *Journal of Religion and Society* 5 (2003).
Goff, Philip, and Alan Heimert. "Revivals and Revolution: Historiographic Turns Since Alan Heimert's 'Religion and the American Mind.'" *Church History* 67, no. 4 (December 1998): 695–721.
Goldman, Marion S. "Continuity in Collapse: Departures from Shiloh." *Journal for the Scientific Study of Religion* 34, no. 3 (September 1995): 342–53.
Gordon, David Frederick. "A Comparison of the Effects of Urban and Suburban Location on Structure and Identity in Two Jesus People Groups." Ph.D. diss., University of Chicago, 1978.

———. "The Role of the Local Social Context in Social Movement Accommodation: A Case Study of Two Jesus People Groups." *Journal for the Scientific Study of Religion* 23, no. 4 (December 1984): 381–95.

Grossberg, Lawrence. "The Affective Sensibility of Fandom." In *The Adoring Audience: Fan Culture and Popular Media,* edited by Lisa A. Lewis. New York: Routledge, 1992.

———. "A Prisoner of the Modern?" *Culture Machine.* http://culturemachine.tees.ac.uk/Cmach/Backissues/j001/articles/art_gros.html.

———. "Putting the Pop Back into Postmodernism." *Social Text,* no. 21 (1989), *Universal Abandon? The Politics of Postmodernism.* Duke University Press.

Harding, Susan. *The Book of Jerry Falwell: Fundamentalist Language and Politics.* Princeton: Princeton University Press, 2001.

Hart, D. G. *Deconstructing Evangelicalism: Conservative Protestantism in the Age of Billy Graham.* Grand Rapids: Baker Books, 2005.

Hartigan, John, Jr. *Racial Situations: Class Predicaments of Whiteness in Detroit.* Princeton: Princeton University Press, 1999.

Hatch, Nathan O. *The Democratization of American Christianity.* New Haven: Yale University Press, 1989.

Hebdige, Dick. *Subculture: The Meaning of Style.* New York: Routledge, 2002.

Held Evans, Rachel. "Why Millennials Are Leaving the Church." *CNN,* July 27, 2013. http://religion.blogs.cnn.com/2013/07/27/why-millennials-are-leaving-the-church/.

Hendershot, Heather. *Shaking the World for Jesus: Media and Conservative Evangelical Culture.* Chicago: University of Chicago Press, 2004.

Hertenstein, Mike, and Chris Ramsey. "Want in the Land of Plenty." *Cornerstone* 12, no. 69: 6–9.

Hodgson, Godfrey. *The Myth of American Exceptionalism.* New Haven: Yale University Press, 2009.

Howard, Jay R., and John M. Streck. *Apostles of Rock: The Splintered World of Contemporary Christian Music.* Lexington: University Press of Kentucky, 1999.

Hunter, James Davidson. *Evangelicalism: The Coming Generation.* University of Chicago Press, 1993.

Ichthus. *The Ichthus Music Festival Is Back! Creation Festivals Helps Keep the Ichthus Festival Legacy Alive!* http://ichthus.org/.

International Council on Biblical Inerrancy. *Chicago Statement on Biblical Application.* Oakland: International Council on Biblical Inerrancy, 1986.

———. *Chicago Statement on Biblical Hermeneutics.* 1982. Reproduced from *Explaining Hermeneutics: A Commentary on the Chicago Statement on Biblical Hermeneutics.* Oakland: International Council on Biblical Inerrancy, 1983.

———. *Chicago Statement on Biblical Inerrancy.* Oakland: International Council on Biblical Inerrancy, 1978.

Jesus People USA Evangelical Covenant Church. *Our Statement of Faith.* http://www.jpusa.org/faith.html.

Joravsky, Ben. "Upscaling Uptown: Can Developers of Subsidized Housing Escape HUD Rules by Prepaying Their Mortgages?" *Chicago Reader*, March 24, 1988. http://www.chicagoreader.com/chicago/upscaling-uptown-can-developers-of-subsidized-housing-escape-hud-rules-by-prepaying-their-mortgages/Content?oid=871958.

Kanter, Rosabeth Moss. *Commitment and Community: Communes and Utopias in Sociological Perspective.* Cambridge: Harvard University Press, 1972.

———. "Supercorp: Book Review and Author Interview." *News Center*, November 3, 2009. Interview. Sean Silverthorne. http://www.moneycontrol.com/news/book-review/supercorp-book-reviewauthor-interview_422139-1.html.

Kantzer, Kenneth S., ed. *Applying the Scriptures.* Grand Rapids: Zondervan, 1987.

Katz, David S., and Richard H. Popkin. *Messianic Revolution: Radical Religious Politics to the End of the Second Millennium.* New York: Hill & Wang, 1999.

LaHaye, Tim, and Jerry B. Jenkins. *Left Behind: A Novel of the Earth's Last Days.* Colorado Springs: Tyndale House, 1995.

Lefebvre, Henri. *The Production of Space.* Oxford: Blackwell, 1991.

LeFevre, Mylon. *Crack the Sky.* Myrrh Records, 1987.

Lindsey, Hal. *The Late Great Planet Earth.* Grand Rapids: Zondervan, 1970.

Lipman, Pauline. *The New Political Economy: Neoliberalism, Race, and the Right to City.* New York: Routledge, 2011.

Loftin, Michael. "Coalition Formed to Fight Displacement." *The Voice Speaks: The Newsletter of Voice of the People in Uptown* (Spring 1987): 1.

Luhr, Eileen. *Witnessing Suburbia: Conservative and Christian Youth Culture.* Berkeley: University of California Press, 2009.

Mankin, Bill. "Peace, Love and . . . We Can All Join In: How Rock Festivals Helped Change America." *Like the Dew: A Journal of Southern Culture and Politics*, March 4, 2012. http://likethedew.com/2012/03/04/we-can-all-join-in-how-rock-festivals-helped-change-america/.

Marini, Stephen A. *Sacred Song in America: Religion, Music, and Public Culture.* Champaign: University of Illinois Press, 2003.

Marsden, George M. *Fundamentalism and American Culture: The Shaping of Twentieth-Century Evangelicalism, 1870–1925.* 2nd ed. Oxford: Oxford University Press, 2006.

———. *Reforming Fundamentalism: Fuller Seminary and the New Evangelicalism.* Grand Rapids: Eerdmans, 1987.

———. *Religion and American Culture.* Belmont, Calif.: Wadsworth/Thomson Learning, 2001.

Marty, Martin. *Pilgrims in Their Own Land: 500 Years of Religion in America.* New York: Penguin, 1984.

Maslow, A. H. "A Theory of Human Motivation." *Psychological Review* 50, no.4 (1943): 370–96.

McAlister, Melani. "Prophecy, Politics and the Popular: The Left Behind Series and Christian Fundamentalism's New World Order." *South Atlantic Quarterly* 102, no. 4 (2003): 773–98.

———. "What Is Your Heart For? Affect and Internationalism in the Evangelical Public Sphere." *American Literary History* 20, no. 4 (Winter 2008): 870–95.

McDannell, Colleen. *Material Christianity: Religion and Popular Culture in America*. New Haven: Yale University Press, 1995.

McLaren, Brian. *A Generous Orthodoxy*. Grand Rapids: Zondervan, 2004.

———. "Needed: Christians Thinking Differently About the Future." June 3, 2010. http://www.huffingtonpost.com/brian-d-mclaren/christian-eschatology_b_598868.html.

———. "Why I'm Voting for Barack Obama . . . and I Hope You Will Too: Reason 4: The Environment." http://www.brianmclaren.net/archives/blog/why-im-voting-for-barack-obama-a-2.htm.

Merriam, Alan P. *The Anthropology of Music*. Evanston: Northwestern University Press, 1964.

"Millennials: A Portrait of Generation Next." February 24, 2010. http://www.pewresearch.org/millennials/.

Miller, Donald E. *Reinventing American Protestantism: Christianity in the New Millennium*. Berkeley: University of California Press, 1999.

Miller, Timothy. "A Communitarian Conundrum: Why a World That Wants and Needs Community Doesn't Get It." Paper presented at the Thirty-Seventh Annual Conference of the Communal Studies Association, New Harmony, Ind., September 30–October 2, 2010.

———. *The 60s Communes: Hippies and Beyond*. Syracuse: Syracuse University Press, 1999.

Morgan, Timothy C. "Dozens of Children Abused at Evangelical Commune, Adult Survivors Allege." *Christianity Today*, February 28, 2014.

Niebuhr, H. Richard. *Christ and Culture*. San Francisco: Harper & Row, 1951.

Noll, Mark A. *The Scandal of the Evangelical Mind*. Grand Rapids: Eerdmans, 1994.

Oldfield, Duane Murray. *The Right and the Righteous: The Christian Right Confronts the Republican Party*. Lanham, Md.: Rowman & Littlefield, 1996.

Pahl, Jon. "Alternatives to What? New Religions and Intentional Communities in Recent American History." Paper presented at the Annual Conference of the American Historical Association, Boston, January 6, 2011.

———. *Empire of Sacrifice: The Religious Origins of American Violence*. New York: New York University Press, 2010.

Pally, Marcia. "The New Evangelicals." *New York Times*, December 9, 2011. http://campaignstops.blogs.nytimes.com/2011/12/09/the-new-evangelicals/.

BIBLIOGRAPHY

Peacock, Charlie. *At the Crossroads: Inside the Past, Present, and Future of Contemporary Christian Music.* Colorado Springs: Shaw/WaterBrook/Random House, 2004.

———. "The Future of Christian Music: Peacock's Prognostication." *CCMmagazine.com.* http://www.ccmmagazine.com/news/stories/11571162/.

Petra. *Not of This World.* StarSong Records, 1983.

Powell, Mark Allan. *The Encyclopedia of Contemporary Christian Music.* Peabody, Mass.: Hendrickson, 2002.

Prater, Jaime. *Born: Growing up in a Religious Commune,* trailer. http://www.bornthefilm.com.

Prothero, Stephen. *American Jesus. How the Son of God Became a National Icon.* New York: Farrar, Straus and Giroux, 2003.

Radmacher, Earl D., and Robert D. Preus. *Hermeneutics, Inerrancy, and the Bible.* Grand Rapids: Zondervan, 1984.

Radosh, Daniel. *Rapture Ready: Adventures in the Parallel Universe of Christian Pop Culture.* New York: Scribner, 2008.

Rev Rag 4 (October and November 1987).

Roll, Jarod. *Religion and American Culture* 20, no. 1 (Winter 2010).

Romanowski, William D. "Rock'n'Religion: A Socio-cultural Analysis of the Contemporary Christian Music Industry." Ph.D. diss., Bowling Green State University, 1990.

Rossinow, Doug. *The Politics of Authenticity: Liberalism, Christianity and the New Left in America.* New York: Columbia University Press, 1998.

Roszak, Theodore. *The Making of a Counter Culture: Reflections of the Technocratic Society and Its Youthful Opposition.* Garden City: Doubleday, 1969.

Schaefer, Alex R. "Evangelicalism, Social Reform and the US Welfare State, 1970–1996." In *Religious and Secular Reform in America: Ideas, Beliefs and Social Change,* edited by David K. Adams and Cornelis A. Van Minnen. New York: New York University Press, 1999.

Schaeffer, Francis. *Escape from Reason.* Downers Grove, Ill.: InterVarsity Press, 1968.

———. *The Francis A. Schaeffer Trilogy: The Three Essential Books in One Volume.* Wheaton: Crossway Books, 1990.

Schaeffer, Frank. "The Only Thing Evangelicals Will Never Forgive Is Not Hating the 'Other.'" *Religion Dispatches* (2009). http://www.religiondispatches.org/archive/rdbook/2097/the_only_thing_evangelicals_will_never_forgive_is_not_hating_the_%E2%80%-9Cother%E2%80%9D/?page=2.

Scharnberg, Kirsten. "Commune's Iron Grip Tests Faith of Converts." *Chicago Tribune,* April 1, 2001. http://articles.chicagotribune.com/2001-04-01/news/0104010382_1_needy-youth-commune-spiritualism.

———. "Exodus from Commune Ignites Battle for Souls." *Chicago Tribune,* April 2, 2001.

BIBLIOGRAPHY

Shenker, Barry. *Intentional Communities: Ideology and Alienation in Communal Societies* Boston: Routledge & Kegan Paul, 1986.

Shires, Preston. *Hippies of the Religious Right.* Waco: Baylor University Press, 2007.

Shupe, Anson. "Jesus People USA." In *Sects, Cults, and Spiritual Communities: A Sociological Analysis*, edited by William W. Zellner and Marc Petrowsky. Westport, Conn: Praeger, 1998.

Shupe, Anson, William A. Stacey, and Susan E. Darnel, eds. *Bad Pastors: Clergy Misconduct in Modern America.* New York: New York University Press, 2000.

Slater, Philip E. *The Pursuit of Loneliness: American Culture at the Breaking Point.* Boston: Beacon, 1970.

Small, Christopher. *Musicking: The Meanings of Performing and Listening.* Middletown, Conn.: Wesleyan University Press, 1998.

Smith, Christian. *American Evangelicalism Embattled and Thriving.* Chicago: University of Chicago Press, 1998.

Smith, William Lawrence. "Urban Communitarianism in the 1980's: Seven Religious Communes in Chicago." PhD. diss., University of Notre Dame, 1984.

Stout, Harry S. "Review Essay: Religion, War, and the Meaning of America." *Religion and American Culture* 19, no. 2 (Summer 2009): 276.

Stowe, David W. "Both American and Global: Jazz and World Religions in the United States." *Religion Compass* 4 (2010): 312–23. doi: 10.1111/j.1749–8171.2009.00212.x.

———. *No Sympathy for the Devil: Christian Pop Music and the Transformation of American Evangelicalism.* Chapel Hill: University of North Carolina Press, 2011.

Stowe, David W., and Malcolm Magee. "David W. Stowe: A Conversation about the Jesus Movement with Malcolm Magee." April 17, 2013. http://uncpressblog.com/2013/04/17/david-w-stowe-a-conversation-about-the-jesus-movement-with-malcolm-magee/.

Streiker, Lowell D. *Jesus Trip: Advent of Jesus Freaks.* Nashville: Abingdon Press, 1971.

Students for a Democratic Society. *Port Huron Statement.* June 15, 1962. http://history.hanover.edu/courses/excerpts/111hur.html.

Sutton, Robert P. *Communal Utopias and the American Experience: Religious Communities, 1732–2000.* Westport, Conn.: Praeger, 2003.

Taylor, Steve. *Bleed into One: The Story of Christian Rock.* Documentary film. Imperial Pictures, forthcoming.

"That American Way." *Cornerstone* 6, no. 41: 15.

Thomas, Alexandar R. "Ronald Reagan and the Commitment of the Mentally Ill: Capital, Interest Groups, and the Eclipse of Social Policy." *Electronic Journal of Sociology* (1998). http://www.sociology.org/content/vol003.004/thomas.html.

———. *Raised by Wolves: The Story of Christian Rock & Roll.* Toronto: ECW Press, 2000.

Thornton, Sarah, *Club Cultures: Music, Media and Subcultural Capital.* Middletown, Conn.: Wesleyan University Press, 1996.

Tipton, Steven M. *Getting Saved from the Sixties: The Transformation of Moral Meaning in American Culture.* Berkeley: University of California Press, 1982.

———. "Is Abuse About Truth or Story: Or Both? One Intentional Community's Painful Experience with False Accusations." http://muse.jhu.edu/books/9780814786697.

———. "Part 1b: Quest for Balance." *A History of Jesus People USA.* http://www.jpusa.org/lessons1b.html.

———. "Part 2: House and Home." *A History of Jesus People USA.* http://www.jpusa.org/lessons2.html.

———. "Part 4: Authority, Freedom and Uptown." *A History of Jesus People USA.* http://www.jpusa.org/lessons4.html.

———. "Part 5: Who Is My Neighbor?" *A History of Jesus People USA.* http://www.jpusa.org/lessons5.html.

———. "Part 6: Cornerstone Festival." *A History of Jesus People USA.* http://www.jpusa.org/lessons6.html.

———. "Part 7: Action—Social and Political, I. *A History of Jesus People USA.* http://www.jpusa.org/lessons7.html.

———. "Part 8: Action—Social and Political, II. *A History of Jesus People USA.* http://www.jpusa.org/lessons8.html.

———. "Progress & Poverty." *Cornerstone,* no. 59: 58, 60.

Tucker, Ruth. "JPUSA Is Family: Observations by Ruth Tucker." *Cornerstone* 22, no. 102/103 (1994): 41.

Turner, John G. "The Christian Woodstock." *Wall Street Journal,* January 18, 2008.

Turner, Victor. *The Ritual Process: Structure and Anti-Structure.* Chicago: Aldine De Gruyter, 1995.

"Uptown." *Cornerstone* 6, no. 40: 4.

Vachon, Brian. *A Time to Be Born.* Englewood Cliffs, N.J.: Prentice-Hall, 1972.

Valente, Judith. "Jesus People Documentary Sheds Light on Religious Community's Darker Stories." *USA Today,* April 7, 2014.

Vanier, Jean. *Community and Growth.* Rev. ed. New York: Paulist Press, 1996.

Wacker, Grant. "The Functions of Faith in Primitive Pentecostalism." *Harvard Theological Review* 77, no. 3/4 (July–October 1984).

Wallis Jim. "The Global Church and America's War." *Huffington Post,* September 14, 2001. http://www.huffingtonpost.com/jim-wallis/the-global-church-and-ame_b_64326.html.

———. *God's Politics: Why the Right Gets It Wrong and the Left Doesn't Get It.* New York: HarperCollins, 2005.

Ward, Hiley H. *The Far-Out Saints of the Jesus Communes: A Firsthand Report and Interpretation of the Jesus People Movement.* New York: Association Press, 1972.

Wasser, Julian. "The New Rebel Cry: Jesus Is Coming!" *Time,* June 21, 1971.

Weber, Max. *The Protestant Ethic and the "Spirit" of Capitalism.* New York: Penguin, 2002.

Weinstein, Deena. *Heavy Metal: A Cultural Sociology*. New York: Lexington Books, 1991.
"Work and Taxes." http://www.jpusa.org/covenant.html.
Young, Shawn. "Apocalyptic Music: Reflections on Countercultural Christian Influence." *VOLUME! The French Journal of Popular Music Studies* 9, no. 2 (2012): 51–67.
———. "Evangelical Youth Culture: Christian Music and the Political." *Religion* 6, no. 6 (2012): 323–38. doi/10.1111/j.1749-8171.2012.00354.x/abstract.
———. "From Hippies to Jesus Freaks: Christian Radicalism in Chicago's Inner City." *Journal of Religion and Popular Culture* 22, no. 2 (2010): 3. http://utpjournals.metapress.com/content/t20838415723558h/.
———. "Into the Grey: The Left, Progressivism, and Christian Rock in Uptown Chicago." *Religions* 3, no. 2 (2012): 498–522. http://www.mdpi.com/2077–1444/3/2/498.
Zinn, Howard. "Marxism and the New Left." In *Dissent: Explorations in the History of Radicalism*, edited by Alfred L. Young. DeKalb: Northern Illinois Press, 1968.

Recordings

Bloodgood. "Crucify." *Shakin' the World: Live Volume Two*. Intense Records, 1990.
Caldwell, Bobby, and Paul Gordon. "The Next Time I Fall." *Solitude/Solitaire*. Warner Bros., 1986.
Doors, The. "Break on Through (To the Other Side)." Elektra, 1967.
Grant, Amy. "Find a Way." *Unguarded*. A&M Records, 1985.
McGuire, Barry. "Eve of Destruction." *Eve of Destruction*. Dunhill, 1965.
Norman, Larry. "I Wish We'd All Been Ready." *Only Visiting This Planet*. Verve Records, 1972.
Roe, Michael. "The Lust, the Flesh, the Eyes & the Pride of Life." The 77s. Exit/Island Records, 1987.
———. "Woody." *Pray Naked* (a.k.a. *The Seventy Sevens*) Brainstorm Artists, Intl., 1992.
Thompson, John. *Cornerstone Festival: Twenty Years and Counting*. Produced and directed by John J. Thompson. Nashville: Floodgate Records, 2002. DVD.

INDEX

✯ ✯ ✯

46th Ward, 42, 52, 57, 65, 105, 116, 118, 263, 268,
920 West Wilson Avenue, 47, 49, 52, 121

Abortion, 12, 47, 110, 118, 148, 150, 152, 157, 163, 170, 174, 176, 228, 286–288
Adult Spanking, 10, 89, 90,
AGAPE, 182
AIDS, 67, 168
Alamo, Tony and Susan, Christian Foundation, 57, 131, 278, 294
Altamont, 180
American Dream, 80, 85, 125, 126
American Family Foundation, 84
Antichrist, 143
Anti-Riot Act of 1968, 108
Apocalypse, 7, 58, 130, 132, 145, 166, 167
Apocalypticism, 25, 101
Apologetics, 17, 32, 106, 134, 137, 138, 139, 145–147, 149, 171,
AudioFeed Festival, 220, 273

Baby boomers, 101, 116, 133, 138, 142, 144, 145, 152, 158, 159, 163, 172, 176, 190, 209, 227, 228, 241, 256, 257, 286

Billboard Guide to Contemporary Christian Music, 198
Black Panthers, 118
Bonhoeffer, Dietrich, 124
Bono, 207, 209
Book of Acts, 11, 23, 37, 123, 125, 257, 258
Brady Street, 29, 30, 39
Bright, Bill, 137, 144, 182
Brown, Ron, 40
Bryan, William Jennings, 104, 163
Bush, George W., 1, 3, 15, 47, 102, 118, 125, 126, 148, 154, 158, 187, 284
Bushnell, Illinois, 35, 186

Cadieux, Denny, 37
Calvary Chapel, 28, 57, 131, 140–142, 145, 146
Campolo, Anthony, xi, 286, 288
Cameron, Tom, 31, 37, 61, 63, 95, 96, 225
Campus Crusade for Christ, 137, 144, 182
Carter, Jimmy, 1, 71, 174
Cash, Johnny, 21, 180, 182, 185
Catholic Left, 110, 112
Catholic Worker, 109, 110, 128; and magazine, 112

INDEX

CCM; and music genre, 13, 174, 177, 179, 180, 184, 185, 191–193, 195, 196, 197, 199, 201–215, 217, 218, 220, 260, 264, 267, 268, 272, 291
CCM magazine, 197
Chapman Hotel, 43
Charismatic movement, 140, 149
Chicago, 8, 10, 11, 23, 24, 34–36, 38–40, 42, 47, 50, 52, 60, 64, 66, 69, 70, 73, 82, 94, 96, 103, 104–108, 110–113, 115–118, 120, 128, 154–156, 171, 177, 185, 186, 216, 226, 239, 246, 251, 255, 263, 268, 282
Chicago Sun-Times, 45, 216
Chicago County Fairgrounds, 185
Chicago Department of Child and Family Services, 73
Chicago Housing Authority (CHA), 156
Chicago Statement on Biblical Application, 106
Chicago Statement on Biblical Hermeneutics, 106
Chicago Statement on Biblical Inerrancy, 106, 255
Chicago Union of the Homeless, 47
Children of God (COG), 29, 55–57, 122, 131, 157, 168, 287, 294
Christ Is the Answer, 29
Christian and Missionary Alliance, 252
Christian band, 14, 192, 196, 203, 207, 209, 215, 221
Christian bookstore, 174
Christian coalition, 16, 118, 119, 152, 176
Christian heavy metal, 192
Christian Legal Society, 152
Christian nationalism, 151, 154, 159–163, 171
Christian punk, 202
Christian Right, 86, 108, 118, 176, 285
Christian rock, 2, 13, 34, 93, 141, 176–178, 181, 184–186, 190, 196, 206, 207, 213
Christianity Today, 24

Christians for Biblical Equality, 150
Chronic Homeless Initiative Grant, 73
Claiborne, Shane, 135, 161, 162, 167
Communalism, 10, 26, 35, 36, 58, 130, 233
Communal Studies Association, xi, 83
Commune, vii, 3, 4, 5, 7, 8, 10–12, 14–16, 18–20, 23–52, 56–64, 68, 70, 74, 76, 79, 81, 82, 84, 86–88, 91–96, 98, 100, 101, 103–105, 113, 115, 116, 122, 123, 125, 129, 130, 131, 136, 139, 140, 143, 146, 148, 150, 157, 158, 163, 168, 169, 171, 172, 190, 219, 221–225, 227, 229, 231, 232, 234, 236, 237, 240, 243, 247, 249, 250, 252–260, 263–266, 268, 269, 286, 295
Communism, 77, 98, 167
Conservatism, 1, 3, 6, 29, 44, 57, 65, 118, 132, 133, 138, 169, 204, 208, 241, 251, 261, 272
Compassion International, 152, 165
Contemporary Christian music (CCM), 4, 5, 6, 13, 33, 133, 174, 175, 177, 179, 180, 184, 185, 191, 192, 193, 195, 196, 197, 198, 199, 201, 202, 203, 204, 205, 206, 207, 208, 209, 210, 211, 212, 213, 214, 215, 217, 218, 220, 260, 264, 267, 268, 272, 291, 290
Cook County, 74, 76, 246
Cornerstone Community Outreach (CCO), 24, 57, 63, 70, 222
Cornerstone Farm, 35, 49, 186, 190
Cornerstone Festival, ix, x, 9, 13, 16, 24, 34, 35, 61, 64, 66, 69, 100, 120, 125, 130, 134, 136, 144, 145–147, 151, 158, 160, 161, 168, 171–173, 179, 182, 183, 185, 188, 197, 206, 208, 211, 222, 254, 256, 257, 259, 266, 269, 295
Cornerstone Magazine, 24, 35, 37, 64, 97, 99, 114, 120, 124, 126, 197, 213, 238, 258, 266
Cornerstone University (now cstoneXchange), 189

INDEX

Council, 14, 36, 37, 48, 49, 51, 62, 66, 73–75, 77, 78, 83, 88, 89, 91, 96–99, 106, 127, 130, 134, 158, 163, 222, 224, 225, 229, 230, 234, 239, 241, 249, 250, 252, 259, 264, 265, 282, 302
Counterculture, 1, 2, 10, 13, 20, 23, 28, 113, 133, 137, 141, 171, 173, 175, 180, 181, 216, 218, 231, 263
Creation Festival, 182, 183
Crisis Pregnancy Center, 47, 69, 77
Cult Awareness Network, 84

Daley, Richard J., 107, 108, 122
Darby, John Nelson, 141, 289
David Letterman Show, 202
Day, Dorothy, 111, 112
Daystar, 90
Days of Rage, 108
Democrat, 6, 104, 108, 128, 147
Democratic Party, 109, 117
Democratic National Convention, 108, 117
Department of Housing and Urban Development (HUD), 73, 277
Department of Human Services (Chicago Department of Child and Family Services), 73
Dispensational, 105, 110, 141, 167
DIY, 207, 216
Dobson, James, 152, 159, 160
Dove Award, 177, 199
Dylan, Bob, 142, 210

Elders, 24, 231
Eldership, 61, 96, 264
Emergent Christianity, 8, 19, 102, 134, 135, 139, 147, 162, 254, 269, 272, 284
Emergent, 8, 15, 19, 133, 135, 146, 147, 152, 162, 166, 169, 213, 257, 263, 270, 272, 274, 285
EMI Christian Music Group (now Capitol Christian Music Group), 176, 177

End-times, 131
Enlightenment, 18, 138, 145, 146, 213, 269
Enroth, Ronald, 49, 81, 82, 84, 86, 92, 96, 106, 140, 235, 259, 280, 289
Environmentalism, 12, 159, 160, 162
Equal Rights Amendment (ERA), 150
Eschatology, 140, 145, 159, 167, 168, 170, 228, 286
Establishment Evangelicalism, 12–14, 17–19, 50, 57, 104–106, 119, 124, 126, 128, 129, 148, 151, 152, 169, 172, 174, 185, 190, 193, 212, 214, 217, 218, 220, 221, 262, 266, 268, 269, 272, 294
Eskridge, Larry, xi, 28, 177, 266
Evangelical Covenant Church, 24, 32, 38, 40, 82, 97, 102, 183, 205, 208, 222, 246, 265
Evangelical Christians, 1, 6, 7, 111, 158, 286
Evangelicalism, 2, 4–14, 17–20, 23, 24, 50, 52, 55, 57, 65, 86, 93, 102, 104–106, 109, 111–113, 119, 124, 126, 128–131, 133–138, 144–148, 150–152, 159, 162, 165, 166, 169, 171, 172, 174, 175, 177, 181, 182, 185, 186, 190, 193, 211–214, 217–221, 241, 254–256, 260–263, 266–270, 272, 286, 288, 289, 294
Evangelical Left, 3–8, 16, 17, 19, 27, 50, 51, 102, 116, 117, 129, 135, 138, 148, 150, 161, 162, 165, 170, 172, 184, 251, 261, 269, 270, 271, 272, 288
Evangelical Right, 46, 204
Evangelism, 39, 51, 55, 63, 69, 76, 86, 94, 95, 99, 120, 140, 160, 182, 189, 238, 239, 255, 278
Explo '72, 21–23, 181, 182

Faith Tabernacle, 36, 39
Falwell, Jerry, 152
Family International, The, 55, 122, 157
Feminism, 12, 149, 150, 152, 162, 166, 174
Finney, Charles, 3, 105, 175,

INDEX

Fishnet, 13, 183
Focus on the Family, 152, 159
Frisbee, Lonnie, 141
Friendly Towers, 49, 52–54, 57, 66, 73, 103, 121, 229, 236
Full Gospel Businessmen's Association, 36
Fundamentalism, 12, 133, 136–138, 269, 278, 287

Gainesville, Florida, 10, 30
Gay rights; 152, 174, same-sex marriage, 12, 148, 170, 229, 230, 288
Geisler, Norman L., 105, 106, 134
Generation X, 257, 270
Gentrification, 42, 45, 46, 47, 57, 72, 113, 115, 155, 156
Gitlin, Todd, 109, 111, 115, 117
Glenn Kaiser Band (GKB), 66, 70
Globalization, 110
Gospel Music Association (GMA), 6, 179, 198, 199, 209, 216, 290, 292
Graham, Billy, 22, 23, 36, 182
Grammy Award, 177, 199, 210, 292
Great Awakening, 2, 20, 175, 217
Greenbelt, 186, 211
Grossberg, Lawrence, xi, 191–193, 194, 195, 211, 212, 214, 220, 271
Grrr Records, 24, 63, 66, 69, 171, 226

Haight-Ashbury, 29
Heart of Uptown Coalition, 47, 115, 116
Heavy metal, ix, 69, 192, 217
Hendrix, Jimi, 33, 180
Herrin, John, xi, 31, 34, 37, 47, 49, 89, 116, 154, 169, 186, 205, 214, 224, 256
Herrin, John Sr.; "Papa" John, 30, 31, 37, 96
Hippies, 2, 3, 16, 19, 20, 23, 24, 27–29, 30, 35, 38, 42, 53, 55, 58, 73, 109, 139, 140, 141, 164, 166, 175, 187, 218, 256, 278
HM magazine, 189, 195, 204

Homelessness, 34, 43, 47, 71, 72, 114, 115, 126, 158
Homosexuality; and same-sex marriage, 12, 148, 157, 163, 170, 228, 229, 230, 244, 288
Howard, Jay, xi, 179, 196, 197, 207
Huckabee, Mike, 182
HULL House, 115
Humanism, 120, 174, 286

Intentional community, 15, 24, 34, 36, 40, 79, 91, 93, 249, 255
International Council on Biblical Inerrancy (ICBI), 106, 282
Institute for the Study of Christianity and Culture, 108
Israel, 99, 141, 142, 143, 153, 159, 167

Jenkins, Jerry, 105
Jerusalem, 143, 160
Jesus freaks, 1–3, 9–11, 13, 16, 20, 23, 24, 28, 29, 31, 36, 38, 51, 80, 94, 101, 108–110, 116, 124, 125, 132, 133, 136–143, 145, 148, 151, 154, 160, 163, 164, 166, 171, 173–175, 218, 223, 256, 257, 262, 266, 269, 272,
Jesus movement, 2, 3, 5, 8–10, 12, 13, 17, 20, 23, 24, 27–29, 31–33, 36, 38, 40, 50, 51, 55, 57, 61, 62, 64, 65, 69, 94, 95, 101, 102, 108–110, 122, 131, 132, 133, 137–146, 148, 149, 151, 152, 154, 157–159, 163, 165, 166, 168, 171–175, 181, 187, 197, 205, 216, 217, 220, 226, 241, 257, 262, 263, 266, 268, 272, 273, 275, 278, 288, 289, 294
Jesus People Army, 29, 131
Jesus People Milwaukee, 29, 30, 36, 131
Jesus People USA Traveling Team, 10
JOIN, 115, 116
JPUSA Covenant, 75, 77, 79, 86

Kaiser, Glenn, xi, 30, 37, 50, 66, 70, 90, 91, 143–145, 151, 152, 164, 169, 196, 197

INDEX

Kaiser, Wendy, xi, 99, 162, 226,
Kanter, Rosabeth Moss, 8, 10, 11, 14, 25, 29, 60, 68, 69, 80, 91, 92, 122, 124, 228, 234, 235, 247, 258–260, 263, 265, 266
Kennedy, D. James, 152
King, Martin Luther, 107, 112, 285
Korn, 180, 185, 189, 203, 207

Lakefront Roofing, 24, 66, 67, 70, 97
L'Arche community, 59, 60
LaHaye, Tim, 105, 168
Led Zeppelin, 33, 203, 210
Lewis, C. S., 134, 139, 229
LGBT, 243, 270, 273
Liberalism; and theology, 2, 6, 7, 12, 24, 132, 137, 138, 146, 169, 218, 255, 260; and politics, 16, 108, 117, 133, 150, 260, 288
Lindsey, Hal, 105, 141, 142, 143, 144, 145, 166, 168, 171, 174
Lombard Bible Church, 252
Lowrey, Bill, 29

Malden Street, 43, 44, 45, 47
Mayan calendar, 58
McDowell, Josh, 134
McLaren, Brian, xi, 135, 161, 167, 168, 169, 284, 285, 288
McPherson, Amy Semple, 3, 175
Megachurch, 7, 151, 152, 288
Meissner, Linda, 29,
Mental Health Systems Act, 71
Middle East; and divine plan, 142, 159; and war, 158, 162, 166, 167
Millenarianism, 94, 140, 143, 166, 288
Millennials, 227, 228, 270
Millennium, 143
Milwaukee, Wisconsin, 10, 29, 30, 36, 37, 131
Missions; and Christianity, 13, 69, 158, 170, 189, 235; and social outreach, 69, 126, 222, 224, 235

Modernism; and philosophy, 18, 134
Monastery, 242
Monterey International Pop Festival, 180
Moody, D. L., 105, 106, 109, 111, 119, 163, 282, 289; and Moody Bible Institute, 104, 282
Moral Majority, 16, 119, 152, 153, 176
Mortimer, Dawn, 30, 37, 76, 77, 95, 96, 251
Mortimer, Curtis, 61, 62, 90, 96, 97, 99, 253
Murphy, Richard, 36, 37
Music industry, xi, 3, 4, 5, 7, 13, 14, 16, 17, 35, 87, 173, 176, 177, 179, 183, 187, 190, 191, 194, 195, 197, 202, 203, 207, 209, 213, 215, 268, 290, 292

Nashville; and music industry, 3, 208, 210
National Association of Evangelicals, 159
Nationalism; and politics, 153, 157, 158, 167; and Christianity, 6, 7, 148, 151, 154, 157–163, 167, 171, 268
Nehemiah American Romania Company (NARCOM), 67
New Evangelical, 15, 137, 146, 151, 166
New Left; and Christianity, 2, 11, 16, 44, 101, 102, 110–113, 116, 117–119, 127–129, 137, 164; and student movements, 2, 11, 16, 44, 50, 101, 102, 105, 107, 108, 109, 110–113, 116–119, 127, 129, 137, 139, 164
New Life Fellowship, 63
New Monasticism, 15
New Testament, 12, 66, 124, 249, 254, 258
New World Order, 110, 132
Niebuhr, H. Richard, 112, 140, 179, 267
Norman, Larry, 141, 142, 175, 177, 210

Obama, Barack, 1, 41, 76, 125, 132, 148; and health care, 41, 286

INDEX

O'Connor, Flannery, 134
Old Left, 26, 111, 112, 119, 137
Old Testament, 32, 141, 153
Oneida Perfectionists, 27
Ozz Fest, 202

Palosaari, Jim, 29, 30, 36
PAPA Festival, 273
Paulina Street, 39, 40
Peacock, Charlie, 209, 210, 268, 292
Pentecostal, 17, 133, 138, 140, 145, 174, 244, 269; and Pentecostalism, 2, 138, 139
Phantom Tollbooth, 147, 198, 214
Pluralism; and cultural, x, 4, 5, 7–9, 19, 27, 41, 49, 60, 75, 80, 93, 119, 128, 133, 135, 146, 148, 157, 158, 161, 167, 169, 170–172, 187, 190, 211, 219, 222, 223, 227, 228, 231, 250, 255, 258, 262, 263, 268, 271, 272, 274, 284, 285
Powell, Mark Allan, xi, 34, 158, 195, 196, 199, 267
Port Huron Statement, 120
Postmodernism; and philosophical, 7, 134, 218, 271
Prater, Jaime, 241–246, 249
Premillennialism, 110, 141
Project 12, 97, 253, 280
Progressivism, 103, 110, 117
Protestantism, 4, 134, 140, 288; and Reformation, 9, 20, 24, 93, 217, 274

Reaganomics, 43, 70, 114
Reagan, Ronald, 3, 43, 71, 102, 109, 110, 114, 115, 133, 153, 154, 174, 186, 190
Reba Place, 60, 61
Religious Right, 51, 64, 102, 105, 109, 118, 119, 132, 135, 148, 152, 160, 161, 163, 166, 171, 172, 174, 230, 270, 274, 275, 282, 284, 286, 287, 288
Rapture theology, 12, 94, 105, 131, 132, 140–145, 148, 151, 159, 160, 162, 163, 165, 166, 168, 171, 173, 174, 197, 262, 263, 266, 285, 289
Republican Party, 110, 125, 251
Resurrection Band, 10, 30, 32, 33, 42, 63, 64, 66, 70, 99, 100, 177, 178, 239,
Revival, 1, 2, 20, 28, 30, 31, 34, 106, 124, 144, 151, 175, 217; and revivalists, 104, 151, 175; and revivalism, 49, 57, 104, 151, 176, 217, 281
Robertson, Pat, 118, 152
Romney, Mitt, 87, 118

Salvation Army, 70, 111, 115, 135
Same-sex marriage, 12, 148, 170, 229, 230, 288
Schaeffer, Francis, 109, 134, 137, 159, 282
Second Coming of Jesus, 110
Secular Left, 4, 108, 117, 118
Shakers, 27
Shiller, Helen, 46, 47, 118, 250
Shiloh Houses, 28, 57, 131; and Shiloh Youth Revival Centers, 28
Slow Church Movement, 271
Smith, Chuck, 141, 142
Socialism, 12, 24, 25, 46, 51, 59, 66, 127, 263,
Social Gospel, 105, 110, 111, 124, 135, 151, 163, 164, 165, 166, 258
Social justice, 4, 11, 17, 35, 36, 44, 60, 68, 69, 76, 95, 102, 103, 105, 107, 108, 110, 112, 116, 117, 120, 129, 130, 131, 140, 145, 146, 151, 152, 158, 159, 160, 161, 165, 166, 169, 171, 172, 207, 221, 237, 252, 263, 268, 269, 273, 278, 289
Stowe, David W., x, 142, 143, 167
Students for a Democratic Society (SDS), 46, 109, 112, 118, 120, 139, 148, 250
Student Nonviolent Coordinating Committee (SNCC), 112

INDEX

Sunday, Billy, 3, 163, 175
Sunshine Gospel Mission, 111

Taylor, Neil, 37, 63, 73, 77, 88, 93, 94, 95, 96, 256, 257
Tone Zone recording studio, 24, 66
Trott, Jon, xi, 30, 31, 35, 38, 43, 44, 45, 47, 70, 84–88, 90, 104, 115, 116, 118, 120, 122, 124, 125, 132, 139, 146, 147, 149, 150, 152–154, 160, 161, 164, 166, 169, 185, 226, 230, 231, 277, 280, 284, 286

U2, 180, 209, 210
Uptown; and neighborhood, 11, 23, 24, 29, 42, 45, 50, 57, 60, 70, 71, 94, 95, 103, 107, 109, 110, 112, 113, 116, 119–124, 126, 128, 226, 227, 232, 250, 252, 253, 257, 263, 264; and homelessness, 73, 76, 94, 103, 107, 113, 114, 115, 116, 120, 121, 219, 222, 232; and *Uptown News*, 43
Uptown Task Force on Displacement and Housing Development, 45
Urban renewal, 45, 71, 126, 154

Vanier, Jean, 59, 60, 88, 89, 93
Van Pelt, Doug, 195, 197, 201, 204, 205, 206
Vineyard, 57, 64, 131, 140

Wallis, Jim, 117, 118, 162, 167, 286, 288
Welch, Brian "Head," 185, 189, 207
West Wilson Avenue, 47, 49, 52, 121
Whitfield, George, 3
Wild Goose Festival, 211, 293
Williams, Victor, 37
Willow Creek, 104
Winters, Jack, 90
World Vision, 152, 165
Wright, N. T., 134

Yippies, 108
Young Men's Christian Association (YMCA), 105, 112, 285
Young Women's Christian Association (YWCA), 105

Zinn, Howard, 50, 59, 127

GPSR Authorized Representative: Easy Access System Europe, Mustamäe tee 50, 10621 Tallinn, Estonia, gpsr.requests@easproject.com

www.ingramcontent.com/pod-product-compliance
Lightning Source LLC
Chambersburg PA
CBHW021934290426
44108CB00012B/837